CHINA'S AFRICAN REVOLUTION

CHINA'S AFRICAN REVOLUTION

Alan Hutchison

WESTVIEW PRESS

Published in 1975 in the United Kingdom
by Hutchinson & Co. (Publishers) Ltd.

Published in 1976 in the United States of America
by Westview Press, Inc.
1898 Flatiron Court, Boulder, Colorado
Frederick A. Praeger, Publisher and Editorial Director

Library of Congress Cataloging in Publication Data

Hutchison, Alan.
    China's African revolution.

    Bibliography: p.
    Includes index.
    1. Africa—Relations (general) with China.
2. China—Relations (general) with Africa. I. Title.
DT38.9.C5H8 1976   327.51'06   75-45233
ISBN 0-89158-025-5

for my mother

CONTENTS

ILLUSTRATIONS

PREFACE

My curiosity about the Chinese in Africa was aroused immediately on arrival in Tanzania in 1969. The excesses of the cultural revolution, which had unfortunate repercussions in many African countries, had caused general resentment against the Chinese throughout the continent. In Tanzania, there was agreement amongst Western diplomats that China was, in an ill-defined way, 'up to no good'. There was also scepticism that she would be able to carry out her commitment to build the Tanzania–Zambia railway. Western embassies, each with their China expert, counted rows of disembarking Chinese in Dar es Salaam harbour with ever mounting gloom, and evolved fanciful theories about China's long-term motives for being in Africa.

But there was a striking discrepancy between what China was actually doing and what her critics said she was doing, and as I watched the relationship between China and Tanzania develop, it seemed to me highly beneficial for the African country. There was no apparent Chinese 'threat', pressure or even influence. My interest in discovering whether Western myth had distorted other Chinese initiatives in Africa was the root of this book.

That does not mean that it is an apologia for China's African policies, however fashionable apologia for every aspect of Chinese life have become. Where, in my opinion, China has made mistakes or behaved with duplicity I have said so; where she was unlucky, or her actions misrepresented, I have also said so. There seems little point in depicting China as better than her admirers make out, or worse than her enemies claim. China *has* been treated unfairly in the past, but it is of service to no one to over-compensate now and claim for her virtues which she does not possess.

But this book is about Africans, as well as Chinese. Perhaps because of the West's colonial relationship with Africa in the past, Western writers have too often ignored the African factor, as if the Cold War, the Sino-Soviet dispute or some other international issue could rage in an African country quite regardless of the government or the people living there. Africans have shown tact and subtlety in their dealings with China, and have made their own contributions to the relationship. As I have said in the book, African leaders who secured the withdrawal of the colonialists have proved themselves equally politically capable of hosting a Chinese presence in their independent countries. As a result, they have benefited from Chinese material help and learned from Chinese experience, flattering China by copying some of her developmental models, not insulting her by aping all of them.

As far as primary sources of information are concerned it would be difficult to imagine two less fruitful areas than China and Africa. African governments are highly sensitive to any – but especially Western – questioning about their relations with China, while China confines her coverage of Africa to cryptic notices of arrivals and departures of African guests, publication of banquet speeches and polemical articles on Chinese aid activities. For certain factual events I have relied on Chinese, Western and African newspaper and magazine reports, as well as on the published sources quoted in the text. Other information has come to me through conversations with private individuals and officials, whose names for obvious reasons have had to be withheld – but whom I should like to thank. My own observations have provided the balance of the raw material.

The dangers of writing a book about the relations of China with a whole continent, especially one as diverse as Africa, are obvious, but it seemed a risk worth taking. China herself, while acknowledging the differences, has treated the entire continent as a more or less homogeneous area diplomatically and administratively. I have therefore made generalizations about Chinese policies in Africa as a whole where I have felt they were justified, but in other instances have been careful to specify certain areas or a particular country where the distinction was needed.

For easier reading I have left out the diacritical mark in the romanized versions of Chinese names, as does NCNA in its English-language dispatches. A word on the order of the book. Part One is a chronological account of China's varied activities in all African countries in the period 1955–74, and also provides a background to such extra-African issues as the Sino-Soviet dispute and Chinese–US hostility, both of which affected China's relations with Africa. Part Two examines in detail specific aspects of the Sino-African relationship, such as personal relations between Chinese and Africans, China's aid and trade with Africa, China's relations with the liberation movements and China's very special relationship with Tanzania. By writing the book in this way I hope that non-specialists will accumulate enough knowledge in the first part to help them better understand, and I hope enjoy, the second half.

Finally, my thanks to Mohamed Amin for permission to reproduce some of his excellent photographs, and especially to Sarah Hawkins, who badgered me so sweetly into finishing the book.

PART ONE

I

CHINA'S FIRST CONTACTS WITH AFRICA

'Let the past serve the present'
MAO TSE-TUNG

IN the twenty-five years since the Chinese Communist party won power, the primary foreign policy objectives of the People's Republic of China have remained constant: to ensure the security of the state of China and to ensure the continued authority of the Communist party within that state. No foreign policy would be implemented unless it contributed to the attainment of those two goals, however well it might serve secondary considerations, of an ideological or even an altruistic nature. China, like the British ruling class, has 'no permanent friends, nor permanent enemies, but only permanent interests' – the survival of the state.

These fundamental goals have in the past been obscured, both by the propaganda of China's enemies, and by her own propaganda. The most obvious example of the former was the United States' presentation of China's revolutionary actions abroad as ends in themselves, and the portrayal of China as a simple 'trouble-maker'. America's policy of 'containing' China and the very real physical threat to China's territorial sovereignty posed by the presence of US forces around her borders were ignored as catalysts. Equally, China's rulers have not wanted to draw their subjects' attention to the weaknesses of the state by emphasizing the diversionary nature of much of their foreign policy. Actions which were motivated by a desire to distract China's enemies have therefore been presented as China's 'internationalist duty' or as China's contribution to the worldwide revolutionary struggle against imperialism. A further smoke-screen has been put up by the polemical, almost theatrical nature of China's pronouncements on world issues. Talk of the 'imminent collapse' of the capitalist system, and of the 'surging revolutionary storms' raging throughout the world may have bolstered the morale of people within China and to a lesser extent the populations of other weak states; but they have also disguised the essential chauvinism of Chinese foreign policy.[1]

The nations of Africa have made important contributions towards the achievement of China's foreign policy goals. Even in the period of greatest isolation, Chinese leaders were able to tell their subjects that China had the full support of such African allies as Tanzania, Guinea, Mali, Congo-Brazzaville etc. That these nations were themselves weak, and in their own way isolated, was not important – nor, probably, was it known to the great majority of the Chinese population. What counted was that their leaders were prepared to recognize China, lend her support on certain international issues such as the nuclear-test-ban treaty and even travel to China to pay tribute to the Chinese leader and to the Chinese way of life. To bolster international morale, and also incidentally the ego of the visitor, these African leaders were invariably billed in the Chinese press as 'great and revolutionary' leaders of 'large and important' countries. In international struggle, they were told, theirs was a strong voice, not a weak one.

Even Africans themselves were sometimes puzzled and flattered by the attention they received from the world's most populous country. But the Chinese constantly emphasized the mutual benefits of these seemingly unequal relationships. The first of their eight principles of aid-giving, for example, stresses that China

... never regards such aid as a kind of unilateral alms but as something mutual. Through such aid the friendly new emerging countries gradually develop their own national economy, free themselves from colonial control and strengthen the anti-imperialist forces in the world. This is in itself tremendous support to China.

The official Chinese line on the mutual benefits of Sino-African friendship was given by premier Chou En-lai on a visit to Mali in 1964:

China and the independent countries of Africa can support and closely co-operate with each other in consolidating national independence, safeguarding state sovereignty, developing national economy, promoting Asian-African solidarity and defending world peace. (NCNA, Bamako, 16 January 1964)

Chou further expanded on this theme during a farewell speech for the Congo-Brazzaville Prime Minister, Ambroise Noumazalay, in 1967, stressing the shared common past of colonial oppression suffered by the two peoples and the need for them both to continue fighting for the liberation of still subjected peoples throughout the world:

Why do the Chinese people cherish such a profound friendship for our Congolese and other African friends? This is not only because the Chinese people shared in the past the same experience with the African people of being subjected to colonialist aggression and oppression and are both now confronted with the common task of struggle against imperialism, but also because the Chinese people who are armed with the great thought of Mao Tse-tung are fully aware of the fact that without the liberation of all oppressed peoples and oppressed nations of the world, the Chinese people cannot win complete independence . . .
Our Congolese friends regard China as a staunch comrade-in-arms at all times, and this is an expression of great trust and support to us . . . The friendship between us is sincere and not false. (NCNA, Peking, 5 October 1967)

Moral support from a handful of small nations might seem little enough return for the considerable investment of effort and money which China has put into her relations with Africa. But the relationship has yielded other benefits of a more substantial nature. It was, for example, the African vote which finally secured Peking's seat in the United Nations; a healthy two-way trade has also been built up, with African nations supplying China with necessary raw materials and in turn buying unsophisticated manufactured goods for which there is not a ready market elsewhere. But no African nation has as yet provided what would, in Peking, be considered the ultimate political payoff: full endorsement of China's viewpoint in the Sino-Soviet dispute.

When China first took an interest in Africa, considerations of how the relationship would develop, and to whose advantage, were well in the future. At the time of the founding of the People's Republic in 1949 only four African countries – Egypt, Liberia, Ethiopia and South Africa – were independent. The method by which the colonial subjects of Britain, France, Belgium, Portugal and Spain were to gain their independence was therefore the paramount consideration.

China was not alone in expressing an interest in the independence movements of African colonies. The Soviet Union, whose primacy in the world communist movement was freely acknowledged by China, had devoted a good deal of thought and effort to the subject. Immediately after the Bolshevik Revolution, Lenin had high hopes that a series of socialist upheavals would be sparked off in the industrialized countries. When they failed to materialize the Soviets hoped for a time that their revolution would spread to China, India and South-East Asia, and Soviet theory emphasized the damage that could be done to monopoly capitalism by the freeing of colonial peoples and the subsequent assumed denial to the industrial countries of their raw materials.

Early on, it was agreed that the right conditions for a full Marxist revolution did not exist in backward countries. But Soviet prescriptions that communism would have to form a temporary alliance with non-communist nationalist independence leaders of colonial countries ('the bourgeois-democratic movement') received a severe setback in 1927 and again later in 1936, when Stalin's encouragement to the Chinese Communist party to cooperate with the Kuomintang gave the latter their opportunity to all but crush their rivals out of existence.

The Soviet Union's dismissive attitude to this disaster was partly explained by the onset of Stalin's policy of 'building socialism in one country alone', asserted in opposition to Trotsky's thesis of world revolution. But it is hardly surprising that it coloured vividly the Chinese approach to the theory of winning independence. From the outset, China made it clear that she felt her own revolution was of particular significance for Africa (and implicitly, therefore, of more significance than the Soviet Union's). As early as 1949 Liu Shao-chi, later China's first head of state, told a Moscow conference of Asian trade-union representatives that the Chinese revolution was uniquely placed to serve as a model for future revolutions throughout the backward, agricultural and colonialist-dominated areas of Asia and Africa. In 1951 Lu Ting-yi, Mao's panegyrist, said,

The November Revolution is the classic type of a revolution in imperialist (that is to say capitalistically developed) countries. The Chinese revolution is the classic type of a revolution in colonial and semi-colonial countries, and its experience is of incalculable value to the peoples of such countries.

The Chinese particularly stressed the value of 'struggle', in promoting political consciousness and national cohesion. Independence too easily won might be too easily lost. It was this emphasis on violent revolution, allied with the Chinese claim that successful revolution in the colonial countries depended, not on the classic Marxist war of the classes but on frustrated nationalism, that was of significance to pre-independence African leaders and which was also to lead China into her bitter dispute with the Soviet Union.

THE INDEPENDENCE ERA

In the event, communist theorizing about the nature of the African revolution proved so much wasted paper. With the notable exception of Algeria, and to a lesser extent Kenya, no African leader had to 'struggle', at least not violently, to win his country's independence. Upsetting communist predictions about 'last-ditch struggles', the European colonial powers simply folded up their flags and went home. The communists, caught unawares and unprepared to take the leading role for which they had cast themselves, at first explained away unsatisfactory situations as imperialist plots. Nasser's seizure of power in 1952 was described by an official Soviet encyclopedia as a manœuvre organized by 'a reactionary group of officers in alliance with the United States'.[2] With just a little more accuracy Nkrumah's party and his first, pre-independence, government were portrayed as 'shields behind which the reality of British imperialist dominance conceals itself'.[3]

Just as it was becoming clear that communist predictions about the nature of independence were not going to be fulfilled, Soviet prestige suffered still further with the defection of a leading Francophone communist and the publication of a highly critical book by a former negro member of the Comintern, both in the same year, 1956.

The Francophone apostate was Aimé Cesaire, leader of the semi-philosophic, semi-poetic négritude movement. Based in Paris, the movement absorbed communist ideas, but, despite the fact that one of its founders, Leopold Senghor, later became president of Senegal, it never gained a political momentum. The end of its flirtation with communism came with the publication of Cesaire's famous Open Letter to Maurice Thorez, secretary-general of the French Communist party. In it he wrote,

I could easily express my feelings towards both the French Communist party and the Communist International as it has been shaped by the patronage of the Soviet Union; the list of dissensions and grievances would be long. Lately, we have had a record-breaking crop; and Krushchev's disclosures concerning Stalin are such that everyone, no matter what the extent of his participation in communist activity, has been thrown – or, at least, so I trust – into an abyss of dismay, of pain and of shame . . .

What I want is that Marxism and Communism be harnessed into the service of coloured people, and not coloured people into the service of Marxism and Communism. That the doctrine and the movement be tailored to fit men, not men to fit the movement.[4]

Similar complaints were voiced by George Padmore, a West Indian, who in the 1930s had worked for colonial liberation in the Comintern. But, disillusioned with communism, he returned to London where he took upon himself the task of educating potential African leaders, notably Nkrumah, to distinguish, in one commentator's words, 'between democratic socialism, Marxism and Communism; and to steer Pan-Africanism into non-violent methods of struggle'.[5] In his book, *Pan-Africanism or Communism*, Padmore drew attention to communist duplicity and opportunism, and wrote,

... Since communists have nothing to lose and everything to gain by fishing in the troubled waters of Asia and Africa, they can afford to pay lip service unreservedly in support of colonial freedom.[6]

CHINA'S IMAGE

In the pre-independence era Africans' knowledge of, and in some cases disillusionment with, communism had thus been shaped by their contacts with the Soviet Union.[7] Of China itself, and of Chinese communism, there was almost total ignorance. There were no communications between the two areas, and in any case, Chinese visitors were barred from travelling to the non-independent countries. There was virtually no mention of Africa in the Chinese press until after the Bandung Conference. The only tenuous connections were effected by contacts between Chinese officials and African delegates at conferences organized by such Soviet 'front' organizations as the International Union of Students and the World Federation of Trade Unions.

Initially at least, African ignorance about China seems to have worked in China's favour. Many Africans were generous in interpreting this ignorance; Aimé Cesaire, for example, in his Open Letter wrote

There exists a Chinese communism. Though I have no first-hand acquaintance with it, I am strongly prejudiced in its favour. And I expect it not to sink into the monstrous errors that have disfigured European communism.

HISTORICAL CONNECTIONS

Although in this century, contacts between China and Africa were few until after 1955, an historical connection linking the two goes back many centuries.[8] Chinese spokesmen have often stressed these historical links; Chou En-lai during his 1964 tour of Africa was constantly referring to 'a shared past', a 'common heritage' and 'centuries' old links'. In view of the nature of those links this emphasis was somewhat surprising, for in the great days of Chinese seaborne exploration, in the

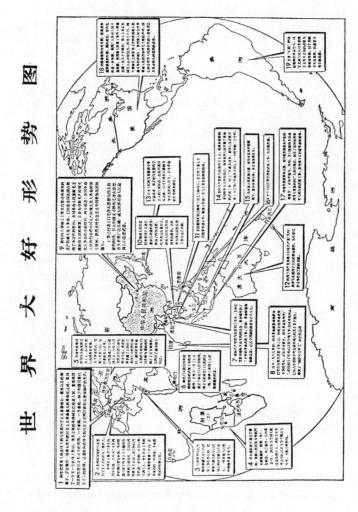

'A MAP OF THE FAVOURABLE WORLD SITUATION'

A Chinese propaganda map printed in the early sixties showing supposed promising revolutionary situations throughout the world.

fifteenth century, the Emperor's Grand Eunuchs were entrusted with great fleets, sometimes numbering over sixty ships and up to 40 000 soldiers, with orders to make known to the 'barbarian' peoples the 'transforming power of the imperial virtue' and in return to receive tribute from them acknowledging his distant authority.

The greatest of these explorers, Cheng Ho, sailed down the east coast of Africa as far south as Ts'eng-pa, or Zanzibar, collecting 'tributes' of ambergris, ivory, gold, tortoise-shell and even animals. On one voyage he managed to return to China with a Tsu-la-fa (giraffe), whose grace and beauty so enchanted the Emperor Yung-lo that he received it in the Hall of Receptions. 'Devil slaves' were also occasionally captured to serve in the imperial court.

But after Cheng's seventh voyage China began to turn in on herself. The Emperor Hsuan-te decreed that 'the building of ships to go to the barbarian countries shall everywhere be stopped'. Within a few years documents relating to the voyages had been burned by imperial officials, anxious that such mistaken policies should not be pursued again. Historians pronounced against expansionism, and the increasing influence of Confucian conformism deadened interest in the world outside the Middle Kingdom.

The last medieval contact between China and Africa recorded in the Ming History, came in 1441 when the ruler of Mi-hsi-erh (Egypt) sent envoys to the imperial court with 'tribute of mules, horses, and various products of their localities'. By one of those extraordinary chains of history the next recorded official contact between the two regions came over five-hundred years later when the premier of the People's Republic, Chou En-lai, shook the hand of the Egyptian president, Gamul Abdel Nasser, at the Bandung Conference of African and Asian nations, thus initiating the modern links between China and Africa.

Notes

1. The literal interpretation placed – both by accident and by design – on Chinese propaganda metaphors accounts for quite a lot of the misunderstanding about China's real intentions and beliefs. This occurs notably

in the Western understanding of the Chinese word Ko-ming, which can have the meaning 'change of fate', but which is invariably translated as 'revolution', with the connotation of violent revolution. But it can also be a peaceful change, as in the English phrase an 'agricultural revolution'. Chou En-lai tried to explain this nuance after the furore caused by his famous remark that Africa was 'ripe for revolution' (see page 68).

2. *Bolshaya Sovietskaya Entsiklopaediya*, 2nd edition, Moscow, 1952.

3. In the book *Narody Afriki* (the Peoples of Africa).

4. A. Césaire, 'An Open Letter to Maurice Thorez', *Présence Africaine*, 1956.

5. Colin Legum, in *The Soviet Bloc, China and Africa*, lectures delivered to the Scandinavian Institute of African Studies at the University of Uppsala, London, 1964.

6. Bukharin had said as much in 1919 when at the eighth congress of the Russian Communist party he openly declared: 'Let us by all means proclaim self-determination for the European colonies, for Hottentots, Bushmen, Negroes, Indians and the rest. It won't cost us anything.'

7. And to a lesser extent with the representatives of the European Communist parties. For example, the French communists successfully established branches of their Confédération Générale du Travail in most French colonies, a policy facilitated by their participation in the Popular Front Government. The British Communist party, however, showed little enthusiasm to dismantle the Empire, and in 1924 the fifth congress of the Communist International heard that 'not one of the official statements of the British Communist party contains any clear and unambiguous demand for the separation of the colonies from the British Empire'.

8. For a fascinating account of China's medieval contacts with Africa see *China and Africa in the Middle Ages*, by Teobaldo Filesi, translated by David Morison, Frank Cass, London, 1972.

2

BEGINNINGS OF THE SINO-SOVIET DISPUTE

The East wind prevails over the West wind.
OLD CHINESE PROVERB

For the first five years of the People's Republic, Chinese foreign policy consisted almost entirely of reactions to pressures exerted by the United States. The hostility of the US towards China was no figment of her leaders' imaginations; it had been amply demonstrated by massive support for the Kuomintang, which in money terms was estimated at over $1 billion, by the continued support for and defence of the Nationalist regime in Taiwan, by US participation in the Korean War, by the oft-pronounced policy of containing and isolating the Chinese 'menace', and by the fervent anti-communism exhibited in America during the fifties, reaching a peak in the notorious Macarthy era. The only other major Chinese foreign initiative taken during this period was the strengthening of the alliance with the Soviet Union and the acceptance by China of considerable Soviet assistance; this was not, properly understood, 'aid' as Soviet supplies had to be repaid with interest. But the Soviets claimed that the relatively low level of interest in fact constituted aid.

The year 1954 was a watershed in the communist world. Stalin died, wars in North Korea and Vietnam were concluded and the Chinese Communist party finally consolidated its authority throughout the land. China's leaders could breathe more easily; Stalin's death emboldened them to take some independent foreign policy decisions and gave China the quiet satisfaction, not publicly expressed, that Mao Tse-tung was now the communist world's elder statesman.

By her international behaviour China hoped to give the lie to American allegations that she was an irresponsible, un-approachable firebrand. That she was partially succeeding was shown in 1954 when, at the Geneva Conference on South-East Asia, Chou earned the somewhat patronizing reputation of being a 'communist one could talk to'. During a recess in the conference he travelled to New Delhi with Jawaharlal Nehru to sign the Panch Sheela, or Five Principles of Peaceful Co-existence, which initiated the short-lived era of 'Chini-Hindi Bai Bai', or Sino-Indian friendship. During this period, which came to be known as the 'Bandung phase' of Chinese diplo-macy, China also signed boundary and friendship treaties with some of her Asian neighbours, such as Nepal, Burma, Afghanistan, Pakistan and Mongolia. China showed herself to be most accommodating, a gesture which she vainly hoped would be reciprocated by the refusal of her neighbours to sign military pacts with the US or, at least, deny the US military facilities on their territory.

The 'Bandung phase' and the 'Bandung spirit' owed their name to the small Indonesian mountain town where, in April 1955, twenty-three Asian states, six African ones – Gold Coast (later Ghana), Liberia, Sudan, Egypt, Ethiopia and Libya – and observers from liberation movements met to discuss common problems.

At the conference Chou En-lai showed considerable flexi-bility and diplomatic skill. Sensing that the mood was moderate and conciliatory, he watered down previously militant demands about the return of Taiwan to China, and, towards the end of the conference, astonished delegates by offering to enter into peaceful negotiations with the US about the island's future. It seems that he altered his prepared text in order to harmonize with the 'Bandung spirit' – an early example of Chinese pragmatism in foreign affairs.

Chou and his deputy Chen Yi[1] do not seem to have gone to Bandung with the specific object of opening up contacts with the African world. Their seeming cultivation of Nasser[2] may have been undertaken for a variety of reasons: he was the only African head of state present, and therefore, apart from Nehru, the only statesman of anything like equal status to Chou En-lai. Of the other African states at Bandung, little could be expected from Liberia or Ethiopia with their close American ties, while the non-independent states – Sudan, Gold Coast and Libya – were represented by second-rank politicians. Chou En-lai's interest in Egypt was also probably roused by her position as an Arab as well as an African country, and there is evidence that at least initially, China was more interested in the Middle East than in Black Africa.

After Bandung, China's interest in Africa quickened. A small Egyptian trade delegation visited Peking immediately after the conference, and in July China agreed to buy 13 000 tons of Egyptian cotton. This was a particularly valuable commercial contract for Egypt because some months earlier traditional Western buyers of Egyptian cotton, which provided 80 per cent of her export earnings, had refused to agree to Egypt's price. In August another Egyptian mission visited China and the two sides negotiated the first Chinese trade agreement with any African country, under which China agreed in the first year to buy 15 000 tons of Egyptian cotton,[3] and Egypt contracted to buy 60 000 tons of Chinese rolled steel. The two countries agreed to set up trade offices in each other's capitals. The momentum of this first important commercial agreement enabled Chinese trade to weather the political crises which later marred Sino-Egyptian relations, and China's trade with Egypt has consistently been at a high level. In fact, throughout this study, we shall see that Chinese pragmatism is nowhere so well illustrated as in commercial relations, which function virtually in a political vacuum.

Diplomatic relations between Egypt and China were established in May 1956, formally re-opening the official ties between China and Africa which ceased when Sayyid Ali, the envoy of Sultan A-shih-la-fy, the ruler of Egypt, left the Imperial Court clutching his gifts of silk stuffs and garments in November 1441.

The importance Peking attached to Egypt was signalled by the appointment as first ambassador of Chen Chia-kang, the assistant minister for foreign affairs, who remained in Cairo until late 1965. His deputy was Chang Yueh, formerly deputy director of the West European and African Affairs division of the Foreign Affairs Ministry.[4]

Throughout the rest of 1956, these two guided China's

expanding interests on the continent. Chinese cultural missions visited Egypt, Sudan, Morocco, Tunisia and Ethiopia, and in the next two years – before the contraction of external trade associated with the failure of the Great Leap Forward – Chinese trade with selected countries continued to expand at a satisfactory rate.[5]

The 'Bandung spirit' still continued to guide Chinese foreign policy decisions elsewhere: at a meeting of Asian and African students held in Indonesia in May 1956 and organized by the International Union of Students, a communist front organization, China raised no objections when the credentials of the more suspect communist 'students' were examined, nor to their subsequent expulsion. The Chinese representatives also demurred when it was agreed that all connections with the IUS should be severed, and further, they agreed not to use the meeting as a propaganda platform for the return of Taiwan.

THE SUEZ CRISIS

In July 1956, just a week after the arrival of the Chinese ambassador in Cairo, President Nasser nationalized the Suez Canal. In the subsequent months leading up to the Anglo-French invasion of Egypt, Chinese statements seemed to be trying to serve the dual purpose of assuring Egypt of her radical support at the same time as allaying Western fears about her militancy. Thus on 15 August France and Britain were even commended for having 'recently taken some actions favourable to the relaxation of international tensions', while two weeks later the New China News Agency was reporting the registration of Chinese volunteers in response to Nasser's request for canal pilots. Even after Anglo-French military action Chinese statements were calling for a settlement of the crisis through peaceful negotiations, and it was only on 8 November, with a ceasefire imminent, that China offered material aid – a £1·8 million loan – and not until the ceasefire had actually been arranged did she make the celebrated announcement that volunteers were being registered in China for action in Egypt. Nevertheless, from Egypt's point of view, China had done everything that could be expected from a new ally, and Nasser expressed his gratitude in a message to Chou En-lai.

From China's point of view, she had won some relatively cheap publicity amongst radical states, without entirely tarnishing, in the West, the image she wished to project of a moderate state bent on internal development.

CHINA'S NEW MILITANCY

This was the last occasion for nearly a decade that China found it necessary to restrain so publicly her revolutionary ardour. From the time of Suez onwards, factors both internal and external pressured her into adopting more radical policies.

Suez itself came as something of a surprise to China. As Chou En-lai himself said in March 1957:

[Suez was] a great revelation to us, showing that although the Asian and African countries are not yet powerful in material strength, all aggression by the colonialists can be frustrated, as long as we maintain our solidarity and firmly unite with all peace-loving forces of the world and wage a resolute struggle. (*People's Daily*, 6 March 1957)

It had never before occurred to the Chinese that the Western powers might back down on an international issue in the face of a communist threat of force – primarily because the communists were aware of the far greater military capability of the West. Suez showed them they had perhaps been wrong, and in August 1957 Moscow's first successful launch of an ICBM convinced Chinese leaders that militarily, the communist powers were entering a period of ascendancy. It was the Soviet Union's supposed rocketry superiority that led Mao Tse-tung to make his famous speech at the Moscow celebrations to mark the fortieth anniversary of the October Revolution later that year:

It is my opinion that the international situation has reached a turning point. There are two winds in the world today, the East wind and the West wind. There is a Chinese saying 'Either the East wind prevails over the West wind or the West wind prevails over the East wind'. I believe it is characteristic of the situation today that the East wind prevails over the West wind. That is to say the forces of socialism have become overwhelmingly superior to the forces of imperialism. (Quotations from Mao Tse-tung, 1st edition, 1966)

It was a theme taken up by Chou En-lai when he reported to the National People's Congress in February 1958:

A decisive change has taken place in the international situation that favours our socialist construction, the socialist camp, the cause of world peace and the progress of mankind. As all the world knows, in October and November 1957 the Soviet Union launched two artificial earth-satellites, while on the occasion of celebrating the 40th anniversary of the great October Socialist Revolution, representatives of the Communist and Workers' Parties of the socialist and other countries met in Moscow and issued two statements of great historic significance demonstrating the unity of the Communist and Workers' Parties of various countries.

. . . Everybody can now see that, compared with the imperialist camp, our socialist camp has definitely gained supremacy in population and popular support, in the rate of industrial and agricultural development and in a number of important fields in science and technology. Even the imperialist aggressors cannot but admit that they stand before an invincible socialist camp headed by the Soviet Union, stronger and more united than ever before.

Both Mao Tse-tung and Chou En-lai felt, or said they felt, that Soviet military superiority would deter the West from undertaking not only general wars but also local ones. The communists could encourage revolution in colonial territories with little risk to themselves. Conditions for the resistance to imperialism and colonialism were said to be 'especially favourable'. Chinese propaganda began to stress, paradoxically, that peaceful co-existence could only be achieved by struggle. Independence itself could only be won through struggle, which had the added advantage of imbuing the masses with revolutionary consciousness. A *People's Daily* editorial, hailing the success of the 1957 Afro-Asian People's Solidarity Conference in Cairo, commented that

The establishment of a lasting peace is inseparable from the national independence movements. Only when the people of all countries have gained independence and equality can a stable and lasting peace come into being. This is a good for which our nations in Asia and Africa should jointly fight.

THE LINES DIVERGE

This more militant line was put forward, not jointly with the Soviet Union, but tacitly in opposition to what China was later to term the Soviet Union's 'gross error of principle' in asserting that socialism could be achieved by the 'parliamentary road'. Krushchev had argued at the CPSU's twentieth congress in February 1956 (the same meeting at which he had denounced Stalin) that the working class of a number of capitalist and former colonial countries, having won a parliamentary majority, could create the conditions needed to secure 'fundamental social changes'. Communist parties need for a time play only a secondary role.

China, as a result of her own disastrous, Soviet-encouraged, experiences of cooperating with such bourgeois elements could not agree. She had to advise that the African struggle for independence should be violent, like her own. There could be no cooperation with non-communists.

Although the CCP's experiences *were* a compelling and genuine reason for China to advocate violent revolution, her harder foreign policy line was also the result of internal factors: Mao's extreme left supporters with their slogan of 'let politics take command' were gaining ascendancy over the more conservative wing of the party, which advocated continued reliance on Soviet aid and guidance. In domestic affairs the extremists' control of power led to the Great Leap Forward, while abroad it led to the adoption of a more radical foreign policy and eventually to the split with the Soviet Union.

Despite the revolutionary rhetoric, China was pursuing two types of diplomacy – the united front from above (state-to-state relations with sovereign governments) and the united front from below (support for revolutionary groups). In the same year – 1958 – that the *People's Daily* editorial enthusiastically commented that 'the tide of the national independence movement has spread from Asia to Africa', China established diplomatic relations with the kingdom of Morocco. In the next two years she expanded both her commercial and her diplomatic contacts with some of the newly independent 'bourgeois' regimes, establishing diplomatic relations with Algeria, Sudan, Guinea, Ghana, Mali and Somalia.

These actions implied a realistic appraisal of the situation, but it was as a champion of revolution that China propagated herself. It was left to the Soviet Union to puzzle publicly over the fact that the first wave of colonial liberation had shown that

2

national leaders could win their independence without violence and without the help of the communists; worse, many of the new leaders appeared to be actually hostile to the communist movement. As early as 1958 a Soviet commentator was surveying the independence scene in these pessimistic terms:

Anti-communism, 'Communist-phobia', the suppression of Marxism–Leninism as a system of thought, the attempt to crush communist organizations – all this is not only a limitation on democracy in Africa. It is no less than a limitation on national development, a weakening of the truest interests of the mass of the people, and an assistance to the imperialists. . . . It is regrettable that some African leaders have picked up this tattered mantle of the dictators and imperialists.[6]

Of course, these leaders were only 'imperialist puppets' and times would change. But in the meantime the Soviet Union would have to put the best face on things, and come to some sort of temporary accommodation. This was the contentious policy of peaceful co-existence. Some nationalist leaders, it was admitted, had 'revolutionary potential'. The more progressive nations were awarded the Soviet title of 'national democracies'. In Africa early examples of these were Ghana, Guinea and Mali.

Central to Krushchev's thinking was his thesis that in a thermonuclear age 'even a tiny spark can cause a world conflagration', and with their greater knowledge of the world balance of power and more realistic appraisal of the relative military strength and technical capabilities of the West, the Soviets had no wish to put to the test their Chinese allies' touching faith in their military superiority. In the long run, the Chinese analysis that in practice the nuclear weapon would never be used has proved the correct one; in Cuba Krushchev had to withdraw rather than risk nuclear confrontation, and the United States did not resort to nuclear warfare in Vietnam. But that is to use the wisdom of hindsight; at the time it seemed that the Soviet approach was the more practical.

Krushchev intensified his search for a détente during 1959. He advised the Chinese not to test imperialism over the Taiwan Straits issue. He visited the United States and came back convinced, he said, that Eisenhower was a man of peace. In

March he left for Paris to meet de Gaulle in preparation for the Four Power talks scheduled to take place in May. The u2 incident, which sabotaged the summit, secretly delighted the Chinese. It showed that their interpretation of the imperialists' real designs was the correct one – the us was 'showing its real colours'. Krushchev had badly misjudged Eisenhower, and the Chinese made veiled references to certain people being 'misled'.[7]

In contrast to the Soviet line, a *Red Flag* editorial of May 1960, far from recommending collaboration with the West, however grudging, called for the formation of a broad united front to defeat imperialism. Africa, where the struggle was only just beginning, was seen as an important battleground for the fight between progressive and reactionary forces; but there was not a great deal of enthusiasm for the newly independent countries:

On the African continent several countries have either proclaimed independence or won a certain degree of independence. They are continuing their fight against imperialism in an effort to consolidate the fruit of their struggle and achieve complete independence. (*Red Flag*, 16 May 1960)

These militant statements, with their inferences that there was struggle still to come, and that true independence was some way off, were hardly designed to appeal to the 'bourgeois' leaders of the newly independent countries, and in an astonishingly short time China had fallen foul of most of the important leaders of the Third World. There was a sharp decline in relations with previously friendly Indonesia over the treatment of Chinese nationals; President Tito's 'revisionist' policies came in for vituperative attack; there was the gathering cloud over Sino-Indian relations, triggered off by the sanctuary offered to the Dalai Lama by India after China's occupation of Tibet. The Tibetan incident was also one of the contributory causes in the deterioration of relations with Egypt. The Egyptian Information Ministry published a sixty page pamphlet condemning China's actions in Tibet, referring to the invasion as 'an Eastern version of the Hungarian revolution'. China in turn took issue with Nasser's treatment of local communists, and his support for anti-communist elements in Iraq.[8]

All these actions marked out China as having a different approach to the world situation from the Soviet Union. Silence on the subject of the 'parliamentary road' signalled dissent, and China instead preferred to refer to the 'Bandung spirit', or that part of it connected with the anti-colonial front. The significance of this was that the Bandung meeting had not included representatives from the Soviet Union and later, when the Sino-Soviet dispute came into the open, China made great efforts to exclude Soviet participation in a 'second Bandung'.

Africans would have been aware of these divergent approaches; they may, for example, have contrasted China's handling of Nasser's attacks on local communist parties with the more tolerant attitude adopted by the Soviet Union. They would have noted, many with approval, Krushchev's attempts to reach some sort of détente with the United States, and China's silent disapproval of the exercise. There were also divergences of view at meetings of the Afro-Asian People's Solidarity Organization, to be discussed later. But China still acknowledged the leadership of the Soviet Union in the socialist camp. These surely were simply minor differences amongst friends. The more charitable observers even referred to the different activities of China and the Soviet Union in Africa as a division of labour policy, carefully worked out by the two partners so that the monolithic communist movement could appeal to both revolutionaries and established national leaders at the same time.

The evidence, however, is that China viewed her foreign policy in a very different light. Since we now know from the Chinese themselves that the origins of their dispute with the Soviet Union go back to the 20th Congress in 1956,[9] it is reasonable to assume that in the years immediately succeeding that meeting, China's leaders were trying to establish an independent foreign policy. By doing so they could then say after the split that they had been defending the purity of the revolution, while the 'revisionist clique' in Moscow had been acquiescing in the dissolution of communist parties, and attempting to come to terms with the imperialists.

Africans who visited China were impressed that there *was* a difference between the policies of the two communist partners. China, it seems, did not wish to appear beholden to the Soviet

Union, and visiting Africans were not told, for example, that the technicians working on various projects were Russian. One visitor, Abu Mayanja, former secretary-general of the Uganda National Congress, commented after a trip to China in 1958:

In external affairs their desire was to be seen as separate from and equal to the Russians; hence their insistence on making separate contracts with Africans, and in giving support to African leaders and movements of their own choice.[10]

Africans could most clearly see this difference of emphasis in the different approaches of China and the Soviet Union to three separate revolutionary situations on the continent at the end of the fifties and the beginning of the sixties – the 'independence era'.

Notes

1. Chou was at this time both Prime Minister and Foreign Minister. Chen Yi was a vice-premier, and did not become full Foreign Minister until 1958. But Chou continued – and continues – to take a controlling interest in foreign affairs.

2. The Chinese delegation met Nasser in Rangoon on the way to the conference, where Chou reportedly asked the Egyptian leader to visit China. The offer was repeated at Bandung, where Chou extended a blanket invitation to all delegations to visit China.

3. This was the original 13 000 tons, plus an extra 2000 tons.

4. The African Department of the division was hived off in September 1956 to the newly created West Asian and African Affairs Department of the Ministry, under the directorship of Ko Hua, later ambassador to Guinea. In 1964 the Department was further divided: a separate African Affairs Department was set up, acknowledging the growing importance of Black Africa in Chinese foreign policy, while Arab Africa became the concern of a new West Asian and North African Department. For a detailed account of the structure of China's Foreign Ministry and an account of the movement of personnel engaged with Africa, see Bruce Larkin, *China and Africa 1949–1970*, University of California Press, p. 229 *et seq.*

5. E.g., in 1957 China's exports to Morocco were worth £3·9 m., her imports from Morocco nil; in 1958 exports were valued at £5·7 m., imports at £1·1 m. Chinese exports to Sudan doubled from £200 000 in 1957 to over £400 000 in 1958, while imports in the same period edged up from £600 000 to £700 000.

6. A. Zusmanovich, *Proletariat Afriki boretsia protiv imperialisma*, Sovremenny Vostok, 1958.

7. There was a certain amount of personal animosity between Mao and Krushchev, not only because they were in some sense rivals, but also because of Krushchev's alleged association with and encouragement for the rightist, disgraced Foreign Minister, Peng Teh-huai, who had advised Mao to rely more heavily on Soviet military and technical assistance.

8. China was on good terms with the revolutionary government of General Qassim. China's criticisms of Nasser's treatment of the Egyptian Communist party should be compared with her silence when the Moroccan Communist party was banned in 1959; China wanted good governmental relations with Morocco because she transported supplies to the Algerian revolutionaries through Morocco.

9. See *On the Origin of the Dispute between the leadership of the CPSU and Ourselves,* Foreign Language Press, Peking, 6 September 1963.

10. *Policies Towards China – Views from Six Continents*, ed. A. M. Halpern, McGraw-Hill, New York, 1965, p. 434.

3

THREE AFRICAN
REVOLUTIONARY
SITUATIONS

Peace can only be won by fighting for it, not by begging . . .

NCNA DISPATCH

THE Algerian War, which was fought from 1957 until 1962, is a prime example of the contrast in policies practised by the Soviet Union and China in the period leading up to open acknowledgement of their dispute. In African eyes, Algerian independence was a crucial issue, a challenge between a European power seemingly determined to remain and Nationalists determined that it should get out. For a time it seemed that on its outcome might well hang the independence of the remaining African dependencies; a successful guerrilla campaign would probably convince the French, and in their wake the British, that African independence was inevitable and that if not granted immediately Nationalists were prepared to fight for it.

For the Chinese the Algerian situation was potentially 'the classic type of a revolution in a colonial or semi-colonial country', for which Lu Ting-yi had written the Chinese model would be of 'incalculable value'. A successful campaign, based on Mao's guerrilla strategy, would validate China's revolutionary methods, and would possibly set an example for the rest of the continent.

The issues were nothing like so clear-cut for the Soviet Union, whose actions were constrained by European and big power considerations. Krushchev at that time was doing his best to encourage France's anti-Americanism and prise her away from NATO, and did not therefore want to confront de Gaulle directly over the less important Algerian issue; he also used as an excuse for not extending initial recognition to the National Liberation Front (FLN) his desire not to offend the Algerian Communist party – which operated separately from the FLN, with very little popular support; finally he adopted an equivocal attitude towards the French Communist party, many of whose members supported de Gaulle's proposals. It was, as one commentator put it, the 'realistic and typically unheroic' attempt of a great power to serve contradictory interests at the same time.

For a short time China demurred, possibly in deference to the leadership of the Soviet Union in the socialist camp, more likely because when it was first considering the issue in early 1956 the lesson of Suez was still in the future. However, once the French Communist party had signalled its support of the FLN China was quick to respond, and throughout the war went into virtual open competition with the Soviet Union in the supply of moral and material support to the revolutionaries.

In the autumn of 1958 the FLN announced the formation of a Provisional Revolutionary Government, which China immediately recognized. Mao sent a congratulatory message to the FLN leader, Ferhat Abbas, and the *People's Daily* said the establishment of the government would

exert a tremendous influence on the national independence movement of the African people. The armed struggle of the Algerian people has always been a source of great inspiration for the other African people under the yoke of colonialism . . .[1] (*People's Daily*, 23 September 1958).

In the next two years four FLN delegations travelled to Peking, the last, in August 1960, including Abbas himself. China agreed to supply the FLN with US automatic weapons captured during the Korean War, as well as Chinese rifles and infantry equipment and an undisclosed amount of money.[2] Throughout the war vast parades in support of Algeria were held throughout China, and volumes of propaganda for the FLN were printed in Peking.

China also offered to send volunteers to Algeria, just as she had the previous year to Egypt; they were to be fighter-bomber pilots and volunteers trained in guerrilla warfare techniques. Like the previous year's offer this was probably intended as a symbolic gesture of support.[3] Nevertheless the 'threat' – however remote – of China physically entering the war was used by the FLN in their negotiations with de Gaulle, so the offer helped in some measure to gain Algerian independence.

The differences in approach of the two communist powers were underlined by their reactions to de Gaulle's proposals for a peaceful solution and a referendum on Algerian independence, made in September 1959. Krushchev told the Supreme Soviet on 31 October that

The recent proposal of General de Gaulle for a solution of the Algerian question on the basis of self-determination and a people's referendum in Algeria can play an important role . . .

He added that a peaceful solution would 'greatly heighten the international prestige of France as a great power'. Without naming China he also warned against the dangers of 'Trotskyite adventurism'.

China's reactions were very different. A broadcast declared that

French imperialism is now engaged in a dark conspiracy . . . The plan for 'cease-fire' negotiations and for a 'people's referendum' in Algeria, proposed by President de Gaulle a month ago, is nothing but a sugared poison draught . . . There is merely a tactical difference in the situation: France is now trying to obtain by a trick what it has not been able to attain by force of arms. (Radio Peking, 17 October 1959).

When the war was finally settled by the Evian Agreement, both China and the Soviet Union could claim some credit for the FLN's success. Both had supplied material assistance. Krushchev had even managed to join the bandwagon of victory by receiving members of the Provisional Government at the UN in the autumn of 1960, an action which he later claimed implied de facto recognition. China had succeeded in establishing her revolutionary credentials and in showing that she was capable of backing up verbal support with hardware. She might have been more fulsome in welcoming the Evian Agreement, even if it did imply the end of immediate revolutionary prospects in Algeria. The *People's Daily*, however, pointed out that the 'fight' (to safeguard independence) would continue, while it also held out the possibility of renewed armed struggle, this time against the new menace of US neo-colonialism in Algeria.

For China, Algerian independence, won by armed struggle, was an encouraging introduction to the continent, presenting possibilities of armed risings in the other colonial territories. China was not to know that, with the possible exception of Kenya, Algeria was to be the only African dependency which had to fight physically for its independence. For the Soviet Union, Algerian independence had been a more equivocal event. Unlike China, the international outcast, she had to weigh all-out support for the FLN against big power and state considerations. In the background was the fear that a localized war could quickly escalate into a global confrontation, with the US intervening to 'contain' communism.

The Soviet Union's almost diffident approach and China's 'reckless attitude', as Krushchev increasingly came to see it, were illustrated in two other revolutionary situations in Africa at the same time.

CAMEROON

French Cameroon's independence, granted on 1 January 1964, was declared 'fictitious' by the communist-led insurrectionary party, Union des Populations du Cameroun, because of the declared intention of the President, Ahmadou Ahidjo, to invite French troops to remain to preserve internal security. The UPC's leader, Felix-Roland Moumié, announced that he would continue to wage a guerrilla war after independence.

These moves polarized Soviet and Chinese attitudes. The Soviets dropped their support for the UPC and moved steadily towards recognition of the legitimate, if bourgeois, Ahidjo government. Accoring to one informed writer,[4] they gave an undertaking to the new government that they would use what influence they had with the UPC to persuade it not to reject out of hand any proposals the government might make for peaceful negotiations.

For China Cameroon seemed a promising revolutionary situation.[5] Moumié travelled to Peking twice and eventually set up his external headquarters in Conakry, where he maintained contact with the Chinese through a special 'Cameroon wing' of the Chinese embassy. UPC members were given training in China and later at Nkrumah's Chinese-run guerrilla camp in Ghana. Captured UPC guerrillas gave details of China's considerable support for the movement.[6]

The Chinese lost much of their influence with the UPC, not all of whose members were professed communists, when Moumié died from poisoning in Switzerland in 1960. Chinese support continued but further setbacks were sustained, first with the establishment of a legal wing of the movement within Cameroon in July 1962, and then with the death of the pro-Chinese vice-president, Abel Kingue, in June 1964. His death revealed serious splits in the movement, for just three months later the UPC rump accused China of meddling in their internal affairs and of assuming a 'hostile attitude' towards them. But by that time the UPC had degenerated into factionalism and scarcely counted inside or outside Cameroon.[7]

THE CONGO

The Congo's strategic position gave the country a peculiar importance in the foreign policies of both China and the Soviet Union. Both saw opportunities for themselves in the widespread anarchy prevailing after the hastily granted independence of June 1960; for China it was especially significant that the Congo was the only African situation in which it seemed possible the US might become directly involved. But both communist powers made the mistake of turning a blind eye towards moderate African opinion, which, as UN voting showed, was in favour of a speedy return to stability. Their opportunism did not go unnoticed.

The Soviet Union made a serious miscalculation when she misjudged the UN's willingness, and even more, ability, to intervene effectively in the Congo crisis. An appeal to the UN had been sent by premier Patrice Lumumba, who enjoyed the support of both Moscow and Peking, after the second hectic week of independence, during which the army had

mutinied, the Belgian army had been called in to protect
Belgian lives and property and Katanga had moved to secede.
Welcoming the appeal to the UN, Krushchev made it clear he
did not expect it to have any result. He incorrectly calculated
that the UN would be unable to act and that Lumumba would
be forced to ask the Soviet Union to intervene to restore order.
His remark that the 'Security Council has been turned by the
USA into an instrument for suppressing the freedom-loving
peoples and keeping the peoples in colonial bondage' looked
rather flat the very next day when that same body authorized
the dispatch to the Congo of an international peace-keeping
force, including soldiers from independent African countries.

China was at first obliged to mute her criticism of the
Soviet-backed UN action; then as the scenario evolved both
China and the Soviet Union cooperated in denouncing the UN
as a Trojan horse for US imperialism. Later still, the Chinese
criticized the misguided Soviets directly for their handling
of the situation:

Some naive people were inclined to believe that the UN intervention
could help the Congolese people . . . They did not realize that the
US has always used the UN as an instrument for aggression, and that
inviting in the UN means letting in US imperialism. (*People's Daily*, 25
November 1960).

In September, President Kasavubu removed Lumumba,
whose deputy, Antoine Gizenga of the extremist Parti Solidaire
Africaine, immediately appealed to China for material support.
Money was sent, but China pleaded geographical difficulties for
not sending the requested volunteers and equipment. The
immediate reaction came from General Joseph Mobutu,
who temporarily seized power and ordered the expulsion of all
communist representatives in the Congo. Later that month
Lumumba was murdered.

Gizenga then set up his own government in Stanleyville,
recognized by both the Soviet Union and China as the legitimate
Congolese government, and to whom they both sent representatives. China was then outmanœuvred, or as she would say
betrayed, by the Soviets who encouraged Gizenga to throw
in his lot with the new, moderate, government of Cyrille
Adoula in Leopoldville.[8] The Soviets established relations with

the central government and moved their mission from Stanley-ville to Leopoldville. The Chinese mission was withdrawn less than two months after arriving in Stanleyville; relations could not be established – 'most regrettably' – with Leopoldville, because the government recognized Nationalist China. Chinese propaganda adopted a somewhat head-in-the-sand attitude by continuing to refer to Gizenga as the rightful leader of the Congolese people. When he was later arrested China insisted he would suffer the same fate as Lumumba, and heaped insults on Adoula. The Soviets invited Adoula to visit Moscow.

When the Sino-Soviet dispute came fully into the open both Moscow and Peking tried to outdo each other in de-nouncing the other's Congo policies. Their accusations provide a summary of their respective attitudes towards potentially revolutionary African situations. The Soviets discovered in retrospect that

The uncontrolled efforts to 'revolutionize' all the processes in Africa without any profound scientific analysis had their effect on the rebel movement in the Congo ... The adventurism of the initiators of the 'super-revolutionary war' produced a crop of light-headed performers ... The tragic events in Stanleyville exposed the whole theory of the adventurist theory of 'certain victory' under any conditions transferred on to unprepared soil. (*Literaturnaya Gazeta*, 2 June 1966).

The Chinese criticized the revolutionary lukewarmness of the Soviet Union and saw in the UN intervention signs of a Soviet-US 'plot':

Again, let us examine the part played by the leaders of the CPSU in the Congo question. Not only did they refuse to give active support to the Congolese people's armed struggle against colonialism, but they were anxious to 'cooperate' with US imperialism in putting out the spark in the Congo. On 13 July 1960 the Soviet Union joined with the US in voting for the Security Council resolution on the dispatch of UN forces to the Congo; thus it helped the US imperialists to use the flag of the United Nations in their armed intervention in the Congo. The Soviet Union also provided the UN forces with means of transportation. In a cable to Kasavubu and Lumumba on 15 July Krushchev said that 'The UN Security Council has done a useful thing'. Thereafter, the Soviet press kept up a stream of praise for the UN for 'Helping the government of the Congolese Republic to

defend the independence and sovereignty of the country', and
expressed the hope that the UN would adopt 'resolute measures'.
In its statement of 21 August and 10 September, the Soviet government continued to praise the UN, which was suppressing the
Congolese people.

In 1961 the leaders of the CPSU persuaded Gizenga to attend the
Congolese Parliament which had been convened under the 'protection' of UN troops, and to join the puppet government. The
leadership of the CPSU falsely alleged that the convocation of the
Congolese Parliament was an 'important event of the young republic'
and a 'success of the national forces'.

Clearly these wrong policies of the leadership of the CPSU
rendered US imperialism a great service in its aggression against
the Congo. Lumumba was murdered, Gizenga was imprisoned,
many other patriots were persecuted, and the Congolese struggle for
national independence suffered a setback. Does the leadership of
the CPSU feel no responsibility for all this? (*People's Daily*, 22
October 1963)

China's brash statements on the Congo and her public optimism
about the fine revolutionary potential there, given 'correct'
policies, contrast sharply with a private Chinese analysis of the
Congolese situation, prepared for members of the People's
Liberation Army, which fell into Western hands.[9] It stated,
in part, that

. . . the situation in the Congo, as seen from the surface, appears
to be very confused and 'very rotten' but actually it is very good.
It has tempered the Congolese people, made them realize who is
enemy and who is friend, enabled them to differentiate right from
wrong, so that they may further consolidate their strength and
prepare to engage in a new struggle for national liberation . . .

But there are certain unfavourable factors in the struggle of the
Congo people. At present the national liberation movement of the
Congo is mainly led by the capitalist nationalist elements. Among
them wavering and compromise prevail and so they cannot under-
take correct and firm leadership. The strength of the nationalist
party is also scattered and there is no single force to unite the whole
country.

As a result of long colonial control there exist in various places
of the Congo the comprador class and the reactionary, feudalistic
tribal influence. They are in collusion with the imperialists to oppose
the people and occupy different places to engage in secession
activities.

The struggle of the Congo people is extensive, severe and heroic, but at present there is no core guidance organized by the workers' class . . .

The situation is favourable but the leadership is weak.

This realistic assessment summarized the objective factors preventing the fulfilment of China's publicly optimistic expectations of African revolutionary situations: the masses were not revolutionarily conscious, guerrilla technique was poor and leadership weak. Even to its own army the Chinese leadership could not admit other considerations: the inability of China, for logistic and economic reasons, to fuel promising situations; the absence of satisfactory opposition groups to back in certain countries; the desire to maintain state-to-state relations with some governments, thus inhibiting support to dissident movements, and the belief amongst leaders who had freed their countries from colonial rule that they had indeed won 'true' independence and they therefore needed no further assistance from China to gain 'further victories'.

In the absence of truly promising examples Chinese propaganda either harped on the one case (Algeria) where armed struggle had been the decisive factor in winning independence, and to a lesser extent on the 'revolutionary storms' blowing in the Congo, or resorted to generalizations. At all times the Soviet theory of peaceful co-existence was challenged:

Peaceful co-existence is [not] possible between the imperialist countries and the countries fighting for and upholding national independence. How can the oppressed co-exist peacefully with the oppressor? . . . How can the colonial peoples live in peace side by side with the colonialists? . . . Peace can only be won by fighting for it, not by begging . . .

In the last analysis, it is not the imperialist forces of war but the daily more awakened people of the world who decide the destiny of the world. The peoples of Asia, Africa and Latin America will hold still higher the anti-imperialist and anti-colonial banner and will continue to win great victories in their struggle to win and uphold national independence and defend world peace. (*People's Daily*, 9 September 1961)

The rhetoric was familiar. But that China's leaders really believed Africa would be of key importance in *realpolitik* as well as in proving the correctness of Peking's prescriptions, was shown by her secret summary of the situation:

Africa is now both the centre of the anti-colonial struggle, and the centre for the East and West to fight for control of the intermediary zone, so that it has become the key point of world interest. The general situation is the forced withdrawal of old colonialism from Asia, and the changing of the last battlefield to Africa.[10]

Notes

1. The same editorial dismissed as 'trifling and impotent' the non-recognition of the Provisional Government by the colonial powers, a fairly obvious dig at the Soviet Union which had not extended recognition either.

2. In 1960 General Qassim of Iraq, praising Chinese assistance to Algeria, referred to support of 'more than $12m. by way of aid and backing for this blessed struggle'.

3. Chinese revolutionary theory, as we shall see later, stresses the paramount importance of self-reliance in struggle – foreign assistance can only be auxiliary. No Chinese soldier or 'volunteer' has ever seen any active service with any African army or revolutionary movement. The offer to supply volunteers has not been repeated.

4. Fritz Schatten, *Communism in Africa*, Praeger, New York, 1966, p. 206.

5. China's hostile attitude towards Ahidjo cannot be divorced from the fact that following a tour by a Taiwanese delegation of West Africa, his government established diplomatic relations with the Nationalist Government in 1960. (Chiang Kai-shek, therefore, now had relations with five independent African countries: South Africa, Libya, Liberia, Tunisia and Cameroon.) This would explain China's unequivocal support for the UPC, in contrast to her lukewarm attitude towards similar movements in Chad and Sudan (with whose government she had good state-to-state relations).

6. See e.g., the *Sunday Telegraph*, 23 July 1961.

7. China eventually established diplomatic relations with the Ahidjo government in April 1971, seven years after the Soviet Union. As late as 1965 Ahidjo was saying the Chinese had not entirely ceased their support for the UPC.

8. The Congolese leaders' reconciliation came at the first meeting of non-aligned nations, held in Belgrade. China, however, was convinced that the Soviet Union connived at the arrangement – see e.g. The Fourth Comment on the Open Letter of the Central Committee of the CPSU, joint editorial of the *People's Daily* and *Red Flag*, 22 October 1963.

9. Known as the *Bulletin of Activities of the People's Liberation Army*, it was captured in Tibet and has been translated as *The Politics of The Chinese Red Army*, by J. Chester Cheng, ed. Stanford: Hoover Institution on War, Revolution and Peace, 1966. See pp. 398–400.

10. Chester Cheng, op. cit., p. 484.

4
THE FRONT ORGANIZATIONS

'Brothers, comrades and friends, lift up your heads'
Soviet delegate at the first conference of
the Afro-Asian Solidarity Organization

THE Sino-Soviet rift, and its repercussions for Africa, was also reflected in the development of the various communist 'front organizations'. For many years the Soviet Union has attempted to hide her proselytizing activities behind the façade of organizations ostensibly committed to such causes as the rights of mothers, student welfare, sport, trade unions and the arts. In countries where communist parties were proscribed these organizations were useful for gathering recruits, disseminating propaganda and so on; it was hoped that their neutralist titles – The International Union of Students, International Journalists' Organization, International Association of Democratic Jurists, World Peace Council etc – would disguise their real intentions and allay suspicions in states where overt communist activities were banned. All this was done with an almost insulting lack of subtlety, with the result that in the West the front organizations soon ceased to have any real value. The annual conferences produced stereotyped resolutions denouncing the imperialists and applauding the democratic and peaceful actions of the Soviet Union, so even to the relatively naive it was clear who was behind the front, so to speak. In the industrialized countries their activities even became counter-productive, provoking criticisms of hypocrisy, 'wire-pulling' and so on. The Soviets therefore began to concentrate the energies of their fronts on the under-developed world, with far greater success. To begin with, Africans accepted the organizations at their face value, and early conferences were attended by delegates representing a broad spectrum of African political life. Political leaders in the West were confident that the organizations would soon be exposed, and hardly bothered to counter their propaganda, far less set up rival organizations. Here they made a miscalculation, and it arose from a fundamental weakness in the West's dealings with Africa, and one which still influences Western attitudes today. They find it very difficult to look at an African situation through African eyes: witness, for example, the slightly hurt indignation of the British at the outbreak of Mau Mau terrorism, or at Nyerere's breaking of relations over Britain's inability to solve the Rhodesian question. From an African point of view, violence in Kenya or severance of diplomatic ties were perfectly logical responses to the particular situations. To the British they seemed nearly incomprehensible.

At the time of independence Africans eagerly sought membership of the Soviet front organizations. The inevitable International part of their title made them feel they were joining an important, worldwide community, while they doubtless found the solicitous attention they were paid very flattering. Fritz Schatten points out how immensely impressed the African delegations must have been at the People's Congress for Peace in Vienna in December 1952, when 2000 delegates from 100 countries sprang to their feet to cheer the Africans for their 'heroic struggle for freedom from the yoke of colonialism'.[1] This sort of treatment was repeated at hundreds and hundreds of similar meetings, international youth days, journalists' seminars, women's rights days, peace conferences and so on. Contacts were established, invitations extended – who could blame the African delegate if he responded favourably to all this treatment, especially if he had also visited the West and found himself a stranger to its cold individualistic philosophy? Schatten asks us to identify with the (fictional) subordinate official of a small breakaway trade union in Sierra Leone, attending a World Trade Union Congress. He hears himself being described as 'an important African trade-union leader', and is invited to sit with the guests of honour on the platform. He receives, and accepts, invitations to visit friendly countries; and he scarcely notices at the end of the conference that he is automatically voting with his new-found comrades for a resolution calling for the total economic independence of Sierra Leone from the West.

The secretariats of the front organizations flooded African countries with reports on numerous meetings, making constant reference to resolutions like the one in the above example, signed by well-meaning but overwhelmed Africans in the name of 'All Africa'. Some of the propaganda was bound to rub off.

Eventually, in Africa as in the West, however, the communist front organizations became counter-productive. Continued manipulation failed to take into account the Africans' increasing sophistication; the communists, in fact, repeated the errors of the West, taking 'African gullibility' for granted. What is more the front organizations became a forum for Sino-Soviet rivalry, as the history of the major African front, the Afro-Asian People's Solidarity Organization, AAPSO, shows.

FOUNDING OF AAPSO

AAPSO was formed as the result of an initiative first put forward at the Conference for the Relaxation of International Tensions, held in New Delhi in April 1955. This, as the initiated would guess from the title, was a Soviet-organized conference, called, the communists tried to claim, as a preparatory meeting for the Bandung Conference. Although China had been invited to Bandung, the Soviet Union had not, and the New Delhi conference, hastily organized by the Asian branches of the Soviet-dominated World Peace Movement, represented the Soviets' attempts to become associated with what they perceived could be an important new movement. In fact, this tactic misfired because India and Indonesia, two of the organizers of the Bandung Conference, made it clear that there was no connection whatsoever between the two conferences. They did not wish to prejudice the non-aligned nature of Bandung by association with 'the true representatives of the people' present in New Delhi. These decided at their meeting to set up a broad front organization covering Asia and Africa, including, of course, the Soviet Union. After the success of the Bandung Conference the Soviets tried to jump on the band-wagon of the 'Bandung spirit', and implied that the Afro-Asian Solidarity Organization (the 'People's' was not added until 1960) was founded as a result of the Bandung Conference; references to the New Delhi meeting were kept to a minimum.

It took over two years to prepare the ground-work for an Afro-Asian Solidarity Conference. A formula had to be evolved to permit the admission of the Soviet Union as a member, eventually achieved by the constitution of a Soviet National Asian Solidarity Committee, which established the Soviet Union's Asian credentials. China initially showed little interest in what she realized would probably become another Soviet-dominated front; the Chinese Asian Solidarity Committee was not established until February 1956, eight months after the Delhi conference – little was heard of it subsequently and a permanent secretariat was never set up.

The first conference was held in Cairo in December 1957, and was attended by 500 delegates from thirty-nine countries in Asia and Africa. Rashidov, the chief Soviet delegate, affirmed that

this Afro-Asian Solidarity Conference, its spirit and its ideas are supported by all honest men throughout the world, because it is anti-imperialist, anti-colonial and anti-militarist and thus at the same time just, progressive and humane . . .

The Soviet people support this consolidation of those forces in the Afro-Asian countries that will henceforth play an important role by extending the zone of peace in the struggle against the rotten system and piracy of imperialism . . . Brothers, comrades and friends, lift up your heads, the end of your enslavement is at hand.

Although this, and similar speeches, made it clear to the ini-tiated, or the cynical, that the Soviets intended AAPSO to be yet another pliant front, Africans did not see it in this light. John Kale, the moderate general secretary of the Uganda National Congress, described the meeting in these terms:

For those of us who were taking part in such an important inter-national conference for the first time and rubbing shoulders with cabinet ministers, presidents and prominent trade unionists, scientists, artists and writers from countries all over the world, Cairo was a tremendous experience. For the first time we felt we were being taken seriously. They all treated us as equals, whether they had won their own independence forty years ago or perhaps only a couple of years back ... Although many of us instinctively and some of us even consciously, rejected Soviet-communist interference in our work, although many of us distrusted the communists, this mistrust was outweighed bv a feeling of real gratitude that a great world power should support our demands.[2]

The Soviets proposed a resolution calling for the establishment of a permanent Afro-Asian secretariat, to see that conference resolutions were carried out, to ensure continuity between plenary sessions and to publish literature on the organization. Elected to the secretariat were the Soviet Union, China, Cameroon, Ghana, Sudan, India, Japan, Indonesia, Iraq and Syria. Youssef As-Sibai, an Egyptian, was appointed Secretary-General. To act as a permanent liaison between the solidarity movements of the two continents it was proposed to set up an Afro-Asian People's Solidarity Council,[3] and it was also agreed to establish local Afro-Asian Solidarity Committees in about forty countries; this plan was implemented in very few cases, although the Soviet Union set up AASC's in eight Soviet republics in 1961.

The appointment of As-Sibai, the personal appointee of Nasser, gave AAPSO a neutralist credibility in its early years, and later represented an obstacle to complete communist domination of the organization when relations between both the Soviet Union and Egypt and China and Egypt deteriorated. Nasser himself had pretensions to leading the African revolution – Egypt subvented numerous African liberation movements, some of whom had their headquarters in Cairo. Nevertheless, from the very beginning the Soviet Union enjoyed considerable influence in AAPSO's administrative bodies. In terms of Sino-Soviet rivalry, which increasingly dominated proceedings after 1960, the Chinese in the more important of these bodies could probably rely only on the support of Japan (represented by the Communist party), Indonesia, the two Vietnams and Pakistan. After 1965 she could only rely on the unqualified support of Pakistan.

Despite these in-built organizational advantages enjoyed by the Soviet Union (and also because after 1961 the Soviets actively opposed Chinese activities inside such traditionally

Soviet-dominated fronts as the World Peace Council, whereas the 'orientation' of AAPSO was not so clear-cut), China was keen to make her weight felt. Her contribution to the budget was greater than the Soviet Union's,[4] her staff at the Cairo secretariat, headed by Yang Shuo, was numerous and initially she appears to have had a leading influence in the AAPSO propaganda machine: early literature, especially the organization's official journal, *the Afro-Asian Bulletin*, was sprinkled with such Chinese-inspired phrases as 'the main enemy, the United States'. The Chinese also used AAPSO machinery to contact students and arrange further education for them in China, and to contact and finance nationalist movements.[5]

In 1959 deteriorating relations between China and Egypt disrupted the smooth working of the organization. China had answered Nasser's criticism of her Tibetan policies by permitting the Syrian Communist party leader, Khaled Baghdash, to attack Nasser's anti-communism at celebrations in Peking marking the anniversary of the founding of the People's Republic. In turn, Nasser threatened to call on African and Asian countries which had relations with China to downgrade their representatives in Peking to the status of chargés d'affaires. In view of these developments China tried at the beginning of 1960 to have the headquarters of AAPSO moved from Cairo to Djakarta, and to have As-Sibai replaced as Secretary-General. These moves were headed off, thanks to Soviet influence in the administration.

However, the communist 'bloc' (the Sino-Soviet split had not yet come into the open) scored a victory over the Egyptians when it was agreed AAPSO should hold its next plenary session in Conakry, Guinea. The very fact that the conference was held outside Egypt put it beyond Nasser's control; and at that time Conakry was the headquarters for nationalist groups beholden, not to Nasser, but to Moscow and Peking. The Chinese sent a twenty-five-member delegation to the conference – the largest present – but the calibre of many of the other delegations left much to be desired. Of the sixty-eight African and Asian delegations, only a handful were truly representative of their national governments. Sudan, India, Japan, Indonesia, Iraq and several others were represented by their communist parties, some of them banned. The illegal

UPC represented Cameroon, while many other countries, including most of the West African Francophone nations as well as the east and central African countries were represented by minority, left-wing splinter groups. These delegates heard, perhaps without much surprise, that the organization was receiving little support from legitimate governments. Internal harmony was just about preserved by the passing of final resolutions condemning imperialism and capitalism, French nuclear tests in the Sahara and apartheid in South Africa.[6]

An important organizational change was effected at Conakry by the establishment of an Executive Committee, to be elected by heads of delegations. The committee, consisting of fourteen African and thirteen Asian representatives, was to meet twice yearly to interpret conference decisions and to decide how to carry them out in practice, control the accounts, fix the dues and appoint the secretariat – so it was in effect the most powerful organ in AAPSO. The committee would clearly circumscribe the independence of the Secretary-General, and thus weaken Egyptian influence in the organization.[7]

But the Conakry Conference marked more than the assertion of Soviet supremacy in AAPSO. Before the meeting there is ample evidence to show that moderate Africans, like John Kale, took AAPSO seriously, and believed that the presence of China and the Soviet Union lent it prestige and dignity. But these people became increasingly alienated by the imposition of the Sino-Soviet dispute on the organization, and by the forcing through of communist-inspired resolutions to which the name of AAPSO gave, to the credulous at least, a neutralist stamp. Many of the moderates, angered particularly by the acrimonious Sino-Soviet exchanges during the preparatory stages of the conference, refused to have anything more to do with AAPSO after Conakry. As a front organization it was 'sprung', and in the ensuing plenary meetings the Soviets were merely preaching to the converted.

OTHER FRONTS

After the Conakry Conference the Sino-Soviet split began to manifest itself more openly in the other front organizations, and at the Stockholm meeting of the World Peace Council in

December 1961 an open vote was taken for the first time between Soviet and Chinese resolutions. The Soviets wished to
convene a World Peace Congress 'for general disarmament and
peace'. The Chinese supported a Guinean amendment, seeking to label it a congress for 'peace, national independence and
disarmament'. Genuine 'fighters for peace' should not tone
down their support for the national liberation movement for
the sake of peaceful co-existence.

To many of the unsuspecting delegates this must have seemed
like semantic time-wasting; but some realized that battle had
been joined. In the words of Velio Spano, an Italian communist
and member of the WPC praesidium, the pro-Soviet majority
realized that

there was a fundamental contrast between the two political lines and
that any attempt at reconciliation would be quite useless.[8]

After the Stockholm Conference, the Chinese muted their
criticisms of the Soviet Union in those organizations where the
Soviets had an overwhelming advantage; they did not, for
example, openly challenge the Soviet line at the 1962 Moscow
World Peace Congress. But they continued to cultivate influence within AAPSO, and later founded Afro-Asian affiliates
such as the Afro-Asian Journalists' Association, the Afro-
Asian Jurists' Association, the Afro-Asian Writers' Association
etc – none of them embodied in the AAPSO constitution and
from which the Soviet Union was excluded.

In February 1962 Chinese influence at a Cairo conference
of Afro-Asian writers prevented a Soviet-backed resolution for
'general and complete disarmament' from reaching the floor;
a Soviet proposal to hold the next meeting in Mongolia was
also vetoed. Delegates complained of the increasing bitterness
of the Chinese and the Soviets towards each other, and it was
at this meeting that the Chinese were first reported to be claiming a racial affinity with the Africans. They even spoke,
according to one reporter,[9] of the need for 'we coloureds' to
band together against the whites.

During the next year, Sino-Soviet wrangling within the
front organizations increased; in AAPSO itself ideological
disputes over the editorial direction of the *Afro-Asian Bulletin*
led to the suspension of publication. Polarization of the various

fronts became evident, with the Chinese encouraging the fringe Afro-Asian organizations, and the Soviets expanding the scope of their well-established fronts. The World Peace Council, for example, founded nine new African National Peace Committees within the space of a few months. The International Union of Students hastily added more African students to its executive, while the World Federation of Democratic Youth arranged for delegations to visit both East and West Africa.

THE MOSHI CONFERENCE

The battleground, for that was how it was coming to be seen by Africans, for the next major Sino-Soviet clash was the small north Tanganyikan town of Moshi, where the third AAPSO conference was held in February 1963. The very fact that it was held in Moshi, and not the capital Dar es Salaam, reflected Tanganyika's concern at the increasing factional strife within AAPSO.[10] In this opening address President Nyerere appealed to the delegates to keep their internal quarrels to themselves. He warned Africans of the dangers of becoming embroiled in international disputes which did not concern them, and added:

I believe the socialist countries themselves, considered as individuals in the larger society of nations, are now committing the same crimes as were committed by the capitalists before. On the international level they are now beginning to use wealth for capitalistic purposes, that is for the acquisition of power and prestige.

If that was meant for Soviet consumption he also had a word for the Chinese:

No one of us should try to do what we so justly accuse the imperialists of doing, intrigue with dissident groups.

The memorable phrase Nyerere coined – 'the second scramble for Africa' – drew unfavourable attention to communist activities on the continent, and became a critical shorthand description of China's and the Soviet Union's African policies.

To be fair, even the WPC made a pre-conference appeal to the delegates to stress the things they had in common, and to try and avoid divisive issues. But the Chinese were in full cry, and scored an early victory when the conference refused official status to the WPC delegation and to other Soviet-backed fronts, allowing only delegations with national mandates from African or Asian states to address the conference. China's chief delegate, Liu Ning-yi, even tried, unsuccessfully, to exclude the Soviet delegates, on the grounds that they were white.

The previous year's Cuban crisis had polarized Russian and Chinese attitudes towards the problems of peaceful co-existence and armed struggle. For the Russians it marked the last stage in a five-year Cold War campaign to probe Western weaknesses, and it had shown them how far the United States was prepared to go in opposing the aggressive designs of communism. It marked the opening of the era of peaceful co-existence. For the Chinese Cuba had been a betrayal. Both sides tried to capitalize on their version of the debacle. In his message of greeting to the conference Krushchev said his Cuban policy had shown how the national independence of a country could be saved while at the same time preserving world peace, a theme stressed by the Soviet delegation during the conference. The Chinese, on the other hand, used the armed struggle of the Algerian people as *their* revolutionary model. They attacked the two-bloc system, in a speech which clearly presaged their later charges of US-Soviet collusion:

The attempt to decide the major problems of the world and to manipulate the destiny of mankind by one or two countries runs counter to the trend of our times and is against the interest of the peoples. (NCNA, Moshi, 11 February 1963)

Liu dismissed as 'deceitful nonsense' the idea that developing countries might benefit from disarmament agreements by receiving increased economic aid. Privately, the Chinese used the Cuban crisis as an example to show that the Soviets had lost their revolutionary zeal, and assured African and Asian leaders, particularly those still fighting for their independence, that this was not the case with China.

Another international issue whose shadow touched the conference was the Sino-Indian border dispute. Africans did not seem too impressed by India's version of the dispute, and only the Indian delegate, Chaman Lall, demanded a resolution favouring the 'unconditional acceptance' of the Colombo powers' proposals for settling the dispute. When this was rejected he walked out of the conference, but returned a few days later to endorse a watered-down resolution whose wording was also acceptable to the Chinese.

The Chinese won an important (for them) semantic point in the wording of the final general declaration, which described the struggle for national liberation as 'a mighty force in achieving peace and disarmament' as opposed to the Soviet formula, which would have had peaceful co-existence and disarmament creating the best conditions for national liberation.

China also scored a bizarre success when the conference was persuaded to adopt a resolution condemning the moderate Congolese government of Cyrille Adoula, a government recognized by the Soviet Union, as well as by a majority of the African governments whose 'representatives' voted for the resolution. More than anything else, this showed how unrepresentative AAPSO had become.

Finally, the Chinese defeated a Soviet plan for the convening of a conference of the three continents – Africa, Asia and Latin America – under which only organizations affiliated to the WPC would have been invited. The Chinese proposal, which was adopted, called for maximum participation of all organizations opposing imperialism, colonialism and neo-colonialism.

The Moshi Conference may have been a victory for the Chinese over the Soviets, but it was a hollow victory, and could more accurately be characterized as a loss for both communist powers. Sino-Soviet in-fighting had exploded the myth of communist solidarity, while Africans began to consider more carefully the *raisons d'être* for other 'international' organizations. Many delegates left Moshi convinced AAPSO had outlived its usefulness.

The first Soviet reactions to the conference came in a carefully worded article admitting to a certain disappointment in AAPSO. In the veiled invective of the ideological war it also criticized the Chinese for their racialist attitudes:

Some of the more chauvinistically inclined leaders would like to direct the solidarity movement, not against imperialism, colonialism and its agents, but against all white people.

These same people, the writer indignantly declared were

prepared to shrug their shoulders at the participation of international organizations such as the WPC.[11]

Later a more specific attack came from the former Soviet secretary of the WPC:

The Chinese try to liquidate peace organizations and replace them with their own exclusive groups. In 1959 their objections began and in December 1961 Liu Ning-yi in Stockholm attacked the whole WPC. The Chinese have practically withdrawn from participation in the activities of the world peace movement and use its meetings merely to undermine it. They aim particularly at the Afro-Asian solidarity movement.[12]

The Chinese were more laconic in their comments. At a Peking rally to celebrate the success of the conference Liu said Moshi 'had repudiated the erroneous arguments of the modern revisionists.'

Notes

1. Schatten, op. cit., p. 227.
2. Schatten, op. cit., p. 274.
3. But AAPSO has never addressed itself, at least practically, to the problems of Asia. It has been primarily an African-oriented movement, and its five plenary meetings have all been held on African soil.
4. According to the Egyptian journal *Rose al Yusuf* (no. 17) China's initial contribution to the budget was $28 000, compared with the Soviet Union's $25 000. Both countries contributed to the travelling and other expenses of delegates to the conferences.
5. E.g. Radio Peking reported in April 1958 that the Asian Solidarity Committee of China and the Chinese Islamic Association had jointly given 500 000 Yuan to the Algerian FLN, through the AAPSO secretariat.
6. Even so, the final resolutions moved away from the Cairo Conference formula of endorsing the Ten Principles of Bandung, and therefore acceptance of peaceful co-existence, to a (Chinese) position of regarding peaceful co-existence only as a distant goal to be achieved after the liquidation of colonialism and all forms of imperial domination.
7. Egyptian influence was weakened still further when the communists succeeded after the Conakry Conference in having the headquarters of the Fund Committee (which had been instituted at the conference to raise and distribute funds to freedom fighters) sited in the Guinean capital. The three directors were the chairman, Ismail Touré, the Guinean Minister of

Public Works, Moroccan opposition leader, Mehdi Ben Barka, and the Chinese nominee, Chu Tzu-chi. According to the *Egyptian Gazette*, initial responses to the Fund's appeal came from Indonesia ($15000), Egypt ($20000), Soviet Union ($20000) and China ($40000 as well as the offer of a number of scholarships).

8. *Unita*, 23 December 1961.

9. Colin Legum, *Observer*, 12 March 1962.

10. The conference had been scheduled to be held in Dar-es-Salaam, but was moved on Nyerere's insistence that he wanted no international quarrelling in his capital.

11. V. Kudryavtsev, 'Thoughts at the foot of Mount Kilimanjaro', *International Affairs*, Moscow, May 1963.

12. V. Chkhidvadze, *Pravda*, August 1963.

5

SINO-SOVIET 'FRIENDLY COMPETITION'

'The Chinese Government strictly respects the sovereignty of recipient countries.'
2nd of China's Eight Principles of
Foreign Aid.

NOT all early Sino-Soviet rivalry in Africa was as drastic as that which ultimately damaged beyond repair the credibility of AAPSO as a front organization, nor was it as fundamental as the divergent ideological views on the situations in Algeria, Cameroon and the Congo. There was a fairly large area in which China and the Soviet Union could indulge in 'friendly competition'; this included distribution of propaganda, by the printed word and by radio, the exchange of students, exhibitions, invitations to groups and individuals to visit communist countries and the allocation of economic aid.

But even in such relatively trouble-free areas, a distinct difference of approach could be detected from the very beginning. For example, the Soviets used a visit to Moscow as a reward for élite groups, whereas the Chinese welcomed to Peking virtually any African who could come – and who could get his government's permission. Thus in 1960, no less than 113 African delegations, including even groups from countries like Gabon, Dahomey and the Ivory Coast, whose governments recognized Taiwan, visited China. They seldom left unimpressed. Their hosts arranged visits to communes, factories and provincial centres, flattered them with banquets attended by leading Chinese politicians, stage-managed huge and impressive welcoming parades and, for early visitors, inevitably arranged a showing of the Chinese documentary film *Hold Aloft the Banner of the Bandung Conference and Support the Struggle of the African People*. Like the imaginary trade-union delegate of the last chapter, who received so much attention at Soviet-organized 'front' meetings, African visitors to Peking were overwhelmed with hospitality.

In 1960 the Chinese-African People's Friendship Association was founded to handle details of these visits, and to organize visits of Chinese officials to African countries. In 1961 a ten-member delegation made an extensive tour of West Africa, visiting Guinea, Ghana, Mali, Niger, Upper Volta, Senegal, Togo and Dahomey. At the same time, Chinese embassy officials in African countries were arranging exhibitions, promoting cultural exchanges and recruiting students – events reported by the New China News Agency, the official Chinese news agency which, by 1961, had offices in Rabat, Cairo, Conakry and Accra. Broadcasting to Africa also significantly increased. At the beginning of 1961 the Soviet Union broadcast forty-one hours per week to Africa, the East European satellites nineteen hours and China thirty-five hours; at the end of that year the Soviet Union had increased her output to seventy-three and a half hours, the satellites to sixty-three and a half and China to sixty-three, including transmissions in the main African native languages.

EARLY AID GIVING

It was in the aid-giving and developmental field of friendly rivalry that China most sought to make a distinction between her approach and that of the Soviet Union. In revolutionary terms we have already seen that China wished to hold up her revolution as the model which independence-seeking countries should copy, seeking to distinguish it from the Soviet experience by stressing its anti-colonial character. Likewise, the Chinese felt that their basically rural developmental experiences since the revolution had more relevance for developing backward African countries than the industrialization of the Soviet Union. Consequently they stressed, and continue to stress, the value of low investment, labour-intensive, cottage industry-type projects.

In their early dealings with Africa the Russians, on the other hand, recommended speedy industrialization, and in their aid projects they tended to become involved in the total economy, a politically dangerous policy because if things began to go wrong, as they did in Guinea, the Russians were blamed for everything – providing, in fact, a convenient scapegoat for local inefficiency. The Soviet Union also put much faith in mighty, prestige projects – showcases like the Aswan Dam and the Bihar Steel-works in India. In contrast, the Chinese concentrated on small projects which showed a quick and maximum return for their investment. These approaches reflected the differences in resources available for aid projects to the Soviet Union and China, but also a different ideological approach: the Soviets calculated that industrialization would produce an industrial proletariat, which in turn would overthrow the existing national bourgeois governments; the Chinese discouraged industrialization for the very reason that their revolution had been essentially a peasant revolution.

The principles of Chinese aid-giving were summarized by Chou En-lai, in the joint communique issued by him and President Mobido Keita of Mali, after the Chinese premier's visit to Mali in early 1964, and subsequently re-stated many times. The 'Eight Principles', which in part summarized Chinese grievances against Soviet aid to China, were:

(1) The Chinese government consistently abides by the principle of equality and mutual benefit in providing aid to other countries. It never regards such aid as a kind of unilateral alms but regards aid as always mutual.

(2) In providing aid to other countries, the Chinese government strictly respects the sovereignty of the recipient countries, and never attaches any conditions or asks for any privileges.

(3) The Chinese government provides economic assistance by giving interest-free or low-interest loans and where necessary extends the time limit for the repayment so as to alleviate as far as possible the burden of the recipient countries.

(4) The purpose of the Chinese government's foreign aid is not to make the recipient countries dependent on China but to help them embark on the road of self-reliance and independent economic development step by step.

(5) The projects which the Chinese government help the recipient countries to build are those which will, as far as possible, require less investment while yielding quicker results, so that the recipient governments may increase their income and accumulate capital.

(6) The Chinese government provides the best quality equipment and material of its own manufacture at international market prices. If the equipment and material provided by the Chinese government are not up to the agreed specifications and quality, the Chinese government undertakes to replace them.

(7) In giving any particular technical assistance, the Chinese government will see to it that the personnel of the recipient country fully master such a technique.

(8) The experts dispatched by the Chinese government to help in construction in the recipient countries will have the same standard of living as the experts of the recipient countries. The Chinese experts are not allowed to make any special demands or enjoy any special amenities.

These principles, which have by and large been observed, were intended to expose the shortcomings of Soviet, and Western, aid. Western aid was – and often still is – regarded by Africans themselves as a 'soft' form of neo-colonialism, designed to consolidate the former colonial trading patterns of raw producer and manufacturer, to the former's disadvantage. For example, all previously French African states, with the exception of Guinea, signed an economic and monetary agreement with France after independence, under which France would continue to buy their raw materials at slightly preferential prices in return for guarantees that they would import the majority of their manufactured requirements from France. (However, the Yaounde Convention of 1964, which made eighteen French speaking states associate members of the European Common Market, did something to weaken that special relationship.) Former British colonies were likewise associated in the Commonwealth preference scheme, and British aid was – and is – too often 'tied' – i.e. the recipient country has to buy British goods, or employ British services, with British aid money.[1] West German aid also came under a

3

cloud when it was used in attempts to enforce the Hallstein Doctrine, notably in Tanzania. As the Secretary of State for Development Aid, Dr Frederick Vialon, said at the time: '*Kein geld fur feinder*' (no money for enemies), a sentiment which Africans interpreted as meaning West Germany thought she could buy African friendship. US aid to Africa was initially welcomed, especially under the administration of Robert Kennedy, who himself had excellent personal contacts with a number of African leaders. But it became increasingly obvious that the largest African recipients of US aid were those countries, like Ethiopia and Morocco, with which the US had defence agreements and in which she maintained military bases. Later, as Vietnam came to have first claim on American resources, aid to Africa declined as US interest in the continent dwindled.[2] Finally the Soviet Union's own aid record came under closer scrutiny, as details of biased barter agreements came to light, and it was discovered the Soviet Union was re-selling on the world market commodities taken in exchange for Soviet goods or services. The relatively harsh repayment terms, and the 2·5 per cent interest usually charged on Soviet loans, were also criticized – a criticism met full on by one Soviet expert who wrote as early as 1960 that

To the USSR, granting of credits and other aid to the backward nations is not a charitable undertaking but assistance on a commercial basis.[3]

Chou's Eight Principles were therefore designed to reflect African grievances against both Western and Soviet aid. China, reluctant to enter into burdensome aid commitments because of her own straitened economic circumstances, nevertheless felt obliged to offer a limited challenge to the Soviet Union.

She initiated her African aid programme in West Africa for a variety of reasons; the unsuitability of North Africa as a recipient of aid was one factor, but the most important was that a number of West African nations were soon, after independence, referring to themselves as socialist states. Even though, politely, denying that status to all of them, including Algeria,[4] China could hardly afford to be seen, in her own euphemistic phraseology, encouraging 'further victories' (i.e. helping to overthrow legitimate governments) in states which she admitted were at least on the way to socialism. A more positive interaction was called for: aid provided the answer.

Throughout China's relationship with Africa the aid programme has been the obverse of the revolutionary image, the 'respectable' side of China's policies. This contrapuntal approach to Africa's problems, the united front-from-above and the united front-from-below policy of cooperating with friends and subverting enemies, is a thread which runs through this book.

China therefore accepted the socialist pretensions of many of the West African governments, particularly those of Guinea, Ghana and Mali, and was prepared to consider government-to-government cooperation. There were also coincidental state reasons for concentrating attention on West Africa, notably worsening relations with Egypt, which made Cairo an unsatisfactory base for China's African operations. Conakry proved an acceptable alternative, both as a centre for cooperative activities and as a base for contacting dissidents and furthering the disruptive ambitions of such groups as the UPC.

COMMUNIST AID TO GUINEA

Guinea was an obvious target for communist blandishments. In 1958, Sekou Touré had organized his people into rejecting de Gaulle's proposals for a Communaute Française, and opting for full independence instead. In an appalling act of spite, and to encourage other French territories not to do the same, de Gaulle withdrew all French administrators and technicians and cut off all aid to Guinea. The withdrawing French are reported to have ripped out telephones, smashed technical equipment and even stripped the police of their uniforms and weapons. The new nation was virtually helpless. Western countries were slow in offering assistance for fear of offending de Gaulle; the communist powers had no such compunctions. They were encouraged anyway by the fact that Touré had studied in Prague, had headed the Guinean branch of the communist-led Confederation Generale des Travailleurs after the war and had formed his own party, the Parti Democratique de Guinée, as a national branch of the Rassemblement Democratique Africain, the mass African party in which the communists had, for a time, enjoyed a certain amount of influence. The first ambassador to arrive in the new republic was from Bulgaria, followed shortly afterwards by ambassadors from the Soviet Union, Hungary, Poland, Czechoslovakia, even Mongolia. China established diplomatic relations in October 1959.

The first two years of Guinea's independence were disastrous, with poor harvests underscoring a rapidly deteriorating economic situation. In this atmosphere Guinea negotiated a 140-million-rouble credit with the Soviet Union in the summer of 1959. Hopes were high that this would solve all Guinea's problems, but when the promised credits did not materialize, Touré himself went to Moscow to talk to Krushchev. The result was Guinea's first three-year plan, heavily tied to Soviet aid and linked with barter trade agreements, under which Guinea exchanged her bananas and other raw produce for bloc-manufactured articles. The plan was to be financed by Soviet credits and put into operation by Soviet technicians. During 1960 over 1000 advisers and experts arrived in Guinea, including Soviet trade-union officials and military advisers. There seemed to be some justification for Western claims that Guinea was rapidly becoming a communist dependency, and a centre for subverting the surrounding region.

The Soviets, however, made serious errors in their dealings with Guinea, which gave the lie to that assessment. Firstly, the long delay in the materialization of their promised credits made it look as if they were holding the country to ransom. Secondly, they miscalculated the type of aid Guinea needed and finally their ambassador, Daniel Solod, was expelled for interfering in the country's internal affairs.

Early Soviet aid to Guinea has long since passed into the canon of awful mistakes. The snowploughs and serried rows of porcelain lavatory bowls on Conakry docks became the unfortunate symbols of the Soviet Union's unhappy knack of blundering around Africa, seemingly determined to do the wrong thing at the wrong time. Apart from wrongly addressing aid packages, the Soviets, in Guinea as elsewhere, catered to the desire of the élite groups for non-productive prestige projects, which seemed to them to symbolize national independence. Allowing for the fact that the author was American ambassador to Guinea at the time, the following account of

Soviet aid projects gives an idea of the extent of the Soviet Union's miscalculations:

Thus by 1961, Conakry was swarming with Soviet bloc technicians and engineers occupied with building a Polytechnic Institute for 1600 students (though there were not more than fifty Guineans qualified to attend); a printing plant that eventually operated at less than 5 per cent capacity; a 100-kw radio station for external transmission (which never worked properly since it was erected over a vein of iron ore); a million-dollar outdoor theatre (half-completed and abandoned); a sea-front hotel (still under construction three years after ground-breaking); a 25 000-seat sports stadium (for a city of 100 000 people); and a national airline equipped with nine Ilyushins (usually grounded), pilots who couldn't speak French and sophisticated radar equipment (there were no fogs) that slowly deteriorated in the damp heat.[5]

At the end of 1961 Soviet diplomacy received a serious setback when ambassador Solod was asked to leave. Although no official reason was given for his departure, apart from a bland an-nouncement that he had been 'recalled to take up another post', it was widely assumed that Solod had encouraged dissi-dent Guinean students and others to march through the streets that November demanding 'pure' communist remedies to the country's problems. Attwood, the US ambassador, claimed that Touré had told him Solod had been caught 'red-handed', and in later speeches in Susu, the local language, Touré admitted that the ambassador had interfered in Guinea's internal affairs and had cooperated with dissidents. Although relations were patched up, it took Soviet diplomacy a long time to recover from the bad publicity attached to the affair. The immediate beneficiaries were the Americans whose offer of a £6·8 million aid package was accepted.

China was not affected by the Soviet Union's misfortunes. Indeed, some of the more spectacular Soviet blunders positively helped to underline the practicality of Chinese aid. In their separate approaches to Guinea, the Soviet Union and China had not, contrary to Western thinking at the time, devised a 'division of labour' policy. In fact, China had been careful to distinguish her aid – through its softer terms and different applications – from that of the Soviet Union. Evidently Guineans were aware of these differences, for Barry Diawadou, the Minister of Education, was saying in 1959 after a trip to Peking:

Since my return I am quite convinced of the efficacy of Chinese methods. I was greatly impressed by the similarity of the economic problems that China has succeeded in solving and those that are now facing the peoples of Africa. In China I saw what can be done if you mobilize the vital forces of a nation. With all due regard to the difference in magnitude we now propose to do the same thing.[6]

The next year, Sekou Touré became the first ever African head of state to visit China, and Guinea, the first African country to receive 'civilian' Chinese aid (Egypt and Algeria had previously received aid for military situations) when China offered a loan of £3·6 million (designated as 100 million roubles). Pointedly, the loan was interest-free, in contrast to the Soviet 2·5 per cent interest rate, and it was agreed Chinese experts would not be paid a salary higher than that paid to an equivalent Guinean official. It was clear that Guineans were intended to draw the contrast between the simple living standards of the Chinese and the 'colonial' style of living for which the Soviet technicians had been criticized locally.

Chinese ideas on collective agriculture were incorporated in the first three-year plan and the Chinese credit was immediately drawn on with the dispatch to Guinea of a rice team.[7] Shortly afterwards construction of a match factory and a cigarette factory in Conakry was begun.

Chinese leaders must have been gratified to note what appeared to be a political dividend for this assistance, for on his return from Peking Touré displayed a noticeably harder, pro-Chinese line, referring in his speeches to the 'imperialist American illegal occupation of Formosa' and opposing the Soviet line on peaceful co-existence. It was in fact a Guinean (implicitly anti-Soviet) amendment at the Stockholm World Peace Council (see p. 42) which caused the first open vote to be taken between Soviet and Chinese lines. Guinea also opposed the giving of Soviet aid to non-socialist African states, criticized the Soviet Union's wavering support for the Algerian FLN and supported the Chinese-backed UPC.[8] These policies could be said to have been independent, flavoured by a certain amount of bitterness towards the Soviet Union. But they had the appearance of being 'pro-Chinese', and were certainly not discouraged in Peking.

Guinea was the first African country to benefit from Chinese aid, and initially it absorbed almost all the resources China had available for this purpose. For however much China may have wanted to contrast her style of aid-giving with that of the Soviet Union, and hold up her own developmental experiences as the model for poor, rural African countries, her ability to do so was circumscribed by domestic economic circumstances.

A severe economic crisis had been brought on by natural disasters, by the withdrawal in July 1960 of all Soviet aid experts and by the failure of the Great Leap Forward. For the first few years of the decade, ideological turmoil, precursing by some six years the stormy events of the cultural revolution, raged in China between supporters of Mao's extreme left ideology – the belief in the power of 'subjective' forces – and those who were later to be labelled the 'capitalist top-roaders', leaders who counselled a certain amount of economic planning and even renewed reliance on Soviet aid.

This preoccupation with domestic affairs, coupled with the depletion of resources available for aid purposes, meant that China had to be very selective in her choice of recipients – scarce resources could not be wasted, and every yuan had to count. Nevertheless, a number of countries other than Guinea did benefit from Chinese aid, although it was noticeable that aid programmes were very slowly implemented, and in some cases it took up to two years before the protocol to an aid agreement was signed. Except in a very few cases, aid was in the form of the provision of Chinese goods and services, usually those of agricultural or technical experts, because of the severe lack of foreign exchange in China. All the same, a number of governments expressed gratitude to China for her aid efforts and there is little doubt that its practical nature was greatly appreciated. The fact that China, herself a developing country, was able to make *any* aid donations was frequently commented on.

GHANA

The identity of views between the Soviet Union and Ghana's

first president, Kwame Nkrumah, was considerable. In the years before the formation of the Organization of African Unity, African nations had split into two blocs, the Casablanca Group, which held radical Pan-African views similar to those held by the Soviet Union,[9] and the more conservative Monrovia Group. Leadership of the Casablanca Group, composed of Ghana, Guinea, Mali, Morocco, the Algerian provisional government and Egypt, was contested by Nkrumah and Nasser, both of whom were cultivated by the Soviet Union, which shared their Pan-African views. Ghana received considerable amounts of aid from the Soviet Union, but China decided to put in a limited challenge.

In August 1961 Nkrumah visited Peking. He arrived directly from Moscow and his opening remark – 'War in our time would be a calamity and would substantially eliminate civilization as we know it' – certainly reflected current Soviet thinking. Nevertheless, he left with a £7 million loan, offered conspicuously interest-free in contrast to the Soviet Union's harder terms, and repayable, in Ghanaian exports or a third-party currency, over ten years with a nine-year grace period. The two countries also signed a trade agreement, under which they would each grant the other a £4 million yearly credit for the purchase, by Ghana, of machine tools, building and road construction machinery and agricultural implements, and by China of industrial diamonds, cocoa, tobacco and coffee.

Ghana's proposals as to how the loan might be utilized proved an early obstacle to the swift implementation of the aid. The Ghanaian side wanted a textile factory built, but that in turn depended on the importation of raw cotton, a measure which Ghana could not afford. No aid project had been decided on by the time of Chou En-lai's visit to Ghana in 1964; he suggested to Nkrumah that China was perhaps better placed to assist with Ghana's agricultural development, and later that year Chinese rice experts arrived with the object of making Ghana self-sufficient in rice within two years.

However, even the idea of Chinese aid had some beneficial results for Ghana. The Chinese insistence on low salaries for their experts, coupled with Ghanaian criticism of the high standard of living enjoyed by Soviet aid-personnel, led in January 1962 to the Soviets agreeing to halve their experts' salaries – all of which had previously been paid by Ghana – and themselves paying half of the new amount.

MALI

Mali also received an interest-free loan of £7 million in 1961, but the implementation of projects seems to have been swifter than in Ghana. China agreed immediately to supply machinery to help Mali build up industries to process her raw materials, mainly groundnuts, meat, rice and cotton. Technical and agricultural experts arrived shortly afterwards, and within a short time the Chinese had established a reputation for their hard work and dedication. In 1962 a public health exhibition was staged by the Chinese in Bamako and in the following year a broadcasting cooperation agreement was signed by the two countries.

OTHER AID

Other early Chinese aid initiatives included the announcement of a loan of £17 million to Algeria in October 1963, the same month that the Soviet Union made a £34 million loan. However, an agreement on how the loan might be utilized was not signed for another year, which annoyed the Algerians as they wanted to assist urgently the depressed Constantine area. By 1966, only £1 million of the loan had been utilized, and it was not until well after the cultural revolution that the Chinese were able to honour fully the commitment they had made some ten years previously.

The first major aid initiative in East Africa was taken in September, 1963, with a loan of £7·2 million to Somalia following the visit to Peking in August of Prime Minister (later President) Shermarke. This was given to balance Somalia's deficit budget, and may have been partly in gratitude for being allowed to beam Chinese radio programmes from the Chinese-erected 60000-watt transmitter near Mogadiscu, one of the most powerful in Africa. Equally, it was also probably a response to a growing Soviet interest in the horn of Africa, itself caused by the withdrawal of Western aid from Somalia. (see p. 89).

Notes

1. E.g. in 1970 48 per cent of British aid was so tied.

2. Africans also took exception to the 'conspicuous consumption' (Chou's eighth principle) of many American aid experts, although the introduction of the Peace Corps blunted some of that criticism.

3. Professor Smirnov in *USSR International Currency and Credit Relations*, 1960, p. 275.

4. The Soviet Union, in her anxiety to cultivate early nationalist leaders, conceded that they were 'candidates for socialism' or even well on the way down the path of socialism, an action which she was later to regret when their socialism, and their friendship for the Soviet Union, became suspect. Now, they are considered to be only 'on the path of non-capitalist development', and the attainment of socialism is decades, rather than years, away.

5. *The Reds and the Blacks*, by William Attwood, Hutchinson, London, 1967.

6. *Le Figaro*, 25 December 1959.

7. According to one report (*Observer*, 11 March 1962) the local inhabitants tried to force the rice team out under the slogan 'The Chinese never leave once they have settled.' This attitude was unfounded, as was a similar Moslem-inspired fear, common at the time when China and the Chinese were an unknown quantity in Africa, that the Chinese were trying to 'convert' Africans to godless communism.

8. The UPC leader, Moumié, travelled on a Guinean passport; Guinea also gave material support to the UPC, according to a statement made by Cameroon Foreign Minister, Charles Okala, to the Yaounde Parliament on 9 December 1960.

9. The Group wanted, for example, to form an African common market and a military high command for the entire continent which would have been based at Accra.

6

CHOU EN-LAI'S
TOUR OF AFRICA

*'Mr Chou En-lai came to Africa wearing two
hats: a silk topper and a guerrilla beret'*
The Observer

FOR six weeks, from 14 December 1963 to 4 February 1964,
with a short interlude to visit Albania, Chou En-lai, accompanied by Chen Yi and about forty Chinese officials, toured
ten African countries.[1] The purpose of his visit, he said, was to

enhance the mutual understanding between China and the friendly
African countries, strengthen the traditional friendship between the
Chinese people and the African people, further develop the relations
of friendship and cooperation between China and the African
countries, increase our knowledge and learn useful things from the
African people. (NCNA, Accra, 17 January 1964)

He came, in other words, to hear what Africans thought about
China, to see for himself how effective the Chinese presence
was and, with the aid of his note-taking entourage, to draw up
if necessary new Chinese policies for the continent. There were
subsidiary reasons for his tour too: it symbolized China's
efforts to break out of US containment and to show that she had
global interests; it was an attempt to explain China's attitudes
towards the 1963 Moscow nuclear-test-ban treaty (which had
been ratified by all African nations with the exception of
Guinea, Congo-Brazzaville and the Central African Republic);
it was undertaken to boost China's image, tarnished as far as
the moderates were concerned by her support for subversion,

and to explain to friends that the flagging aid effort was caused by the temporary Chinese economic crisis and would be expanded when circumstances permitted. Finally, Chou was seeking African support for the convening of a 'Second Bandung' – a meeting of African and Asian nations without Soviet participation – before the holding of a proposed second non-aligned summit (a 'Second Belgrade'), which China could not attend since she considered herself aligned – on the side of 'progressive' nations.

The tour emphasized the dichotomous nature of China's African policies, with Chou playing in different places on the themes of peace and struggle, progress and poverty, weakness and strength, cooperation and opposition. He stressed the similarities between China and Africa, and played down the differences; he patiently explained China's state policies and tactfully propagated her ideology. For a 65-year-old man, attended constantly by a doctor and two nurses, the 53-day tour was a diplomatic *tour de force* which few other statesmen in the world could have carried off. Personally, the tour was a great success for him and his diplomatic skill and tact were widely commented on. In Cairo he even gave away prizes to Islamic theological students; everywhere, according to a Western reporter who accompanied him, he managed to 'hug babies without looking like a politician and pump hands without a trace of humbug'. His own international standing was considerably enhanced.

But he could not have failed to have seen the difficulties facing China in Africa, and his attention was constantly being drawn to the shortcomings of Chinese policies. In Egypt he was shown the great Soviet-built Aswan Dam,[2] reminding him of the limited resources with which China could attempt to compete with the Soviet Union in the aid field. In Tunisia and Ethiopia he was closely questioned about what those countries interpreted as China's obstructive attitude towards the nuclear-test-ban treaty. In Algeria he learned that Africans resented Chinese pretensions to lead the revolutionary struggle; China's help was welcome – but Africa's revolution should be won, and led, by Africans, he was told. In Morocco he learned of King Hassan's fears that Algeria was to become a communist bridgehead, and even as he was talking of the growing friendship between the peoples of China and Morocco, members of the (admittedly pro-Soviet) communist party were being tried in Rabat on charges of subversion. In West Africa, particularly in Ghana, he saw signs of considerable Soviet influence, and had to compare large-scale Soviet aid schemes with China's more modest programmes. In East Africa he had to face the fact that China had yet to make any impact at all. Everywhere he would have sensed African resentment at the intrusion of the Sino-Soviet dispute on African and international affairs, for which China was held primarily responsible. He was also made aware of the intense distrust felt by moderate, 'bourgeois' leaders for revolutionary Chinese ideology. As *Jeune Afrique*, the left-wing African weekly, pointed out:

If, for leftist militants . . . China appears to be a model for development . . . the country has quite another image for African governments. For them, China is the standard-bearer of part of their own opposition. By giving Chou too much honour they reinforce this oppositional fringe.

The most forceful critic of China's policies was President Bourguiba of Tunisia who stunned dinner guests with a critical speech at a farewell banquet for the Chinese premier. Afterwards, he recalled what he had said:

I told him straight that 'accepting your existence does not mean accepting your ideas . . .' I told him what shocked us in his manner, style and conceptions. I said: 'You come to Africa as the enemy of the capitalist states, of the West, of the socialists, of the neutralists and the non-aligned, of India, of Tito, of Krushchev, of everybody. You haven't chosen a policy of facility, I'll say that. Don't expect to score much in Africa. Others won't tell you straight; I will – you won't get far in this continent . . . We don't like your way of arranging frontier issues.'[3]

NORTH AFRICA

In North Africa Chou had to concede the enormous difficulties in the way of an effective Chinese policy. Independence had been won, bourgeois leaders were in power, extremists were in jail and Chinese revolutionary theory was rejected. What these countries needed most was economic assistance; being relatively rich, and with pretensions to industrialization, they wanted to purchase on easy terms sophisticated capital equipment, they wanted help in constructing steel mills, dams and petro-chemical plants and they wanted to import technical know-how. China was simply not in a position to satisfy these wants. The cottage industries and rice schemes which constituted the strength of Chinese aid to West Africa were in North Africa simply symbols of backwardness. Here the two old-fashioned propeller-driven charter aircraft, piloted by two Dutchmen, that transported Chou and his team were objects of ridicule. In West Africa they were symbols of brotherhood. In North Africa Chou was also introduced to the complexities of Islam and Arab nationalism, two supra-national forces which did not easily fit into the Chinese world view.

In these countries Chou was at his most conciliatory. In Cairo he saw the 'daily strengthening and development of the friendly relations between China and the UAR' as providing 'an eloquent proof that countries with different social systems can live together in peace and on the basis of the five principles of peaceful co-existence and the ten principles of Bandung'.

In Tunisia he praised that country's 'new, great victories in recovering from the hands of the colonialists its own territory of Bizerta', and he turned away Bourguiba's brash criticisms of Chinese policy by declaring that: 'We can certainly march forward arm-in-arm in the spirit of seeking common ground between us while reserving our differences.'

In Morocco he praised the people's efforts to 'safeguard their national independence and recover foreign military bases' and the government's support 'for the independence struggle of the African people still under colonial domination'.

Chou was also conciliatory about two international issues on which China's position had caused misunderstanding and in some cases resentment: the Sino-Indian border dispute and the nuclear-test-ban treaty. On the latter he repeated China's argument that in her view the test-ban treaty had been concluded by Britain, the US and the Soviet Union with a view to monopolizing nuclear weapons; it was in effect nuclear 'blackmail' against the non-nuclear powers. China believed in the complete prohibition and destruction of all nuclear weapons, and opposed the creation of an exclusive, big power nuclear club. She would continue her own nuclear research, but would never be the first to use a nuclear weapon. Greeted on arrival in Ethiopia by Haile Selassie's statement that Ethiopia had 'eagerly associated herself' with the treaty, Chou quietly agreed that: 'Our countries differ in systems, and the policies we pursue are not completely the same, but since we are getting together our aim is to seek common grounds and to try and eliminate or reserve our differences for the time being.'

On the Sino-Indian dispute Chou emphasized that China's disengagement had gone beyond the proposals made by the Colombo powers, and he repeated the historical reasons for Chinese claims.[4]

ALGERIA

Considering China's unequivocal support for the Algerian revolution, Chou could have expected a better welcome than he got in Algiers. But on the eve of his arrival the official government newspaper *Le Peuple* carried a full-page interview with Krushchev, in which he fully explained his idea that peaceful co-existence and struggle for liberation were compatible. This compares with the six inches of space devoted by the same newspaper to Chou's arrival, the sparse turn-out at the airport and the poor crowds on the route into the city, blamed by officials on 'cold rain and short notice'.[5] One experienced observer blamed the poor reception on the bad personal relations between Chinese and Algerians:

Despite constant indoctrination, and despite China's very real help during and after the Algerian war, the Chinese are not popular in Algiers. The ways of the Chinese embassy here, with its quota of bossy, trousered, utterly sexless Chinese women, baffle the Algerians. Few Chinese diplomats speak French, but entertainment habits and thought processes here are still predominantly French.[6]

The same reporter noted that Chen Yi spent an entire lunch sitting between two Algerian officials without saying a single word.

But despite the lukewarmness of the reception Chou felt he was on firmer revolutionary ground in Algeria. In a speech to the FLN cadres he referred to 'revolution, the locomotive of history', which would 'break all barriers and speed onward at all events'. He even struck a glancing blow at the Soviets whose support for the Algerian revolution had been so opportunistic:

The Algerian revolutionaries have been able . . . to bring the national liberation struggle from victory to victory because they are under a correct leadership, have confidence in the strength of the people, despise the strength of the enemy and uphold the anti-imperialist revolutionary line, and combat the capitulationist line which does not oppose imperialism but is opposed to revolution. (NCNA, Algiers, 27 December 1963)

But Algeria, for so long the darling of Chinese African policy, was herself anxious to lead and inspire the African revolution[7] and Chou learned of resentment at Chinese claims that her revolution was the true model for Africa. In turn, Chou could not agree with the Algerian claim that Algeria was building socialism. After hours of wrangling the final communiqué admitted only that Algeria had 'decided to take the socialist road' (which compared with the Soviet formula that Ben Bella was 'transforming Algeria on the basis of socialism').

WEST AFRICA

In West Africa, which Chou visited after a ten-day interlude in Albania, peaceful co-existence and revolutionary violence were stressed equally. In Guinea he touched on a theme which Lin Piao was later to develop into his famous theory of the developing nations, the world's countryside, surrounding and defeating the world's 'towns', the industrial nations:

The world situation today is favourable to the struggle of the peoples to win and preserve independence and freedom and unfavourable to imperialism and new and old colonialism. The national liberation movements in Asia, Africa and Latin America have formed an irresistible torrent pounding the embankment of imperialism and colonialism. The powerful national democratic revolutionary movements in these areas are effectively hitting at and weakening the imperialist forces of war and have contributed immensely to the cause of the people throughout the world in opposing imperialism and defending world peace. (NCNA, Conakry, 24 January 1964)

In Guinea Chou's attention was drawn to China's seemingly contradictory foreign policy. The Yugoslavian embassy distributed a pamphlet entitled 'The Two Chou's' which juxtaposed remarks Chou had made earlier in his tour about peaceful co-existence with a vitriolic attack made on the 'Tito revisionists' during his stay in Albania. Which Chou should Africa believe, the pamphlet asked? Chou also broke the diplomatic rule of not referring to third parties when he made a speech in Guinea attacking US policies in Panama. The Ministry of Information had not given clearance for the speech, and his remarks about the US were cut out of newspaper and radio reports.

Another pamphlet, 'Friends and Comrades in Africa', was distributed to the crowd at Mali's Bamako airport as Chou's aeroplane came in to land. Prepared by the Soviets, it purported to be a recitation of Soviet aid and friendship, but was in fact a thinly disguised attack on the Chinese. Mali was not a good place to mount such criticisms, for in fact Chinese aid was widely appreciated, a fact acknowledged by President Keita when he paid

warm homage to the People's Republic of China for the low cost of its technical assistance, for the readiness of its technicians to adapt themselves to the lives of our people, for the speed and competence with which the projects . . . are carried out one by one, and all these are done without the slightest attention of interfering in our internal affairs. (NCNA, Bamako, 16 January 1964)

Chou seemed anxious in West Africa to disarm criticism. In every country he visited he recited the eight principles of Chinese aid-giving, and reassured his hosts that political relations would continue to be based on the principles of Bandung. In Ghana he agreed to a new £8 million loan to help Nkrumah's seven-year plan, but, in keeping with the low profile he was adopting, the two sides agreed that an announcement of the offer should not be made until he returned to China.

CHOU'S SUMMARY

Chou waited until the last country of his tour, Somalia, before

making his definitive summary of Chinese prospects in Africa.
He told a mass rally in Mogadiscu that

The African continent, which has given birth to a brilliant, ancient
civilization and suffered from the most cruel colonial aggression and
plunder, is now undergoing earth-shaking changes. More than thirty
African countries have become independent, and those African
peoples still under colonial oppression and partition are waging
heroic struggles to win independence and freedom. Revolutionary
prospects are excellent throughout the African continent. (NCNA,
Mogadiscu, 3 February 1964)

Chou's last phrase (sometimes translated as 'Africa is ripe for
revolution') reverberated round the continent. It seemed to
confirm the worst fears of such moderates as Bourguiba and
Haile Selassie, to give credence to exaggerated claims about the
'Chinese menace', and it gave Western journalists for years a
convenient shorthand way of describing China's African
policies. They could not, or more likely would not, see that by
'revolution' Chou meant 'change' – not necessarily violent –
and that he would hardly crown a goodwill tour by alienating
friend and foe alike by implying that independent African
governments should be overthrown by force. Asked at a press
conference the next day to amplify his remark, Chou, perhaps
already alarmed by the unfavourable publicity it had attracted,
said he had been referring to the 'national democratic revolution' which meant the struggle for complete independence. In
his terminology, Morocco's action in forcing the US to remove
her military bases from Moroccan soil was 'revolutionary'.

Chou's parting remarks tended to obscure the previously
conciliatory tone of his tour. China, as he had told several of
his hosts, had different views to them on various problems –
they must quietly agree to differ, and instead stress the ideas
they held in common. But it was a fairly bleak message that he
had to take back to Peking with him. He had failed to win a
single word of endorsement for China's position in the Sino-
Soviet dispute, and with the solitary exception of Mali no
country had agreed to China's insistent suggestion that a
'Second Bandung' of Asian and African nations be held before
a 'Second Belgrade' of non-aligned nations. And although he
had cemented relations with the radical states, Chou had

further alienated the moderate ones, not even necessarily by anything he had said or done, but simply by his very presence on African soil, which was regarded in some way as 'ominous'. This arms-length attitude was typified by an editorial in the Lagos *Daily Times*, which called him 'one of the world's most dangerous men' and continued

China, like most communist countries, believes religiously that Africa and Africans are the victims of imperialism, plagued by abject poverty and clamped in chains. This image has been so successfully conjured up for them by their propagandists that there is total blindness in communist countries to the realities of under-developed states . . .

We do not know what Chou En-lai has learned from his hosts in the course of his present tour. But Nigeria should have seized the opportunity to invite him to Lagos and tell him that what Africa wants is bread, freedom from ignorance, eradication of disease and speeded enlightenment. Africa does not need guns, bullets and bombs. Secondly we should have given Chou En-lai ample oppor-tunity to see for himself and understand that Africa does not necessarily have to solve its problems by adopting Chinese methods.[8]

This was a typical moderate reaction to Chou's tour, summariz-ing the suspicion with which China was viewed, both as a result of her activities and of hostile propaganda. During the next few years, when Chinese diplomats and journalists were expelled from a number of African countries for supposed subversive activities, this Chinese 'bogey' school of thought had plenty of material on which to work. Some even assumed a new 'revolutionary policy' had been initiated *during* Chou's tour. Referring to the army mutinies in Tanganyika, Kenya and Uganda, Lord Colyton tabled in the House of Lords the cryptic question: 'Is it a coincidence that Chou En-lai is in Africa?' The answer was certainly an equally cryptic 'yes', but the question summarized Western suspicion about China's African policies at that time.

However, the facts do not allow us to deduce that Chou's tour led him to advocate a more subversive role for China in Africa. Chinese policy continued to exhibit those schizophrenic qualities which characterized her activities in the period before Chou's tour: cooperation with, and aid to, certain selected radical governments in whose countries the Chinese behaved with impeccable correctness, and support for opposition groups in other countries, where that support did not conflict with China's state interests.

What did emerge gradually – and one must assume that it came about as a result of what Chou had learned – was a change in geographical emphasis. He had been able to assess the difficulties posed to China in North Africa by such factors as Arab nationalism and by competition in the aid-giving field from the West and the Soviet Union. He had found there – and elsewhere – that Africans did not want to become embroiled in the Sino-Soviet dispute. Tunisia, Morocco and even Algeria had been overtly suspicious of China's motives. A gradual slackening of Chinese interest in this region is perceptible after 1964, and the focus of Chinese attention moved from North, and to a lesser extent, West Africa towards the eastern half of the continent.

Notes

1. The Chinese showed considerable flexibility in the planning of the tour. Their first announcement said Chou would be visiting Egypt, Algeria and Morocco; a later one said invitations had also been extended by the West African countries with which China had relations. While Chou was in Morocco, Tunisia was added to his itinerary. In early January, thanks to diplomatic efforts by Ho Ying, the Chinese ambassador in Dar es Salaam, it was announced Chou would also be visiting Tanganyika, Uganda and Kenya – but these plans were later cancelled when the armies of all three countries mutinied in mid-January. At the end of January, within days of Chou arriving there, China sought, and received an invitation to visit Ethiopia. It seems this was so that the Emperor could put his side of the Ethiopian-Somali border dispute before Chou arrived in Mogadiscu. The patched-up nature of the visit was emphasized by Chou being received, not in the capital Addis Ababa, but in Asmara.

2. This was very much against his wishes. The Chinese side suggested strongly that additional talks with Nasser would be preferable to a visit to the dam, but the Egyptians insisted on going ahead with the planned programme. Thus on his first few days on African soil Chou unwillingly had to make propaganda for the Soviet Union; he had no chance of propagating Chinese propaganda as Egyptian newspapers were under strict instructions not to print any of his remarks that could be construed as either anti-Soviet or anti-American.

3. *Jewish Observer* and *Middle East Review*, London, 3 April 1964.

4. Proposals for a peaceful settlement of the dispute had come from Guinea, Egypt and Tanganyika. Most African states lacked information about the situation, but this did not prevent Niger from accusing China of outright aggression, or Ethiopia, Tunisia, Nigeria, Malawi, Egypt and even Mali from making lesser criticisms – an example of African opinion being shaped by Western reporting. However, the Africans were afraid that Nehru's acceptance of aid from the West would jeopardize his neutrality – Nkrumah even wrote to Harold Macmillan deploring the British offer of arms to India – and were therefore cautious about lining up with India and the imperialists. To its credit, the Tanganyikan government asked the Chinese and Indian envoys in Dar es Salaam to submit more information about the dispute: while the Chinese embassy produced maps, photostats of treaties, plans showing troop dispositions etc., the Indians could provide no documentary evidence to back up their case – see Cornelius Ogunsanwo, *China's Policy in Africa 1958–68*, unpublished thesis for Ph.D. (London), kept at the London School of Economics, p. 146. At a rank and file level, in East Africa at least, Africans were not unamused by the humiliating defeat suffered by India, the mother country of the unpopular Asian minorities. China tried to make capital out of this mood and produced a propaganda film called *Zanzibar marches forward* which in crudely rigged shots depicted Africans being exploited by ruthless Indian 'taskmasters'. Asian organizations in Kenya collected money for the cause, offered to send volunteers to fight and the women resolved to knit warm clothes for the Indian troops.

5. There were poor crowds at most of the places Chou visited, probably because governments did not want to draw too much attention to the arrival of a revolutionary 'firebrand' in their midst.

6. Edward Behr, *Sunday Times*, 29 December 1963.

7. In a report on Algeria while Chou was there, NCNA said Algeria had trained over 1000 freedom fighters from colonial territories. There are still training camps in Algeria today, and most of the liberation movements have branch offices in Algiers.

8. A comment by the same newspaper, after China and Nigeria had established diplomatic relations in 1971, illustrates the effectiveness with which China had changed her image: 'China's new leadership defeated events. They conquered fate. This is an important lesson for those of us in the poor nations of Africa and Asia who prefer to remain poor imitators of some developed nations.' (*Daily Times*, 22 January 1973.)

7

A 'SECOND BELGRADE'
OR A
'SECOND BANDUNG'?

*The Chinese seem to have become obsessed
with the need to hold the meeting as scheduled*

AN AFRICAN FOREIGN MINISTER

DURING, and immediately after, Chou's tour of Africa,
China's main foreign preoccupation was the convening of a
'Second Bandung' of Asian and African nations, excluding the
Soviet Union.

China's need for this conference was directly related to the
events of 1963, in the course of which her dispute with the
Soviet Union had come to a head. The Communist parties of
the two countries met to discuss their differences in Moscow in
July. In August the US, Britain and the Soviet Union signed
the nuclear-test-ban treaty. This proved to be the last straw,
convincing the Chinese leaders of Krushchev's duplicity. The
Cuban missile crisis had shown him to be a weak adventurist;
his lack of support for Peking over the Sino-Indian border
dispute showed he was anti-China. Now there was the nuclear-
test-ban treaty – 'nuclear blackmail' as it was described by
Chinese spokesmen – a plot to prevent China from acquiring
her own means of defence. Chinese statements began referring
to a Soviet-US alliance aimed at China and Chen Yi told an
interviewer that the Sino-Soviet Treaty of Friendship, Alliance
and Mutual Assistance was invalid – 'these sort of promises are
easy to make, but they are worth nothing'.[1]

China's foreign policy objectives were clear. She had to put herself at the head of a broad united front of all the world's anti-imperialists (and if possible anti-revisionists[2]) to combat the isolation she felt creeping in on her. She embarked on an offensive on all fronts, diplomatic, economic and revolutionary, to win friends.[3] Chou's tour, and his canvassing of support for a new Bandung Conference, were important components of the new strategy.

A preparatory meeting for the proposed conference was held in Djakarta in April 1964, during which China successfully argued against Soviet participation. During the next few months the Soviet Union's credentials for participating were widely debated, with China investing a considerable amount of diplomatic effort into winning support for her views. Some bizarre horse-trading took place: on a visit to Pakistan Chen Yi said China would not raise at the conference the question of the Sino-Indian border dispute, and urged Pakistan not to raise the Kashmir question – in an apparent effort to neutralize Indian support for Soviet participation. And when even Indonesia indicated she might not be able to oppose Soviet participation, China hinted she would in that case be unable to support the Indonesian view on Malaysia (although previously she had vigorously supported Indonesia's 'Crush Malaysia' campaign). Chou himself travelled to Africa twice in three months in an attempt to enlist support.[4]

Propaganda on the subject gives an idea of the intense hostility between the former allies. In a note to participating governments, the Soviet Union accused the Chinese of 'trying to do violence to geography in order to cause estrangement between the Soviet Union and the other Afro-Asian countries'. It observed that the Chinese government was 'harping more and more on race as the factor which, it contends, should determine community of political interests and the possibility of joint action on the international scene' and added that an attempt was being made

... to instill little by little an attitude of suspicion towards many peoples of socialist countries merely because they are 'whites' ... The CPR government's preaching of race is no more than a false cloak for its ambitions of hegemony among the Afro-Asian countries. (*New Times*, No. 19, 1964)

The Chinese reply, contained in the *Peking Review* of May 1964, described the Soviet Union's charges as 'drivel and nonsense'. The racial accusation was false; there were, after all, white people in Africa and Asia too – what united African and Asian peoples was not race, but their common desire to safeguard their independence against old and new imperialism. The accusation that China had manipulated the Djakarta Conference showed scant respect for the other twenty-one countries present. Finally, the Soviet Union would make itself a 'laughing stock' by her attitude.

The Soviet Union pressed her claims insistently. When Krushchev visited Egypt in May the joint communiqué started: 'The Soviet Union, being a Euro-Asian power, again confirms its solidarity with the UAR, an Afro-Asian country . . .'

Nevertheless she appeared to be adopting a reasonable attitude, insisting in her note that she would not 'allow the question of [her] invitation to be embarrassing to other African-Asian countries'.

While these arguments were going on China received a rebuff when all her African friends – with the exception of Mali – attended a meeting in Colombo in March 1964 to plan the next 'non-aligned' summit. Chou had made it plain during his tour that China wanted the African-Asian conference to precede a non-aligned meeting and it was therefore a blow to China's prestige when the Colombo meeting decided a 'Second Belgrade' would be held in Cairo that October, six months before the 'Second Bandung' was due to be held in Algiers. China's prestige further suffered when the Cairo meeting endorsed the idea of peaceful co-existence despite the advocacy of China's more militant formulas by her protegé, Indonesia.[5]

Meanwhile, the 'Second Bandung' itself was running into difficulties. In February Algeria asked for a postponement of the conference until June, which was granted. China had not in the meantime been able to secure in advance a guarantee that the Soviet Union would be excluded.

All the pre-conference manœuvrings were in any case negated when, ten days before the conference was due to open, Colonel Houari Boumedienne overthrew the government of President Ben Bella. The Chinese delegation of thirty-five were already on their way to Algiers, but their aeroplane was refused permission to land and they had to return to Cairo. However, the Chinese ambassador in Algiers immediately called on Boumedienne, indicated that China would recognize the new regime and urged that the conference be convened as scheduled.

China also pressed this course on her African friends. One foreign minister, well-disposed towards China, said

The Chinese seem to have become obsessed with the need to hold the meeting as scheduled. I have seldom before encountered such heavy pressurizing tactics as on this occasion.[6]

The immediate reaction of the majority of participants was to request an indefinite postponement; fifteen African and Asian members of the Commonwealth then meeting in London urged this course. China, however, still believed it could be held, for Chen Yi arrived in Algiers expressing confidence that the conference would be a success. But at the preparatory Foreign Ministers' meeting, attended by only thirty-six of the expected sixty-four participants, the conference was finally postponed until November.

During the ensuing months China's attitude to the desirability of holding a 'Second Bandung' became noticeably lukewarm. There were several good reasons for this: many[7] states said during this period that they would not attend the postponed conference, so there was a danger that a conference which China had so vigorously supported would be a failure; secondly, Chinese missions had been expelled from three African countries in the first half of 1965 and she had been involved in the abortive coup in Indonesia – actions for which she might well be censured at an African-Asian conference; thirdly, her high-handed actions in trying to have the conference held at all costs had alienated previously neutral countries; finally, there was now a live danger that the Soviet Union would be invited to participate.

China therefore decided against the conference. Policy statements gradually made Peking's real position clear. In September Chou said it would be 'useless' to hold the conference unless the nations involved decided beforehand to condemn US aggression in Vietnam. China now insisted that not only should the Soviet Union be excluded from the conference, but

also UN Secretary-General U Thant – 'an agent of US imperialism' – who had been invited by Ben Bella. In October
China announced that she would boycott the conference, and
on 1 November it was finally cancelled by the Foreign Ministers
meeting in Algiers.

It is possible to argue that since China had made it clear
after the June postponement that she was opposed to the
holding of the conference, its final cancellation reflected her
wishes and was therefore in some way a diplomatic triumph.
This was not so. Many moderate African leaders were shocked
at the cynical way in which the Chinese had first recognized
the new Algerian government in order to have the conference
held as planned, and then imposed impossible conditions to try
and secure its cancellation when they found holding it would
not suit them. According to Colin Legum

Their role in this matter did the Chinese more damage in the eyes of
African leaders disposed to friendship with them than any single
action of theirs since they arrived on the African scene.[8]

AAPSO

The prolonged debate about a second African-Asian conference
did not prevent the holding of a fourth AAPSO conference, at
Winneba, Ghana, in May 1965. The conference was preceded
by a meeting of AAPSO's Executive Committee in Algiers during
March, a meeting which was so marred by Sino-Soviet squabbling that a neutralist bloc was formed, which presented the
Soviets and the Chinese with the ultimatum to keep their
dispute out of AAPSO, or leave the organization. After the
meeting a delegation from the neutralists travelled to Cairo
to wrest an assurance from the secretariat that in future
ideological debate would be excluded from AAPSO's meetings.
Ben Bella himself, looking forward to the Winneba Conference,
pleaded that 'debate should first and foremost be on Africa
and Asia; the next conference should be more positive and its
character limited to the Afro-Asian sphere'.

This was to be a pious hope. The disruptive processes begun
at Moshi were continued at Winneba, and the non-representa-
tive nature of many of the delegates reflected the disenchant-
ment of legitimate governments with AAPSO. Once again, the

Sino-Soviet dispute dominated proceedings, with the Soviets mounting an anti-Chinese photo display outside the conference hall and the *People's Daily* claiming that 'a struggle between two lines ran through the whole conference'. The fact that China seemed to have imposed its 'line', as measured by the tone and content of the final resolutions,[9] did not at all impress African leaders. Most of them were alienated by China's militancy, contrasting it unfavourably with what they saw as the Soviet Union's reasonableness. The (pro-Soviet) Algerian Communist Party newspaper, *Alger Republicain*, attacked the Chinese for 'making a scandal', and said: 'Only the Chinese delegate did not understand the importance of calm debate. The Chinese delegate's speech did not contain a single fact or proof to support his accusation that the USSR should be likened to imperialism.'

The Winneba Conference attracted more than usually strong criticism in the African press, much of it stressing points which should by now have become obvious to the Chinese: first, Africans were very bored by the imposition of the Sino-Soviet dispute on their problems, and for which they primarily blamed the Chinese; second, the majority of African nations were by now independent, and their leaders were concerned, not with the problems of revolution, but those of economic development.

It had been decided at Winneba that AAPSO's next conference should be held, for the first time, on Asian soil – in Peking. Several nations, including the Soviet Union and India, made it immediately clear that they would not attend such a conference, and in February 1967 an Executive Committee meeting in Cyprus officially reversed the Winneba decision. This in turn was denounced by China as 'null and void'. The Cyprus meeting decided to expel from AAPSO the Chinese-oriented South-West African National Union, and it also substituted on the Executive Committee pro-Soviet factions of the Japanese and Ceylonese Solidarity Committees for the previous pro-Chinese representatives. Clearly, the Soviet Union's organizational advantages in AAPSO were now being translated into practical domination. The Chinese withdrew from the secretariat and, effectively, from the organization.

LATER HISTORY OF AAPSO

Soviet control of AAPSO was demonstrated when AAPSO, in conjunction with the WPC, held conferences in 1969 and 1970, in Khartoum and Rome, in support of African liberation movements (see also p. 238). Chinese-oriented groups were excluded. AAPSO's fifth conference was held in Cairo in 1972; but African interest in the organization had by then almost completely evaporated. A leader in *Pravda* commented that

The success of the anti-imperialist struggle would be greater were it not for separatist and great power actions of the Maoists, brought about by their chauvinist aspirations. (*Pravda*, 19 January 1972)

Factionalism was also evident in two of the Chinese-dominated AAPSO subsidiaries – the Afro-Asian Journalists' Association and the Afro-Asian Writers' Bureau. AAJA had been a Chinese creation, but its headquarters were in Djakarta. After the change in the Indonesian government in late 1965 working conditions became very difficult, with government supervision and police surveillance. The secretariat therefore announced it was moving, temporarily, to Peking. But one part of it remained in Indonesia, and a dispute arose over who were the true representatives. The Peking organization is still from time to time used as an instrument for inviting friendly journalists to Peking, either for a visit or to study. But it, too, has effectively ceased to exist.

The Chinese relied for their control over the AAWB on the pro-Chinese Ceylonese Secretary-General. But in June 1965 the AAPSO secretariat convened a meeting of the organization, without consulting the Secretary-General and excluding Chinese participation. A pro-Soviet segment was formed, which decided the next conference would be held in Baku, in the Soviet Union. Peking described the Cairo meeting as illegal and 'splittist', denounced the new Secretary-General, moved the headquarters from Ceylon to Peking and convened a conference in mid-1966 in Peking. By this time the cultural revolution was under way, and the conference was used merely to publicize writers' endorsements of the achievements of the cultural revolution and the brilliance of Mao Tse-tung's thought. Since then little has been heard of the organization;

but the Chinese-run front organizations, like the Soviet Union's, have lost all pretence at credibility.

Notes

1. Quoted in Arthur Huck, *The Security of China*, London, Chatto and Windus, 1970, p. 65. Transcript of an interview with John Dixon, an Australian television producer, in 1963.

2. From now on China began to canvass for statements condemning revisionism. An early example was the joint statement put out by the Chinese trade unions and the Tanganyika trade unions in November 1963, which stated that 'in order to fight imperialism and colonialism effectively, it was necessary for the people of the various countries to oppose modern revisionism'.

3. The diplomatic offensive could be somewhat undiscriminating – relations were immediately established, for example, in December 1963 with the newly independent Sultan of Zanzibar, who was overthrown just one month later. His usurper, Abeid Karume, was also immediately recognized.

4. He went to Algiers briefly in March after a visit to Rumania. In June he visited Tanzania to compensate for the cancelled visit of the previous year; on his way he called in at Khartoum and Cairo.

5. The meeting also adopted a resolution calling on all nations not to produce, acquire or test nuclear weapons. Six days later China exploded her first nuclear device.

6. Halpern, op. cit., p. 433.

7. They included Dahomey, Ivory Coast, Niger, Upper Volta, Togo, Cameroon, Chad, Gabon and Madagascar; the Congo said she would not attend unless Moise Tshombe was invited – which was unlikely.

8. Ibid., p. 433.

9. One, for instance, referred to the 'armed struggle being waged by the peoples of the Cameroon and Niger (two independent African states) against French imperialist aggression camouflaged behind the regimes of neo-colonialist dictatorship'. Calls for internal revolutions in such sovereign countries as Congo-Kinshasa, Malaysia, Morocco and South Vietnam, as well as in still-colonial areas, were also made.

8

CONSTRUCTIVE
POLICIES 1964–1966

'I was treated like a king'
President Massemba-Debat of Congo-
Brazzaville, on his return from China.

CHINA's interest in eastern Africa by no means began with
Chou En-lai's tour, but the quickening of her activities in
that area immediately afterwards suggests that he advised
greater priority should be given to eastern Africa, at the expense of the rest of the continent. There were sound reasons
for this change of direction. As we have seen, Chou had been
able to assess for himself the challenges posed to China in North
Africa, not only by the greater aid-giving capacities of the
Soviet Union and the West, but also by Islamic resistance to
any form of communist proselytizing.[1] Although as a result of
Chou's visit Tunisia recognized China in January 1964,
China's political relations with the Arab states went into a long
period of quiescence until after the cultural revolution. Both
Algeria and Egypt drew closer to the Soviet Union, and both
held China responsible for dragging the Sino-Soviet dispute
into international and African forums. Algeria, particularly,
must have been a disappointment to the Chinese. The Algerian
revolution was still held up as *the* African revolutionary model,
but China's relations with the Algerian government went into
a period of decline. In what appears to have been a deliberate
slight, Algeria waited until January 1966, four years after the
formal establishment of diplomatic relations, before naming
an ambassador to serve in Peking. Chinese aid programmes

either did not materialize, or were implemented very slowly, a complaint also voiced by Egypt.[2] Immediately after Chou's visit, Ben Bella signalled his alignment by making a four-month trip to the Soviet Union, where he negotiated important aid and military agreements and was made a Hero of the Soviet Union. Asked on his return about Algeria's attitude to the Sino-Soviet dispute, he said: 'Algeria had no desire to take sides ... Algeria would have to balance its policy so that these differences in no way affected her independence.'

Nevertheless economic and military logic made it certain that for some time ahead Algeria would look to the Soviet Union, rather than to China.

To a lesser extent, the difficulties in the way of an effective Chinese presence in North Africa also existed in West Africa. There was the same unequal competition in aid-giving, there were the same Islamic objections to communist 'penetration'. In addition, there were considerable logistical difficulties in maintaining contact with West Africa, although the inauguration in 1964 of Air Pakistan flights between some West African cities and Shanghai made communications a little easier. More importantly, there were very limited prospects of expanding trade between China and the West African nations, and thus of indirectly financing the aid programme. In this region China became more selective with her aid, and as discussed later, counted on expanding her political influence, notably in Ghana.

Many of these difficulties did not exist in East Africa. Logistically, with an entire coastline exposed to China, East Africa presented less of a communications problem. One friendly port – Dar es Salaam – could serve almost the entire region, making aid programmes and assistance for dissident groups much easier to implement. The countries of East Africa also grew a commodity – cotton – and produced a mineral – copper – both of which China needed, thus opening up the possibilities of a beneficial trade.

Whatever their public pronouncements China's policy makers must have by this time realized that the majority of African states had won their independence by non-revolutionary means. Communist exhortations about 'further victories' and 'true independence' had no appeal for the 'bourgeois' leaders firmly in power. But it was quite clear that neither the Portuguese nor the minority regime in South Africa would surrender their authority without a fight. Just at the time of Chou's tour, it became quite obvious that the focus of the real African revolution had moved south, to the white 'redoubt'. Revolutionary fronts were being opened up in Angola and Mozambique, Rhodesia was moving inexorably towards her UDI, South Africa was continuing to insist on her right to administer South-West Africa and was herself as far away as ever from acknowledging the principle of majority rule. The headquarters of Africa's support for the oppressed majorities of southern Africa became Dar es Salaam, where the OAU sited its Liberation Committee; the liberation movements themselves also set up headquarters or branch offices in the Tanzanian capital. If China was to have any chance of guiding this most promising of African revolutions she had to have good government-to-government relations with the host country. This then was a further reason for shifting the emphasis of Chinese activities eastwards.

The Soviets, too, were expressing considerable interest in East Africa. The Soviet Union had also recognized by now that communist revolutionary prescriptions had been discredited by events. The Soviet Union's reluctance to support dissident opposition groups and her desire to establish relations with legitimate independent African governments of almost any political hue led her, earlier than China, to look for other situations in which she could exhibit her revolutionary ardour. The liberation movement in southern Africa suited her purposes admirably and it was recognized that the independent countries of eastern Africa were the front line of this new struggle. China was bound to follow this lead.

CHINA'S EARLY INTEREST IN EAST AFRICA

Although China had not mounted any major political initiatives in eastern Africa, Sudan and Somalia had been amongst the first African countries to establish diplomatic relations with her (respectively in February 1959 and December 1960), and relations had been cordial if a little distant. But a diplomatic push in the area was initiated in 1961 with the appointment of

Ho Ying, the astute director of the West Asian and African Affairs Department, to the post of ambassador to Tanganyika.[3] In the next three years he played the central role in establishing a Chinese presence in eastern and central Africa.

At the end of 1962 China established relations with newly independent Uganda, and Ho himself was appointed ambassador in absentia. In December 1963 Ho and Chen Yi attended the celebrations marking Kenya's independence, at which it was agreed the two countries should establish diplomatic relations. That same month Ho succeeded in winning recognition for China from Burundi and from the Sultan of Zanzibar's short-lived government.

In January 1964 Ho made yet another journey – to Lusaka, to congratulate President Kaunda on Zambia's newly won independence; diplomatic relations were established in October. During the course of 1964, China also succeeded in establishing diplomatic relations with Congo-Brazzaville and the Central African Republic. By the end of 1964 there were therefore only three independent African states in the region with which China did not enjoy government-to-government relations: Rwanda, Congo-Leopoldville and Malawi. Rwanda recognized Taiwan, received aid from the Nationalist government, and was the only country in Black Africa to have a specific anti-communist clause written into the constitution. There was clearly no possibility of China trying to establish any sort of contact with the Leopoldville central government, but ambassador Ho did try and persuade President Banda of Malawi to recognize China. He travelled to Blantyre in January 1964, after his visit to Zambia, but met with no success; in September Dr Banda dismissed four ministers and told Parliament they had been plotting against him, guided by the 'steering hand of the Chinese ambassador in Dar es Salaam'. Banda also said the Chinese had offered him financial inducements to secure Malawian recognition of China, allegations dismissed by the Chinese embassy in Dar es Salaam as 'groundless fabrications and lies'. A little later, Banda amplified his charges, and borrowing Nyerere's phrase described the modern scramble for Africa, which he said was for the soul, rather than for the body, of the continent. Referring to the alleged Chinese bribes, he said: 'My allegiance cannot be bought, not for

4

£6 million, nor even £18 million. That is not the sort of language an Elder of the Church of Scotland can understand.'

Banda's resistance to the real or imagined financial blandishments of Ho Ying was a minor setback compared with China's initial successes in eastern Africa. These were often the reward for the Chinese policy of selecting promising groups or individuals, subsidizing their trips abroad or simply paying them outright, and hoping they would eventually be in a position to repay this generosity in political kind. There was nothing new in this 'seed approach', as it was called – the Soviets had practised it widely in eastern Asia in the 1920s – but the Chinese placed perhaps too much faith in its efficacy. The defector Tung[4] has said the Chinese believed every African had his price – 'The people of Burundi were so poor and ignorant that they could be made to do anything for a little money' – and they despised them for this, a view which does not take into account the fact that an African often does accept a bribe, but as often is not influenced by it. Put more cynically, one could say the Chinese had not learned the old settler saying, that 'You can't buy an African. You can only hire him.'

The Chinese were particularly anxious to gain influence in this way with Africans connected with the information media. A high proportion of visitors to Peking at this time were officials in African Information Ministries, newspaper editors, radio producers etc. In eastern Africa recipients of seed money included senior officials in the Somali Ministry of Information, Burundi politicians, dissident Kenya trade-union officials, branch chairmen of the ruling Kenya African National Union (KANU) party, pre-independence rivals of Nyerere in Tanganyika and, further south, leaders of the Swaziland Progressive Party and the Basutoland Congress Party. Important individual 'catches' included Oginga Odinga, the Kenyan Vice-President, and Abdulrahman Babu, founder of the Zanzibar Umma Party.

An important Chinese link man in these operations was Kao Liang, the NCNA correspondent in Dar es Salaam.[5] Kao had been expelled from India in 1960 for unjournalistic activities, and had worked in Zanzibar before being assigned to the mainland. In 1962 he was reported in Burundi, where he contacted Rwandan Tutsi refugees and reportedly distributed bribes to prominent Burundian politicians, notably building up a

Chinese constituency amongst a left-wing Tutsi group in the ruling UPRONA party.

Soviet enthusiasm for the newly independent territories of East Africa was less marked than it had been for Guinea, which de Gaulle, by cutting off all aid, had virtually presented to the Soviet Union. Despite the Mau Mau uprising in Kenya (which neither the Soviet Union nor China subsidized), independence eventually came as a garden party sort of affair. In all three East African territories, European settlers continued to farm and in Tanzania and Kenya to hold high office in the government. Substantial quantities of Western aid flowed to the new governments and Britain continued to dominate the trading patterns of all three countries. All the same, there were certain parallels with West Africa; one was that the establishment of diplomatic relations with the communist countries was virtually mandatory for national leaders striving to assert their non-alignment. The Soviet Union, her East European allies, and, as we have seen, the Chinese took advantage of this desire to establish relations within a few months of independence.

Soviet commentary increasingly began to stress the importance of East Africa, both because the independence of the three territories was seen as a factor in expediting the independence of other colonies, such as Northern Rhodesia (Zambia) and Nyasaland (Malawi), and because, in the Soviet view, the area was now the 'front line' in the continent's liberation struggle against the white south. Of course, Soviet theoreticians could not allow that 'true' independence had yet been won – that depended, as one writer put it, on further 'consolidation' of independence; while continental liberation, naturally, depended 'on the swift and resolute uprooting of the remnants of colonial rule'.[6] Ironically, in view of future developments, Kenya was singled out as having the best opportunity of following the non-capitalist road of development because of the non-capitalist nature of inter-African relations in Kenya. 'The path East Africa takes will largely depend on what happens in Kenya,' wrote Yu Tomilin in

January 1964.[7] The same analyst had more difficulty in predict-
ing the likely course of events in Tanzania,[8] because of the
disparate development between the mainland and Zanzibar,
with the latter making the revolutionary running. Uganda was
given the worst chance for 'healthy' development, being a
'republican monarchic constitutional patchwork', a structure
presenting obstacles to the development of a centralized, one-
party system; in addition there were reactionary elements in
the Uganda People's Congress party.

CONSTRUCTIVE POLICIES IN EAST AND CENTRAL AFRICA
1964–1966

In eastern and central Africa during this period, China continued to exhibit the schizophrenic qualities which had
characterized her activities in the west – subversion and revolution from below, cooperation and aid from above. I shall refer
to them as the 'constructive' and 'disruptive' approaches.
Disruptive policies, especially those which had a chance of
diverting the forces of the main enemy, the United States,
were still of paramount importance, and we shall examine them
in detail in the next chapter. The constructive approach was
useful, although not essential, in dealing with legitimate
governments. Sometimes the two policies were complementary:
for example, in order to nurture the Congolese, Angolan and
Mozambican rebellions, it was essential to have guaranteed
supply-lines and a permanent base; this entailed cordial and
correct relations with the governments of Tanzania and Congo-
Brazzaville, the two countries singled out for special treatment.
Very often the disruptive activities were regarded with favour
by the host governments – support for the southern African
freedom fighters, for instance, coincided with the views of
Presidents Nyerere of Tanzania and Massemba-Debat of
Congo-Brazzaville, just as in West Africa, attempted Chinese
subversion of the Entente states from Ghana served the interests
of Nkrumah.

PATTERNS OF THE CONSTRUCTIVE APPROACH

The form and implementation of cooperative interaction with

friendly governments of eastern and central Africa were not markedly different from those employed in the west. Loans were given conspicuously interest-free, aid projects were practical and China shunned the showy prestige projects for which the Soviet Union had been censured in West Africa. Partly to offset the (mainly Western) criticism that her aid was tied to the provision of Chinese goods and services and that she could not give the African recipients what they really needed – hard currency – China also made a number of small hard currency grants, usually to help balance deficit budgets. This kind of aid was given to Uganda, Kenya, Somalia, Zanzibar and Tanganyika. China also responded quickly to appeals for the relief of victims of natural disasters, with medicines and small hard currency grants; countries to benefit included Somalia (flood relief), Kenya (drought) and Zambia (copper mine disaster). Gifts were also given, often to celebrate the establishment of diplomatic relations: for Congo-Brazzaville there was 1000 tons of rice and over 5 million CFA francs for the 'relief of persecuted Congo-Brazzaville nationals expelled by Congo-Leopoldville'; Zanzibar was given fifteen Chinese buses while Tanzania received forty army vehicles and a consignment of armaments ('only two years old' according to second Vice-President Kawawa, which must have rankled somewhat with the Kenyans who were at the same time preparing to return some Soviet World War Two equipment, rejected as too old-fashioned).

China was also prepared to tolerate an unfavourable balance of trade with many of her new friends in the area, which directly helped their economies. Partly this reflected China's own trading needs, notably the import of cotton and other raw materials, and her inability to replace traditional suppliers; partly, it was a political gesture of goodwill. In 1965, for example, China was Uganda's fourth largest customer, importing £6·24 million worth of goods, mainly cotton, but exporting only a meagre £970000 worth. In the three years 1964–1966, Tanzania exported a total of £10·34 million worth of goods to China, but imported only half that amount. In 1964 China's imports from Zambia were worth over £1 million, but her exports were a token £16000.

Friendly relations were cemented by friendship treaties, by

economic, technical and trade agreements, by visits of cultural, sporting and professional delegations and, above all, by an official visit of the African head of state to China. From eastern and central Africa during the period under review, visits were made by Prime Minister Ali Shermarke of Somalia and Presidents Aden Osman of Somalia, Abboud of Sudan, Nyerere of Tanzania, Kaunda of Zambia, Obote of Uganda, Massemba-Debat of Congo-Brazzaville, and even the Queen of Burundi. The only figure of any importance (except of course Mobutu of the Congo) not to pay an official visit to China was President Kenyatta, which partly reflected Kenya's disenchantment with the Chinese (discussed in the following chapter) and partly Kenyatta's well-known dislike of travel.

The Chinese also invited heads of armies, men just under the leadership, and ministers, notably those connected with the information services, like Achieng Oneko in Kenya and the Somali Minister of Information, Ali Mohammed Hirave. Visitors of this sort would certainly have helped China to build up a picture of African conditions – social, political and military – at a time when she was anxious to increase her knowledge of the continent. Some, like Kawawa of Tanzania or Kenyan Vice-President Oginga Odinga, were possibly chosen because it was felt that one day they might occupy the highest office. But most of those normally regarded as 'China's friends' were of direct use to China, and were cultivated for immediate, practical reasons. Ministers of Information controlled the output of news and could therefore influence attitudes towards China, either by suppressing unfavourable news about China's activities or by feeding what amounted to Chinese propaganda to their media. This happened in a number of countries where China was on good terms with Ministers of Information, notably Somalia and Tanzania – where Radio Tanzania staff had standing instructions not to carry stories damaging to China. Odinga, in his capacity as Home Minister, controlled Kenyan immigration policies and after his fall it was revealed he had smuggled out several hundred Kenyan militants to train in China. Kawawa was in charge of the all-important Ministry of Defence (and therefore presumably protected Chinese supplies for the Congolese rebels as they were transported across Tanzania); his ministry also controlled the activities of southern

African freedom fighters. Clearly, people like this, responsible for the day-to-day running of a country, were practical figures for China to cultivate.

SOMALIA

A good example of the constructive approach, and a country which also to a certain extent benefited from Sino-Soviet rivalry, was Somalia. Both China and the Soviet Union had shown an interest in Somalia soon after that country's independence in July 1960.

The Soviet Union's interests were partly strategical: placed on the Horn of Africa, Somalia commanded access to the Suez Canal; in addition, it seemed a promising country for oil exploration. Soviet agents in Cairo had established pre-independence contacts with dissident Somalis, and the Greater Somalia League, which contested the country's first elections, had the backing of Moscow. Both China and the Soviet Union established diplomatic relations with the Shermarke government shortly after independence.

Both communist powers must have seen possibilities in Somalia's irredentist claims on territory in Ethiopia and Kenya and her stated ambitions for a 'Greater Somalia'. Raids by Somali 'shiftas', as the bands of irregulars were known, led to a virtual state of war with her two neighbours on a number of occasions. Peaceful negotiations were conducted under the auspices of the OAU after its formation in May 1963, and also on a bilateral basis, but without much initial success. While Chou was in Mogadiscu at the end of his 1964 tour, the jingoistic Radio Somalia was urging its listeners: 'Freedom is not achieved by remaining seated, it is achieved by throwing bombs. If you are brave men . . . rise against the hyena who is picking flesh from your bones.'

It might be supposed that the message, down to the metaphor, was pitched to revolutionary Chinese ears. Shermarke and Osman, in fact, were considerably astute in using the Chinese to lever concessions from the Russians. As Somalia's expansionist ambitions became more evident, and as Western nations showed less and less willingness to underwrite them, Shermarke announced his intention of seeking aid from Peking. He visited

China in August 1963 and came back with a hard currency grant of £1·05 million to help to balance the budget and an interest-free loan of £7·2 million, repayable over seventeen years with a seven-year grace period.

Reaction from the Soviet Union was swift. She made aid offers worth £20 million as an immediate counter, and in October 1963 concluded an estimated £15 million military agreement with Somalia, which topped by some £5 million a military aid-package offered by the us, West Germany and Italy. Somali officers were sent to the Soviet Union for training (including those who were to carry out the 1969 coup) and Russian equipment began to arrive.[9]

The Soviet Union also moved swiftly to implement her aid offers: a team arrived to survey the Juba river valley; a modern hospital was built and given to the nation as a gift; heavy equipment, including lorries, water pumps and tractors, were distributed throughout the country and Soviet experts carried out a survey of a proposed deepwater port at Berbera. She also offered more scholarships to Somalia than to any other single African country – at the end of 1964, Tass quoted a Ministry of Education official as saying that the Soviet Union had granted Somalia in one year alone more scholarships than Italy, Britain and France had offered in sixty years of rule. In April 1965 over 600 Somalis were studying in the Soviet Union.

China experienced more difficulty in getting her aid projects off the ground, partly because of her economic crisis, partly through difficulty in identifying suitable projects. There was in Somalia, as there was initially too in Guinea, a slightly irrational fear of the Chinese – of their strangeness, of their intentions (which always included colonization, according to their detractors) and of their godlessness. Thus China's offer to build a strategic road was turned down when it was discovered this would involve the importation of a Chinese workforce of some 3000.[10] Somalis were even surprised when 200 Chinese workmen arrived to start work on the first major aid project – construction of a national theatre. But the government appreciated that China could not spare hard currency or capital goods, and that her aid had to be labour-intensive, while the population, especially in the rural areas, as in Mali, showed increasing appreciation of the practical nature of Chinese assistance. Chinese water surveyors bored water-holes for remote villages, while Chinese medical teams visited areas where doctors had never been seen before. In Mogadiscu itself great publicity was given to a successful hole-in-the-heart operation performed by a Chinese surgeon on a young boy.[11]

As in West Africa, the Chinese concentrated most of their aid on the sector they knew best – agriculture. A state farm set up with Chinese help was contrasted favourably with an experimental farm established with us aid and run by Mormons, hardly a tactful gesture in a Moslem country. Not surprisingly it suffered from bad labour relations. China also scored obliquely off the us when a Chinese team asserted it would be possible to grow commercially acceptable tobacco at Jowhar, a site abandoned by the British American Tobacco Company on the grounds that there was too much salt in the earth. This was denounced by the Chinese as an imperialist plot to deprive Somalia of revenue. A plantation was established and later, in 1970, a cigarette factory was built near Mogadiscu to process Jowhar tobacco. Chinese experts also introduced two new varieties of high-yielding rice to the country.

Somalia was one of those target countries where Chinese behaviour was impeccable: as far as possible requests were complied with and no known assistance was given to opposition groups. This was partly to meet squarely the Soviet challenge in the field of friendly cooperation. But another explanation was given to me by a senior government official of the time, who shall have to remain anonymous. He said the government was sure that the Chinese embassy in Mogadiscu, which occupied a large house on the outskirts of the capital, surrounded by a high wall, was one of China's most important staging and training posts in the whole of Africa. Its main task was the training of Chinese in local and African languages – teachers of the local Somali dialects of Afar and Qoti were employed by the Embassy, while foreign experts were imported to teach the more widely used Swahili and Amharric. My informant said that in 1963 there were 230 officially registered Chinese embassy staff, obviously far more than could be justified by the modest aid programme being carried out in Somalia, and that the Mogadiscu embassy was virtually China's African headquarters, before that position was taken over by the embassy in Dar es Salaam. Certainly, Mogadiscu was a strategic and convenient haven for China; if it *was* used by the Chinese for a time as a centre of their operations good relations with the legitimate government were clearly essential, and could not be jeopardized by support for dissident groups.

TANZANIA AND CONGO-BRAZZAVILLE

The constructive side of China's state relations with African countries during the period was seen to best advantage in Congo-Brazzaville and Tanzania. As we noted earlier China needed good relations with the governments of these two countries in order to use them as supply lines to important revolutionary situations. Brazzaville was used as a base for assisting dissident Leopoldville politicians and supplying Congolese rebels with arms, as well as for establishing contact with Angolan freedom fighters. Tanzania was also used as a supply link to the eastern Congo, while Dar es Salaam was the headquarters of most of the liberation movements fighting in southern Africa. It would have been foolish to have jeopardized China's position in this promising revolutionary situation by encouraging internal subversion, and as far as I am aware it was never attempted (although in the pre-independence era China had supported Nyerere's extremist rival Zuberi Mtevu). Relations were exemplary, probably deliberately so to demonstrate the undoubted benefits for a friendly African government flowing from a cooperative relationship with China. Tanzania and Brazzaville in east and central Africa, and Mali and Guinea in the west, have always been showpieces for the Chinese 'constructive' approach, just as the Congo was in some senses a 'model' of the revolutionary, disruptive side of Chinese foreign policy.

Tanzania and Brazzaville received considerable commitments of aid from China, and partly because the political will was there and partly because by the time these agreements were signed China was recovering from her economic crisis, projects were swiftly implemented. In June 1964, Kawawa returned from Peking with a £16 million aid package, of which part was to be supplied in the form of armaments. In the same month

China extended a separate interest-free loan of £5 million to Zanzibar. The speed with which the credits to Tanzania were utilized can be gauged by an *East African Standard* newspaper report of June 1966, which said the major part of the original loan had already been committed. In the same month China made an additional loan of £4 million of which £1 million was a direct grant. One of the major reasons for the success of Chinese aid to Tanzania has been Nyerere's desire for progress in the rural sector, an area in which he believed Chinese technical assistance would be of particular value. Amongst the first Chinese-aided projects was a 5000-acre state farm, staffed with Chinese experts. Until it was self-supporting, the recurrent costs were to be met by Chinese loans. At the end of 1964 the Chinese offered to build two high-power radio transmitters, possibly intended to be contrasted with the mere 50-kW transmitter offered to Kenya by the Russians; half of the estimated £350 000 cost was to be met by a grant and the other half by an interest-free loan. Other projects under active consideration included a highly labour-intensive textile mill (the Chinese wished to call it the Mao Tse-tung Mill, but since this was considered too political by the Tanzanians it was eventually named the Friendship Textile Mill – a good example of the way Tanzanians succeeded in 'de-politicizing' the Chinese presence in their country); the creation of a Sino-Tanzanian shipping line, for which China lent Tanzania's initial capital of £750 000 and finally the preliminary survey for the Tanzania – Zambia railway. All these projects are discussed in more detail in the special chapter on Tanzania.

A similar pattern of constructive friendship emerged in Congo-Brazzaville, with which diplomatic relations had been established in February 1964. A government mission to Peking in July of that year was offered an immediate £1·8 million loan to help balance the budget. In September President Alphonse Massemba-Debat visited China, where he signed an economic cooperation agreement providing for an interest-free loan of £7 million, to be used in establishing consumer goods industries.[12] The aid was evidently committed with speed, for in November the Prime Minister was saying:

We will continue to rely, for a long time to come, on the bilateral aid of all countries of the world, particularly France, whose cultural and technical assistance we appreciate, and the China People's Republic, whose material aid has already proved as effective. (*Brazzaville Radio*, 7 November 1965)

In July 1965 the Chinese held an economic exhibition in Brazzaville, where Chinese heavy machinery was on display for the first time in Africa. In September China agreed to build a major 'flagship' project, the Kisoundi Textile Mill, whose projected 1800 workforce would make it the biggest industrial employer of labour in the country. As elsewhere, the Chinese medical teams made a considerable impact on the rural populations.

Both Nyerere and Massemba-Debat went out of their way to stress the effectiveness and disinterestedness of Chinese aid, partly from a desire to give credit where it was due, partly to counter hostile Western press criticism. This was at its severest, and silliest, over Chinese military aid, although, as both presidents pointed out, this only amounted to a fraction of the assistance their armies received from Western sources.

The arrival in Tanzania in August 1964 of eleven Chinese military instructors was greeted knowingly. Nyerere had clearly 'sold out'. The presence of Chinese mortars, anti-tank guns and heavy machine-guns (these were the 'only two years old' gifts) was duly, and gloomily, noted at a military parade in Arusha, northern Tanzania, in February 1965. Nyerere answered the alarmists by pointing out that his army was also being trained by Canadian, West German and Israeli instructors. It was put to him at a press conference that the West was asking if he realized the risks he was running. Patiently he explained

The maximum risk is that the army will revolt. My army revolted in January. It was not trained by the Chinese . . . This simple request is a little attempt to show that we are non-aligned, but when it comes to actual facts this country is completely Western, in government, in business, in the schools, in everything. The influence of this country is Western.[13]

He then produced figures to show that there were 246 Chinese in Tanzania – and 16 000 British. This irrational, paranoid fear of the Chinese was also noted by Massemba-Debat, who on his return from Peking, criticized newspaper reports

about the Chinese 'invasion' of Brazzaville. Like Nyerere, he
effectively contrasted the number of Chinese in the country,
with the numbers of French, British and Americans.

Good relations between Tanzania and China were strengthened in 1965 with Nyerere's first visit to China, in February,
followed four months later by Chou En-lai's visit to Tanzania,
to compensate for the visit cancelled in 1964 due to the army
mutiny. Nyerere was enormously impressed by what he saw in
China, and his visit – during which he received in principle
the Chinese commitment to build the Tanzam railway –
marked the beginning of a very special relationship between
the two countries. Nevertheless, he was careful to emphasize
Tanzania's non-alignment and her right as a sovereign state
to choose her own friends and enemies. In a major speech he
warned that neither Western propaganda about China, nor
Chinese propaganda about the Soviet Union, would be allowed
to affect Sino-Tanzanian relations – 'the fears of others will
not affect Tanzania's friendship with China any more than our
friendship with other countries would be affected by what their
opponents say of them'.

Chou was less reticent in proclaiming the good relations
between the two countries, referring, at a public rally shortly
after his arrival in Tanzania, to the 'profound and militant
friendship' which had always existed between the two peoples.
He continued:

An exceedingly favourable situation for revolution prevails today,
not only in Africa, but also in Asia and Latin America. That
national liberation movement in Africa converging with that in
Asia and Latin America has become a mighty torrent pounding
with great momentum on the foundations of the rule of imperialism,
colonialism and neo-colonialism. The revolutionary storms in these
areas are vividly described in Chairman Mao Tse-tung's famous
verses: 'The four seas are seething, clouds pouring and waters
raging, the five continents are rocked by storm and thunder.'
(NCNA, Dar es Salaam, 5 June 1965)

By this time the Tanzanians had become used to the Chinese
sense of theatre, their need to dramatize and overstate in a
world which barely recognized their existence, and could
therefore afford to ignore the surface meaning of a speech like
this (thereby showing more political sophistication than many

Western countries, which continued to take the Chinese literally). Not so neighbouring Kenya, whose government issued the somewhat prim riposte that

It is not clear to the Kenyan government what type and what form of revolution he has in mind but the Kenyan government wishes it to be known that Kenya intends to avert all revolutions irrespective of their origin . . .

Kenyan MPs introduced a motion condemning Chou's 'destructive' statement and called on the government to sever relations with China – 'in view of the many coups, crises and assassinations which had taken place'. The wording was later amended to read 'any foreign government found participating in such activities in Africa'. But, pointedly, the Kenyan government avoided asking Chou to visit Kenya after his visit to Tanzania.

CONSTRUCTIVE POLICIES IN WEST AFRICA
1964–1966

In West Africa the friendly radical countries of Guinea and Mali continued to benefit from the constructive approach. With China's domestic economic crisis over, there was a greater ability to fulfil old aid commitments and to enter into new ones. China's insistence that aid was mutually beneficial seemed to be borne out by the pro-Chinese stands taken by the leaders of the two countries on certain world issues. Guinea, as we saw earlier, was one of the only seven countries to have refused to ratify the 1963 Moscow nuclear-test-ban treaty, while at the end of President Keita's visit to Peking in 1965 the Sino-Malian communiqué noted with pleasure 'that the situation is most favourable for revolution throughout the continent of Africa'.

While this sort of payoff was welcome, it would hardly seem to be a fair return for China's considerable material assistance. However, the Chinese aid programme also served an important internal purpose: considerable space was devoted in the Chinese press to the exploits of aid personnel. Their 'selfless and devoted' services to humanity in a distant part of the globe were extolled, and their dedicated hard work was held up as an example for all the Chinese people to follow. Alive they were heroes, dead (a few were killed in the course of duty) they became martyrs. NCNA correspondents were assiduous in collecting tributes to the hard work and devotion of Chinese doctors, agricultural experts and technicians, and this was interpreted in China as being a tribute to the Chinese way of life and the communist party's political system. With the onset of the cultural revolution, both aid personnel and recipients were quoted as attributing successful results to the study of Mao Tse-tung's thought. If the aid programme thus contributed towards both the authority of the CCP and to the belief within China that her aid personnel, and therefore China herself, were respected and admired in the outside world, the assertion that aid benefited both donor and recipient was perfectly correct.

GUINEA

Aid projects to Guinea were speedily implemented, and there seems little doubt that the original £3·5 million credit extended in 1960 would have been utilized by 1964. Guinea has been reticent in publishing aid figures, although the US State Department estimates Chinese aid to Guinea in the period 1954–1971 at about £24 million. There were initial criticisms that the People's Palace was being built by Chinese labour with Chinese materials (even, according to one rumour, with Chinese sand in the cement), and that there were therefore no job opportunities for Guineans. The strong Chinese 'presence', estimated at 3000 in 1967, worried some Guineans initially too, but in general there was nothing but praise for the quality of Chinese aid. In January 1966 the minister for economic development cited as model development projects Chinese-built match and cigarette factories and a tobacco plantation, and praised progress on the Pita dam and hydro-electric plant.

MALI

As in Guinea, the Soviet Union was the biggest aid donor to Mali. China, however, decided it was worth competing in the aid field, reasoning perhaps that in a poor, backward country like Mali, most of it desert, her rural technical assistance and simple, labour-intensive factories had a good chance of making a greater impact than the more sophisticated aid of the Soviet Union. (The Soviet Union had in fact already been criticized for building an unnecessarily large sports stadium.) China's calculations were correct, as the increasing scale of her aid activities shows: by 1965 there were some fifteen Chinese projects, including a tea plantation, a sugar-cane growing scheme, rice plantations and several light industrial projects, such as a ceramics works, a match factory, a textile mill, a sugar refinery and a brick factory. The Malians were delighted, and Keita praised the quality and aptness of Chinese aid during his visit to Peking. In July 1966, the Foreign Minister, Ousmane Ba, said

In Mali we have no fear of cooperating with the Chinese, whose technicians have a great respect for our people, are most courteous and discreet, act with dignity, and have at no time interfered with our internal affairs, which is more than can be said for many other agents of foreign technical assistance.

The good relations between Chinese experts and Malians is testified by less partial observers than pro-Chinese Malian ministers and NCNA correspondents. A French journalist visiting Mali in 1964, for example, wrote of the great esteem in which the Chinese were held, and he noted that the Chinese experts spoke good French.[14]

These excellent relations were cemented in June 1966, when China took the unusual step of giving a foreign exchange advance of £1·4 million to Mali to help her repay certain debts.

GHANA

Aid was not an important ingredient in China's relationship with Ghana; China calculated, rather, that her ability to further Nkrumah's political ambitions would be a more effective challenge to Soviet influence. However, although few aid projects had been implemented, a further £8 million loan was offered in 1964, suggesting that at least some of the original funds had been utilized. This was for the establishment of a textile mill and a pencil factory, both of which were abandoned after the coup which overthrew Nkrumah in 1966.

The only other country in West Africa to benefit from Chinese

1. and 2. Chinese instructors train African dissidents at guerrilla warfare camps in Ghana. The post-Nkrumah government published these photographs, and a booklet entitled *Nkrumah's Deception of Africa*, to clear the way for better relations with the neighbouring states he had been helping to subvert.

3. A Chinese acrobatic team in the grounds of State House, Dar es Salaam. Cultural visits were a feature of China's early relationship with Africa.

4. Chou En-lai (centre) and Foreign Minister Chen Yi (left) with King Hassan II of Morocco during Chou's 1963/64 tour of Africa. In North Africa the Chinese leaders learned of Islamic resistance to communist initiatives, but the tour was a great personal triumph for Chou.

5. The first Chinese ambassador to Tanzania, Ho Ying (centre), was responsible for securing diplomatic recognition for China from most of the East and Central African nations. He has risen to become a Deputy Foreign Minister.

6. In 1965 Chou En-lai paid his second visit to the African continent. Here, flanked by Tanzania's Second Vice-President Rashidi Kawawa (left) and President Abeid Karume, he drives through the streets of Zanzibar.

7. and 8. A visit to China and a meeting with Chairman Mao Tse-tung often sealed the relationship between China and African countries. In 1968 President Julius Nyerere (above) was the only head of state to visit China during the turmoil of the Cultural Revolution. (below) General Numeiry of Sudan arrives in Peking.

aid before the cultural revolution was Mauritania. An agricultural mission had been sent to help with a rice scheme in
1964, before diplomatic relations had been established.[15] A
further team, to start a rice scheme in the Senegal river valley,
was dispatched in 1966.

OTHER CONSTRUCTIVE ACTIVITIES

China continued to expand her propaganda activities throughout the continent. In mid-1964 Radio Peking was beaming on
average seventy-one hours of broadcasting per week to Africa;
by February 1965 this had risen to 108 hours. Both the Radio
and NCNA had agreements with most of the countries recognizing China for the free exchange of news material. (In
fact, NCNA correspondents were even prepared to *pay* local
newspaper editors to publish their articles and photographs –
it happened to my knowledge on at least one occasion in the
case of a Tanzanian newspaper.) The previously noted preoccupation with the communications sector was underlined by
considerable Chinese technical assistance in this field: by 1966
China had constructed or strengthened short-wave transmitters
in Somalia, Tanzania, Congo-Brazzaville and Mali; had
established direct telecommunications links with Guinea;
signed a telecommunications agreement with Algeria; was
building a cinema in Mali and was exchanging film and news-
reel with most of the countries with which she had diplomatic
relations.

Distribution of the printed word also increased. Copies of
the *Peking Review* in French, English and Spanish were available
in Africa; with a subscription to the magazine, readers were
promised a free copy of a booklet entitled *The Long March*.
Other glossy Chinese propaganda publications, exceptionally
well printed and presented, were sold at 'Friendship Bookshops'
or mailed directly to subscribers from Peking.

Chinese embassies held parties, usually to celebrate anni-
versaries, at which, invariably films were shown extolling
Chinese achievements. But there is little evidence that these
efforts met with any great success. Embassy film shows, for
example, have never been very popular with Africans. Firstly
the films themselves are rather boring and secondly the Chinese

do not serve alcoholic drinks at their parties. American functions are inevitably better attended: liquor is freely available –
and the films are more entertaining. It is more difficult to assess
the impact of Chinese publications and radio broadcasts, but
it seems reasonable to assume that the absence of any entertainment content must lessen their appeal. Pure propaganda is
hardly of compelling interest to anyone, least of all to Africans,
who are very politically conscious. Chinese broadcasts and
publications give them neither entertainment nor information
nor well-informed comment about African affairs, which for
all their faults Western magazines and radio broadcasts
generally do. African audiences, according to reliable listening
statistics, have shown remarkable loyalty to the radio services
of the old colonialists; when they have 'switched' it has often
been to the Voice of America, whose African service has been
very strong, certainly in quality of transmission, and in my
opinion in content too.

A stronger impression may have been made on Africans by
China's apparent desire to make an impact with a strong
physical presence. In Dar es Salaam, for example, their embassy staff numbered over forty, which was twice as many as all
the other diplomats combined. In Kenya at one time they
fielded twenty embassy staff as well as five NCNA correspondents
– in a country where they had no aid projects. In Burundi
there were forty-five embassy staff, as opposed to the Soviet
Union's four. Their embassy buildings, too, were large and
impressive. In Kenya and Somalia they occupied large buildings, surrounded by high walls, on the outskirts of the capital.
In Burundi, they reportedly gave £40 000 for an impressive
house belonging to the Mwami (King). In Tanzania, they
bought from the Aga Khan what was probably the most luxuri-
ous house in the country, complete with swimming pool and
private beach. In Lusaka they bought an ostentatious house
from a South African businessman. In all these countries senior
staff drove impressive cars – Mercedes, Peugeots and, in Zambia, large, blue, capitalist Chevrolets. This style of living came
under attack by Red Guards during the cultural revolution, but
it was presumably a deliberate policy decision to impress on
local people China's presence in their country and to show them
that she was not the pauper her enemies made her out to be.

SUMMARY

China's constructive activities, practically overlooked by her critics, were as important an ingredient in her relations with African countries as the better publicized disruptive ones. Admittedly, the scale of her aid was small,[16] but, as a developing country herself, it was remarkable that she was able to offer any at all. Her policy was to make as large an impact as possible on a small number of politically satisfactory recipients; this was done by the quality and aptness of her aid, as well as by an excellent sense of timing: loans to Tanzania, Zanzibar, Somalia and Guinea when they had been discriminated against by the Western world; medical teams, medicine and quickly-given cash grants to areas suffering from drought and famine, and practical assistance in the one sector – agriculture – relatively neglected by the major donors. It was a skilful and economical offensive.

Notes

1. The CIA has for long believed in the efficacy of Islam as a bulwark against communism. When Colonel Ghadaffi of Libya 'recognized' China (but relations have never been established) on 11 June 1971, he said that as a country on which atheism had been imposed, China was a stranger and her influence would never be allowed to spread. For a fuller discussion of African religious objections to communism see p. 285.

2. The *New York Times* reported in February 1966 that Egypt had either been unable or unwilling to draw on *any* of the £28m. Chinese credit extended in December 1964.

3. As noted previously, the Department was subsequently subdivided into a West Asian and North African Department and an African Affairs Department. But some time during the cultural revolution and not later than September 1969, the two sections were re-combined, with Ho Ying once again as director before his appointment as vice foreign minister.

4. Tung Chi-ping, the only Chinese diplomat to have defected while serving in Africa, was briefly assistant cultural attaché in Usumbura before handing himself over to the American Embassy in the spring of 1964. He has given useful information about the structure of the Foreign Ministry and details of its African corps, and has written a book *The Thought Revolution*, New York: Coward-McCann, 1966, with Humphrey Evans.

5. Kao caused a sensation when he turned up in the advance party of

the Chinese UN team in 1970. It was widely assumed in the Western press that he would be 'up to his old tricks again' – in New York.

6. V.Kudryautser, *International Affairs*, No. 12, 1964.

7. *International Affairs*, No. 1, 1964.

8. The union between Tanganyika and Zanzibar was effected in April 1964, just four months after Zanzibar's independence and three months after the revolution. The union covers such joint matters as defence, currency, foreign policy, etc., but each partner manages its own internal affairs. To avoid confusion I shall refer to the mainland as Tanzania, to distinguish it from the island of Zanzibar.

9. African reaction to the Soviet–Somalia military agreement included an Ethiopian-Kenyan defence pact concluded in December 1963. The Soviets appear to have been worried about the hostility which the agreement aroused – the Soviet ambassador in Addis Ababa assured the Emperor that the degree of military assistance had been grossly exaggerated; the Soviets also reportedly sought assurances that the Somalis would use their Russian equipment only in self-defence and not against other African states (see *Africa Confidential*, No. 1, January 1964).

10. But by 1973 China had successfully shaken off the old image, and her offer to build a £25m., 700-mile highway between Beledwin and Hargeisa in the north of the country was gratefully taken up, and the army of Chinese 'coolies' warmly welcomed.

11. Medicine provided a strange little side-show of the ideological war: a Chinese doctor examined the much-loved commander of the army, General Daud Hersi, diagnosed cancer and gave him less than three months to live. The Russians picked up the medical gauntlet and sent the general to the Soviet Union, where he underwent three major operations. He died immediately after the last one.

12. On his return he announced that he had been 'treated like a king'. This may have puzzled his hosts in the People's Republic of China, although presumably they must have recognized it as a compliment!

13. Press conference, Dar es Salaam, 24 February 1965.

14. *Le Monde*, 9 December 1964.

15. In July 1965. Tung Chi-ping told Bruce Larkins (*China and Africa*, op. cit., p. 87) that he had seen cables in Peking indicating that Mauritania had wished for some time to establish relations, but that China had delayed the decision for fear of offending Morocco, with whom Mauritania had a territorial dispute. It has also been suggested that traditionalist, Islamic Mauritania wanted recognition to establish more radical credentials among neighbouring states. An equally valid suggestion is that President Ould Daddah's wife, who continues to have a great admiration for the Chinese, persuaded her husband to establish formal relations.

16. But not as small as her critics would have had. Although statistics are unreliable it was certainly greater in terms of percentage of GNP – the normal comparative yardstick – than the Soviet Union's and possibly some Western donors.

9
DISRUPTIVE POLICIES
1964–1966

Long Live the Victory of People's War.
LIN PIAO

CHINA's disruptive policies in Africa, and elsewhere, during the mid-1960s were understood in the West in the context of Lin Piao's celebrated thesis *Long Live the Victory of People's War.* The core of his argument was that

Comrade Mao Tse-tung's theory of the establishment of rural rovolutionary base areas and the encirclement of the cities from the countryside is of outstanding and universal importance for the present revolutionary struggles of all the oppressed nations and peoples, and particularly for the struggles of the oppressed nations and peoples in Asia, Africa and Latin America against imperialism and its lackeys . . .

Taking the entire globe, if North America and Western Europe can be called the 'cities of the world', then Asia, Africa and Latin America constitute the 'rural areas of the world.' Since World War II, the proletarian revolutionary movement has for various reasons been temporarily held back in the North American and Western European capitalist countries, while the people's revolutionary movement in Asia, Africa and Latin America has been growing vigorously.

In a sense, the contemporary world revolution also presents a picture of the encirclement of cities by the rural areas. In the final analysis, the whole cause of world revolution hinges on the revolutionary struggles of the Asian, African and Latin American peoples who make up the overwhelming majority of the world's population. The socialist countries should regard it as their internationalist duty to support the people's revolutionary stuggles in Asia, Africa and Latin America. (*Peking Review*, 3 September 1965)

This document, published in 1965, was treated with surprising seriousness in the West, as though it represented an actual Chinese plan of action. In defending the US presence in Vietnam, Dean Rusk said that to ignore such statements would be to repeat 'the catastrophic miscalculation that so many people made about the ambition of Hitler', while Robert McNamara cited Lin's thesis in urging heightened NATO unity and military preparedness.[1] Such reactions were surprising in view of the known objective limitations which prevented China from effectively supporting such an 'encirclement'. Even to the uninitiated it should have been obvious that this was the talk of a weak state puffing itself up – that Lin's thesis was, in fact, a 'paper tiger'.[2]

Contemporary analysts could be more forgiven, however, for not identifying what, with the benefit of hindsight, was another perhaps more important factor in Lin's thesis and other aggressive foreign policy statements. This was that these were the years directly preceding the cultural revolution, when Chinese internal propaganda constantly referred to the possibility of war in order to 'mobilize the masses' and 'revolutionize consciousness', and stressed the importance of the army. Thus it seems likely that China helped infiltrate Pakistani irregulars into Indian-held parts of Kashmir to help inflame that situation, while for internal reasons Chinese propaganda exaggerated the dangers to world peace and Chinese security during the 1965 Pakistan-Indian war. Spectres were raised, not because the government genuinely foresaw widespread war (the fact that, along with Vietnam, Chinese commentators singled out Venezuela and the Congo as being in the forefront of world struggle showed how few 'promising' situations there really were), but because the possibility of war was an integral part in preparing the Chinese people for the cultural revolution.

But, particularly in Africa, far more serious analytical mistakes were made in the field. A reading of newspaper articles and semi-clandestine reports put out by governments (usually 'leaked' to journalists in the hope they will include government thinking in their articles), shows clearly that journalists were misleading their readers and diplomats their governments. Both seemed happy to accept Chinese propaganda at its face value and assign to China the role of 'baddie' in the

African drama. For journalists the temptations were obvious – stories about the 'yellow peril' or the 'red menace', about sinister Chinese agents paying out dollar bills under palm trees, made more popular reading than statistics on Chinese aid and details of new strains of rice introduced to Africa by Chinese agronomists. Headlines of the period give a flavour of the sort of alarmist writing that was common: *Chinese Dragon in Africa (The Times)*, (did *The Times* not know that in China the dragon is a friendly rain-bringing beast?), *Aims Behind the Acrobats (Economist)*, *China Fans the Flames (Reporter)*, *Red China Points Trumpet at Africa (Christian Science Monitor)* and the rather ponderous *Red China Slips into Africa, Planting the Seeds of Influence (National Observer)*.

Where possible, emotive words were used to rouse the reader – thus 'penetration' or 'infiltration' turns out on closer inspection merely to signify the establishment of diplomatic relations; 'threat' is used indiscriminately to denote 'presence'. In the absence of explanations by China herself for her interest in Africa other than to use it as a 'rural base', editors evolved their own theories, some of them preposterous. Mr Seymour Freidin, an executive editor of the *New York Times*, obliged the 'pro-Soviet communists', whom he quoted as his source, by giving his readers the benefit of this theory: 'The Red Chinese drive in Africa ... involves a long range effort to dominate the continent totally and populate it with Chinese.'

Far-fetched Western theories about China's motives for being in Africa had two important consequences. The first was that moderate African leaders, who often had little else by which to judge Chinese policies, were misinformed. Western newspaper reports inevitably provided much of the raw material for decision-making in countries lacking a sophisticated diplomatic service or intelligence-gathering network. Leaders like Banda or Houphouet-Boigny, who in any case had a long-standing prejudice against communism, were only too glad to have their worst suspicions confirmed by headlines like the ones already quoted; others, perhaps less biased (for example Haile Selassie) but subjected to a barrage of anti-Chinese propaganda and with no corresponding material in favour of China, would play safe and defer establishing diplomatic relations with these seemingly dangerous people. The second consequence of these Machiavellian theories, supported to an extent by China's own militant propaganda, was that it prevented journalists and diplomats from seeing the real reasons for Chinese setbacks and from arriving at a more balanced judgement of China's motives and policies. Naturally, not all diplomats were deceived and some doubtless propagated exaggerated stories about the Chinese as a wider campaign against communism. But the expulsion of a Chinese diplomat or NCNA correspondent, or the severance of diplomatic relations, was generally written down as yet another example of the Chinese getting caught red-handed. Statements like Lin's thesis or Chou's 'Africa is ripe for revolution' speech were gratefully taken at their face value, with little consideration given to their real significance in the context of China's actual situation, or to the likelihood that a nation feeling itself threatened might resort to extravagant language. If observers had examined each example of a Chinese setback on its merits and not been blinded by their prejudices, they would have discovered that, far from having revolution pure and simple as its driving force, China's African policy was pragmatic, somewhat cautious and depended for success, like all other nations' foreign policies, on good timing and on good luck. When those were absent it failed. Nor was any credit given for, or even notice taken of, China's constructive policies. When they were mentioned they were regarded simply as devices for furthering disruptive policies – the Tanzam railway was a Trojan Horse for Chinese influence, Tanzania was a 'communist bridgehead', technical experts were either spies or soldiers, and aid was bribery.

But perhaps the worst aspect of the 'Chinese bogey' school of thought was the assumption that African governments were quite incapable of handling a Chinese presence in their countries. The European powers still felt they 'knew what was best' for their former colonies, that they would 'rue the day' they had asked the Chinese in and that nothing good could possibly come from a relationship with such dangerous and unstable partners. They ignored the fact that leaders, who were successfully able to manipulate them, the colonialists, out of power were also quite politically mature enough to deal with the Chinese. At worst, the Chinese could be asked to leave – as they were from a number of countries. In others, such as Kenya, where Kenyatta's handling of them was masterly, they could be comfortably contained. Finally, although few people in the West were able to see it, there were several countries where the Chinese were positively welcome, for sound political and economic reasons.

President Nyerere summed up many Africans' resentment at Western implications that they were incapable of looking after themselves when he complained at a London press conference in 1965 that Westerners appeared to be scrutinizing Tanzania to see if it had become 'contaminated' by contact with China.

> I gather that even the suits I wear have been adduced as evidence of pernicious Chinese influence . . . Sometimes I wonder whether the Western countries are not rapidly developing an inferiority complex towards the Eastern countries, and China in particular.

We will now examine those countries in which China suffered setbacks in her African diplomacy, and which, taken together, were regarded in the West as ample proof of her intention to subvert the whole continent and thereby further her supposed ambitions for world revolution. What emerges, however, is not a pattern, but a patchwork.

EAST AFRICA AND ZANZIBAR

The 'Chinese factor' was widely believed to be the link between the three East African army mutinies and the Zanzibar revolution, which all occurred at the beginning of 1964. As we saw earlier, Lord Colyton in London's House of Lords even managed to persuade himself that they were all 'something to do' with Chou En-lai's presence in the area. There was general talk in the West about an 'African Cuba' (two of the Zanzibari revolutionaries had in fact been trained in Havana), and East Africa was immediately labelled a 'communist bridgehead'. In the absence of a shred of evidence of Chinese involvement in any of the four affairs, the hysteria aroused in the West did seem to lend credibility to Nyerere's claim that Western countries were developing an inferiority complex towards China.

The mutinies, in rapid succession, of the Kenyan, Ugandan

and Tanganyikan armies can be dealt with quite simply. They were concerned exclusively with pay claims and with African soldiers' grievances over the slow rate of Africanization of the armies – all three were extensively officered by British personnel. Neither during the mutinies (which were quelled by the speedy arrival of British troops, requested by the respective governments) nor during the subsequent trials was any evidence given that there had been outside interference or encouragement. And at the OAU emergency meeting held in Dar es Salaam in February to discuss the mutinies, Nyerere stated quite categorically that 'There is no evidence to suggest that the mutinies in Tanganyika were inspired by outside forces–either Communist or Imperialist.'

ZANZIBAR

Suspicion that China might be involved in the Zanzibar revolution hinged on the fact that Kao Liang was NCNA correspondent on the island immediately preceding the revolution and his place – as a 'stringer' – was taken by Babu, a political activist and leading light of the radical Umma Party, whose public utterance at any rate marked him out as fervently pro-Chinese. But, except for 'sightings' of Chinese 'soldiers' during the revolution (in fact overseas Chinese laundrymen), no hard evidence of direct Chinese involvement was produced.

The revolution in any case hardly needed incitement from outside – it came about as a direct result of an electoral system under which the African Afro-Shirazi party consistently won an overall majority of votes, but because of the peculiar electoral boundaries was unable to win a majority of the National Assembly seats. In the last elections before independence the ASP polled 87402 votes against the 47943 registered by its main rivals, the Arab-dominated Zanzibar National Party; yet in the Assembly the ASP had only thirteen seats out of a total of thirty-one. The ASP concluded that the departing British colonial administration and the Arab ruling élite had evolved a system under which the Africans would perpetually be a suppressed majority. Few countries enjoyed a less auspicious Independence Day, with the Africans refusing to participate in independence celebrations and referring to the occasion simply as 'Uhuru wa Waarabu' (Arab Independence Day). The ASP leader, Abeid Karume, still hoped for a peaceful, constitutional transition from Arab to African rule, but an extraordinary character, 'Field Marshal' John Okello, the assistant Secretary-General of the Zanzibar and Pemba Paint Workers' Union, decided independently that only force would propel Africans into power. According to his own account[3] he trained a force of irregulars 'in the use of axes, bows and arrows, chisels, throwing stones and other materials useful for fighting', and persuaded the ASP leadership to back him. On the night of 11 January he launched his revolution, and within nine hours the island was his. Early on, his force had captured the Ziwani police headquarters and used the weapons they found inside. These were the only modern weapons they had.

It would be difficult to imagine a more homespun revolution, arising out of genuine local grievances. Okello himself denied any outside involvement:

I am no one's agent ... the revolution in Zanzibar which I led was not 'approved from above' or supported from outside, but it may have foiled those who were planning such revolutions with leaders they knew and could control. But I was unknown throughout the world, my resources to lead and win the revolution were unknown and my plans for Zanzibar were unknown.[4]

With his reference to 'those who were planning such revolutions with leaders they knew and could control' it is probable that Okello was thinking of China and Babu; but even if the assumption is correct, it seems Okello bore Babu a certain amount of personal animosity. There is also no reason why he should have had any special knowledge about Chinese intentions. Babu, incidentally, the Chinese 'link' man of Western mythology, was in Dar es Salaam during the three days of the revolution he was supposed to be co-ordinating.

Somewhat ironically it was through the Western press that Chou heard of the Zanzibar revolution. Questioned in Mogadiscu before he left for China about alleged Chinese involvement in the revolution, he declined to take the credit in a statement foreshadowing many similar denials of Chinese revolutionary activities over the next few years:

It is an honour for us when it is said that a people which is alive and is able to rise to defeat colonialism has done so at the instigation of the communists. This is an honour for us, but I must tell you that we had nothing to do with the events in Zanzibar. It was through the press that I heard a revolution had been staged in that country. (NCNA, Mogadiscu, 3 February 1964)

THE CONGO

China's Congolese policies epitomize the difficulties into which she was led by trying to pursue simultaneously united front-from-above and united front-from-below tactics: one could almost say, as it was said of the Soviet Union's policies in Algeria, that it was an unheroic attempt to serve contradictory interests all at the same time. On the one hand were the brash assertions that the Congo was a highly promising revolutionary situation, and in the forefront of the worldwide struggle against imperialism; on the other were denials of direct Chinese involvement to avoid scaring governments with which China enjoyed normal relations and to avoid embarrassing the governments through which China did actually assist the rebels.

However, that China did regard the Congo as an important and promising situation we know both from her published propaganda on the subject and from the captured PLA *Bulletin of Activities*, already referred to. Because of the size of the Congo, and her key geographical position, Chinese policy makers had high hopes that a successful revolution there would induce a 'domino effect' throughout the continent:

Among the independent countries in Africa, if only one or two of them complete a real national revolution, solving their own problems of resisting imperialism and reaching an internal solution of a democratic national revolution, the effect will be very great, the time ripe for action, the revolutionary wave will be able to swallow the whole African continent, and the 200 million or more Africans will advance to the forefront of the world. We should take longe-range views of this problem. (Bulletin of Activities, p. 485)

Corroboratory evidence comes from Tung Chi-ping who has related[5] that he attended a briefing for the ambassador-designate to Burundi, Liu Yu-feng, at which a Chinese Foreign Ministry official told him to concentrate most of his activities in the Congo, where 'the revolutionary situation is very good for us.' The same official quoted Mao as saying: 'If we can take the Congo, we can have all of Africa.'

If this really was China's view of the Congo it was, objectively, a mistaken one, arising out of her inexperience of African politics and her inability to see the Congolese rebellion for what it was – an isolated incident unlikely to spread over the Congo's borders. But it seems likely that the apparent importance attached to the Congolese situation served subsidiary purposes. Within China herself, considerable radio, newspaper and magazine comment on the Congo, as well as disproportionately large public parades in support of our 'Congolese brothers', served both to underline China's self-styled important role in the outside world and acted as a diversion from the economic crisis from which China was still recovering. And in the context of the Sino-Soviet dispute adoption by the initially successful guerrilla bands of Chinese methods ('correct policies' as they were called by the PLA bulletin) proved the superiority of Chinese over Soviet revolutionary theory.

For the two years after Gizenga's 'defection' to the moderate Adoula, and the humiliation of having to withdraw her ambassador to Stanleyville immediately after his arrival (see p. 31), China was unable to find a satisfactory opposition group within the Congo to support. However, contact was maintained, and training reportedly given, to various dissident individuals. These included Pierre Mulele, a former Education Minister in Lumumba's government, who visited China for a period of about two months, and Gaston Soumailot, who had been Minister of Justice for Kivu Province in Gizenga's 1961 government. In 1963 Mulele turned up in Kwilu Province, where he organized a youth movement – for which he was expelled from the PSA-Gizenga party. At the end of the year he launched a guerrilla operation in the province, based partly on the Chinese model; his men, for example, were issued with eight Mao-type instructions on how to conduct themselves, including the need to buy food honestly, avoid trampling on crops, treating women and prisoners of war humanely and so on.

At the same time a convincing opposition group, composed of the Gizengist rump, dissatisfied Leopoldville politicians and provincial rebel leaders, was set up in Brazzaville as a government-in-exile (CNL). After a time the CNL, as was inevitable with so many disparate elements, became factional, split along ideological, as well as tribal, lines. The pro-Soviet group was led by Christophe Gbenye, who with Soviet aid[6] had tried to oust Adoula in November. The failure of the attempted coup led to the expulsion of the Soviet embassy from Leopoldville for the second time in three years and to the discredit of the Soviet prescription of liberation by coup.[7] Meanwhile, the Chinese model received a boost by the apparent success of Mulele's rebellion, which even Radio Moscow had to characterize as a 'patriotic uprising'. The Soviet Union also gave Mulele material support.

In the first bout of Congolese troubles immediately after independence China had been hampered from lending effective support to her protégés by logistical problems. As we saw earlier, she had been able to respond in September 1960 to the Lumumba-Gizenga government's request for volunteers, munitions, helicopters and money only with a cash grant of £1 million. She pleaded geographical difficulties for not sending the volunteers and material.

In the meantime China had established a physical presence in the area, and was capable of sustaining Congolese guerrilla bands – from Tanzania, Brazzaville and Burundi. Supplies were shipped either through Brazzaville, or from Dar es Salaam to Kigoma on Lake Tanganyika and onwards either directly or through Burundi to eastern Congo. Guerrilla training was given, probably at camps in Tanzania and certainly at the Gamboma and Impfondo camps in Congo-Brazzaville, reportedly by General Wang Ping, an expert in guerrilla warfare, according to Western legend. Tshombe, now recalled to restore order, attacked this new axis in a radio broadcast:

The Burundi kingdom and the Congo republic are giving constant aid to centres of the rebellion. There are three training camps in Congo-Brazzaville territory. Burundi is giving open assistance to subversion in the east of the country. In both countries the Chinese embassies are active in the co-ordination of subversion and the support of it with supplies and men. Communist China wishes to exploit the anarchy in certain regions of the Republic to create a new centre of international tension. (Radio Bukavu, 18 August 1964)

Shortly afterwards Tshombe broke diplomatic relations with the two African countries.

The effective end of the second Congolese rebellion came with the fall of Stanleyville, to a combination of Belgian and American paratroopers and mercenary ground forces. Without success the Soviet Union, Egypt and Algeria tried to keep the flames of revolution alive by an airlift of supplies to the Congo and by a crash guerrilla training programme in the Sudan, where many of the insurgents had fled.

In the next two years there was sporadic trouble in the Congo, mostly on ethnic lines. But China's ability to fuel the situation was circumscribed by the expulsion of her embassy from Burundi at the beginning of 1965 and curtailed completely in January 1966 with Tanzania's promise to stop aiding the rebels, or allowing aid to be transported to them through Tanzania.

In retrospect, the most notable aspect of China's activities in the Congo was its conservatism, particularly China's desire to keep secret her material support for the rebels. In a statement reminiscent of Chou's disclaimer of involvement in Zanzibar, the Chinese embassy in Nairobi denied the 'slanderous charge' that China had interfered in the Congo, but added: 'We regard it as our unshakeable and honourable internationalist duty to support the struggle of all oppressed nations and peoples.' It seems in any case that China's material support for the rebels *was* minimal, a reflection not only of the logistical difficulties but also of China's thesis that revolution was not for export.[8] Certainly, compared with the resources made available to the central government by the US, including helicopters, transport aircraft, bombers and even paratroopers, China's support was very sparing. She was sparing too in her diplomatic support, for despite the fact that the CNL could claim to be as representative as Tshombe's government, and at one time its forces controlled nearly half the country, China never afforded it recognition.[9]

It is interesting that, mostly because of extravagant Western press claims about the extent of Chinese involvement in the Congo, as well as a 'quieter' approach by the Soviet Union, it was China which received most censure amongst African moderates for her support of the rebels – despite the probably greater material help supplied by the Soviet Union. In some ways the Soviet Union's big power status, as well probably as her greater aid-giving capacity, gave her a somewhat spurious respectability. Nigeria, for example, established diplomatic relations with the Soviet Union in October 1963, just as Adoula was discovering the Soviet-backed plot to oust him. But Nigeria's Prime Minister, Sir Abubakar Tafewa Balewa, gave as his reasons for not extending recognition to China her revolutionary actions in the Congo. China's revolutionary images cultivated by the West and partly by herself, often had deleterious consequences.

BURUNDI

China's expulsion from Burundi was a visible diplomatic failure. It drew attention to the disruptive side of her activities, without producing any compensating gains, and lent credence to the belief that she was simply creating trouble in her own interests without pursuing any consistent ideological goal.

From Burundi China not only supported the Congolese dissidents, which, as we saw, led to a rupture in relations between the Congo and Burundi, but also Tutsi refugees from neighbouring Rwanda. The Tutsis had been the traditional feudal overlords of Rwanda, but had been ejected by the Bahutu peasantry, who formed 85 per cent of the country's population, shortly before independence in 1962. Many of the Tutsis fled to Burundi, whose politics were dominated by ethnic kinsmen of the overthrown Rwandans. Here they formed themselves into guerrilla bands known as Inyenzi, or Cockroaches, from their habit of raiding at night.

Kao Liang's exploratory trips to Burundi had included contact with these groups, and it was also believed the Chinese had discussed the Rwandan situation with the deposed Mwami (King) Kigeri V, who was living in exile in Kenya. Tutsi guerrillas were subsequently given training in Peking[10] and 'money and encouragement' by the Chinese embassy in Bujumbura.[11] The Rwandan authorities implicated the Chinese in the stepped-up Inyenzi raids of late 1963, which were repulsed only with Belgian assistance.

News of China's support for the Tutsis naturally elicited

charges of cynicism against the Chinese, for neither Rwanda's recognition of Taipei nor the anti-communist clause in her constitution could really justify China's efforts to help feudal overlords reassert their authority over a peasant majority. The comparison between China's encouragement for a genuine peasant-type revolution in Kwilu, and her efforts to undermine Africa's only peasant government in nearby Rwanda, did not go unnoticed. This was pragmatism taken too far, for not only did Chinese support for the Tutsis alienate moderate African opinion, it must also have caused some concern to China's admirers as well. How were they to explain such actions? The silence of men like Nyerere and Sekou Touré on this must surely be taken to signal disapproval.

Within Burundi, Kao Liang had bought a considerable amount of influence for China; recipients of his largesse included the Prime Minister, Albin Nyamoya, and other senior government officials. But Mwami Mwambutsa had American leanings, which he signalled by refusing to see the Chinese ambassador-designate, Liu Yu-feng, although he received the Soviet chargé. In a gallant attempt to improve international understanding, he sent a note to the Chinese embassy informing them that 'the accreditation of the representative of the People's Republic of China to Burundi will take place as soon as the policies of the United States and China have become somewhat harmonized'.[12] Luckily Liu did not have to wait that long, eventually presenting his credentials in September, the day after Burundi had signed a much-publicized technical and financial agreement with the US.

In December 1964 Nyamoya was removed from office by a vote of censure in Parliament, after claims that he had allowed his government to become too close to China. He was succeeded by Pierre Ngendandumwe. Ten days later Ngendandumwe was assassinated. His successor, Joseph Bamina, while not implicating the Chinese in the murder, said the Chinese ambassador was 'seriously involved in sabotaging efforts at reunification among the population of Burundi', and diplomatic relations were indefinitely suspended. Bamina was probably referring to known Chinese support for the trade-union movement, which favoured a republican constitution (its slogan was 'Bread, Peace and Burundi' as opposed to the national slogan of 'God,

5

Mwami and Burundi'), and to Chinese money for extremists in his own administration.

China's policies in Kenya too were opportunistic, badly conceived and not successful. The fact that the Chinese were prepared to subvent opposition to Kenyatta, one of the elder statesmen of African politics, once again made them suspect in the eyes of moderate leaders, while the ease with which they were exposed cast some doubt on their technical subtlety.

For neither China nor the Soviet Union was Kenyatta a particularly satisfactory leader – his country was too obviously in the Western orbit and he made no great pretensions about leading Kenya towards socialism. However, diplomatic relations were established and early offers of Soviet aid earned this tribute from Kenyatta:

I am aware that the Soviet Union, from the very beginning of its existence, has been in the front ranks of the struggle against colonial oppression. (*Pravda*, 10 July 1964)

Less than a year after independence 300 Kenyan students were studying in the Soviet Union. In November 1964 an agreement was signed for the disbursement of a 40-million-rouble credit, offered at the customary $2\frac{1}{2}$ per cent interest rate. The loan was to cover costs of constructing hydro-technical installations in the Kano Plains Valley and of erecting a textile mill, sugar refinery, short-wave radio station and a fish cannery. The Soviets also agreed to build as a gift to the Kenyan people a hospital and a technical institute.

From then on Soviet-Kenyan relations went steadily downhill. In April 1965 a group of students returned from the Soviet university of Baku, complaining of ideological indoctrination and racial discrimination, complaints which received wide publicity in the Western-owned Kenyan press. In the same month Kenyatta rejected a consignment of Soviet arms, complaining they were too old-fashioned and 'would be of no use to the modern army of Kenya'.[13] The next month Parliament approved a motion for the government to take over the Patrice Lumumba Institute in Nairobi, whose Soviet instructors had been attempting to indoctrinate pupils. Later still, after look-ing at the small print of the aid agreement, the government rejected the Soviet Union's offer to finance the Kano Plains scheme because it depended on Kenya's ability to sell Soviet goods to the value of £6 million over four years, which the government could not guarantee. A Soviet bush-clearing scheme was also cancelled, and the Kenyans insisted on a 200-kW radio transmitter rather than the 50-kW one specified in the agreement.

The parallel with Guinea was obvious, but China was not in Kenya, as she had to a certain extent been in Guinea, the bene-ficiary of Soviet blundering. She had, it is true, tried to contrast the generosity of her aid with the Soviet Union's 'commercial' assistance, by giving a cash grant of just over £1 million in January 1964 to help balance the budget, and followed this up with an interest-free loan of £5·3 million. But the loan was never drawn on, and China showed more in-terest in competing with the Soviet Union for the favours of Oginga Odinga, Kenyatta's 'number two' – but implicitly his arch rival – than in making an impression with her aid.

The open competition for Odinga, coupled with disenchant-ment over Soviet aid, led Kenyatta to make a strong attack on communism. He was not concerned with drawing fine lines between the Chinese and Soviet variety; both, as far as he was concerned, were as bad as each other – both were tarred with the brush of subversion. He warned them that

We welcome genuine friendship, but we detest flattery. We welcome cooperation and assistance, but we shall not be bought or black-mailed.

I warn those in our country who seek to create confusion. It is true that we have passed through many years of Western imperialism. It is natural that we should detest Western colonialism, and associate the word imperialism with the West . . . It is naive to think that there is no danger of imperialism from the East. In world politics the East has as many designs upon us as the West and would like us to serve their own interests. That is why we reject communism. It is in fact the reason why we have chosen for ourselves the policy of non-alignment and African socialism. To us communism is as bad as imperialism. (*East African Standard.* 27 June 1967)

Odinga, a prosperous Luo businessman, had lent Kenyatta

money during the emergency, helped to secure his release from detention and worked for his victory in the 1963 elections; he was rewarded by being made Home Minister and later Vice-President. Before and after independence, he visited both Moscow and Peking and received money from both. He was an obvious target for communist blandishments – not only did he appear to be Kenyatta's successor, but – dressed in his Mao suit – he even professed vague socialist leanings. In practice his socialism involved rapid Africanization and a reduction of British influence in Kenya, a message with obvious attractions for Kenya's landless and urban unemployed.[14] That Kenyatta was perfectly aware of Odinga's affiliations and ambitions was made clear as early as June 1964 when he appointed Joseph Murumbi, the Minister of State, to be Prime Minister during his absence at the Commonwealth conference, in preference to Odinga, the obvious choice.

During the next year Odinga's constitutional, and effective, powers, were whittled away. In a new republican constitution he was named Vice-President, but Parliament was given the right to choose a successor in the event of Kenyatta's death. In February 1965 Odinga suffered a more serious loss with the death of his able Goan lieutenant, Pio de Gama Pinto, who had acted as his go-between with the communist embassies and had advised him on political strategy. Odinga became rudderless; whereas Pinto had cautioned a low profile Odinga now began to behave as if the only way he could succeed Kenyatta was by emphasizing the differences between them. He became more open about his communist affiliations, in one speech referring to communism as the people's 'food'. This rapid polarization alarmed the Russians who, despite their setbacks, still believed in government-to-government diplomacy. Odinga therefore came to rely more and more on Chinese advice and finance. Again, Kenyatta knew quite well what was going on – on one occasion he told the American ambassador[15] that Kenya had a new tourist attraction, the Chinese embassy, hidden behind its high walls. 'We now have the Great Wall of China here in Africa. Our police will have to use helicopters to see what those people are doing . . .'. Partly to placate those of his supporters who wanted to sever relations with China over her support for Odinga, Kenyatta expelled

Wang Teh-ming, the NCNA correspondent, in July 1965.

But the crisis came in February 1966 with the surprise announcement of a conference to restructure the ruling party, KANU. In the weeks leading up to the conference Odinga spent a great deal of (presumably Chinese) money trying to buy votes. The day before the conference the government expelled two Soviet diplomats and Yao Chua, a third secretary in the Chinese embassy. At the same time 100 Members of Parliament issued a statement denouncing Odinga and his group as 'agents of rapacious international communism'. Odinga left KANU and formed his own party, the Kenya People's Union. Kenyatta warned the communist embassies that financial support for the new party would be construed as subversion and would lead to severance of relations.

Kenyatta's containment of the Chinese, admittedly with the help of a competent European-officered security force, was admirable. Internally, it probably suited him to have his rival associate with the Chinese, whom he could characterize as the 'baddies'. That was one reason for not completely breaking relations; another was the fear that if they were expelled from the country the Chinese might attempt a more dangerous form of subversion, Cameroon-style, from outside the country. Certainly the unsettled conditions in the North-West Frontier District, with sporadic warfare going on between the Somali shiftas and Kenyan tribesmen, and with a separatist group within Kenya itself, would have offered an excellent opportunity to ferment disruption under the pretext of helping Somalia.[16] But Kenyatta, as he himself said, liked to have the Chinese 'under his nose' where he could see them – and the opportunity for widespread disruptive activity in Kenya therefore never presented itself.

ETHIOPIA

Ethiopia also believed, incorrectly, that China was aiding the Somali shiftas. Partly for this reason, partly because of Chou's reference in Mogadiscu, at the end of his 1964 tour, to US pressure on Ethiopia applied to frustrate relations between China and Ethiopia, Haile Selassie did not fulfil his pledge to establish diplomatic relations. Chou had also added gratuitously

that Ethiopia, like Morocco, should 'throw off outside control'.
A small amount of Chinese aid therefore went, via Syria, to
the Eritrean Liberation Front, a Moslem separatist group
fighting for the independence of Eritrea from Ethiopia.

SUDAN

Disruptive opportunistic activity of a minor sort was reported
in Sudan during the 1964 rising, when China was believed to
have offered arms, not to the pro-Soviet Communist party,
which had little mass backing, but to the pro-Western Umma
party, the only party with any popular following that opposed
President Abboud.[17] Pragmatism like this has brought its
rewards in Sudan, where the Communist party has been
proscribed frequently and Chinese acquiescence (presumably
joyfully given, since the party has inevitably been pro-Soviet)
has been taken by the Sudanese government to indicate
approval of itself and its policies (see p. 171).

EGYPT

A small group of Egyptian dissidents, who were known to have
had contacts with the Chinese embassy, were arrested in 1965
on a charge of trying to overthrow Nasser and establish a
people's republic. The case was held privately, but according
to a *New York Times* reporter, an NCNA correspondent and a
Chinese military attaché were asked to leave as a result of their
part in the conspiracy. The affair was hushed up, and clearly
neither China nor Egypt wished it to interfere with normal
relations.

CENTRAL AFRICAN REPUBLIC

In most of the above examples there was a certain amount of
evidence of Chinese subversion; or, as one Western reporter
put it, the 'crafty hand of the Chinese' could be detected
behind attempts to cause disruption. In some cases the Chinese
denied it, in others they proclaimed it. But in two countries
from which their missions were expelled, the Central African
Republic and Dahomey, cases regarded in the West as crown-

ing the inglorious disruptive achievements of two years and cited frequently as epitomizing the 'failure' of China's African policies, there was absolutely no credible evidence to suggest that China had in any way behaved subversively. But in some ways China had only herself to blame; she had become the victim of her own propaganda, and her actions were suspected even when there were no factual grounds for suspicion.

The establishment of diplomatic relations with the Central African Republic in September 1964 must have been particularly welcome in Peking, with an embassy in Bangui compensating for the loss of facilities in Bujumbura and ensuring a Chinese presence in the heart of Africa. An interest-free loan of £1·4 million was conditional on the recognition and expulsion of the Taiwanese representative. This bazaar diplomacy was taken a stage further with the arrival of the new ambassador Meng Ying, formerly consul in Zanzibar, who tried to reduce the cash element in the loan, previously half of the total, to a third, while the balance would have been supplied in the form of Chinese goods over a period of five years. This uncharacteristically mean gesture was rejected outright by the government.

After this somewhat unpromising start China rapidly expanded her activities in the CAR, and gave every appearance of wishing to establish a constructive presence; certainly, from a strategic point of view, it made sense to try and remain in the country, which formed a useful link between Congo-Brazzaville and eastern Africa, a sort of arm round the Congo. Chinese agronomists arrived, as did an NCNA correspondent, and at the time of the coup China was building an exhibition of economic reconstruction in Bangui.

In January 1966 President David Dacko was ousted by his cousin, Colonel Jean Bokassa, who said Dacko had become a prisoner of pro-Chinese elements and that he had staged the coup to save the President, and the country, from Chinese-inspired chaos. Six days later diplomatic relations with China were broken, following the production of documents purportedly proving that China had been supporting a subversive 'People's Army of the CAR'. Among those implicated were Dacko's principal political secretary, M. Nzallat, who had just returned from Peking, and Jean Mourioumbai, the former Director of

Internal Security, who was arrested by the army as he tried to escape to the Congo. Chinese arms-caches and documents on people's wars were also found in the state house.

Although some elements in the army with pro-Chinese leanings had been noted before the coup, there was no evidence to show they were being groomed by the Chinese for subversive purposes; nor could the presence of Chinese material in state house be described as 'subversive' since presumably the President himself must have asked for it.

One writer sees as a more likely cause of the coup the 'political and economic malaise of the country' at the time.[18] Another contributory factor would have been Bokassa's experiences in fighting for the French in Indo-China, which had strongly prejudiced him, and many other Africans in the French army, against the Chinese. His seizure of power gave him, however remotely and unjustifiably, a chance to settle old scores.

DAHOMEY

General Christophe Soglo of Dahomey had also fought against the Vietcong in Indo-China, and may well have nursed similar grievances against the Chinese. He was propelled into power by a military coup, the third in two years, in the same month that Bokassa took over in CAR. Like Bokassa he immediately expelled the Chinese mission, but offered absolutely no reason for doing so. Not unnaturally China characterized this as 'an unreasonable unilateral action'. Soglo may have just felt generally uneasy about the Chinese communists and decided life was safer without them; he does, however, seem to have been impressed by the Taiwanese, who had undertaken various agricultural schemes in Dahomey before relations were established with the CPR (in November 1964), and relations were re-established with them within three months of the expulsion of the mainland Chinese.

China was understandably frustrated by these two undeserved setbacks, which were eagerly seized on by her critics. Part of this frustration shows in her official explanation of the two events:

The two incidents in the wake of military coups d'etat in both countries were by no means accidental. Imperialism headed by the US is trying to stir up an adverse anti-China current in Africa so as to bring about a breach in normal relations between China and the African countries and undermine the militant friendship and solidarity between these two peoples. Dahomey's ending and the CAR's severance of diplomatic relations with China under the manipulation of imperialism are part of this adverse anti-China current. (*People's Daily*, 9 January 1966)

UPPER VOLTA

Yet another military coup occurred in Upper Volta, where the new President, General Lamizana, had also fought against the Vietcong in Indo-China. China had no diplomatic relations with Upper Volta, but during the demonstrations which preceded the coup, President Yameogo claimed that 'subversion inspired by communists has entered the country'. He accused Joseph Ouedraogo, a former President of the National Assembly, of trying to 'hand over the country to Ghana, thus to the China of Peking'.

GHANA

Nkrumah's political ambitions and his willingness to countenance subversive activities against neighbours he found ideologically unsatisfactory led him to seek the assistance of the Chinese, who must have seemed 'natural allies' in this task. But in fact China was curiously circumspect about claiming any credit for her cooperation, and when sending military experts to Ghana at the end of 1964 asked that their arrival be kept secret – 'because of imperial allegations that the Chinese were encouraging subversion in certain countries'. Even Nkrumah himself had a somewhat ambivalent attitude towards the Chinese, and appointed an officer to keep them under surveillance in case, presumably, they decided he too was dispensable. This officer has said that

Nkrumah believed that China had to have a conspicuous position in the world of Ghanaian ideology, because he suspected that in the final analysis they were right in their view of the liberation movement.

But basically he feared them. He instinctively trusted Russians, he instinctively distrusted Chinese. He was, simply, scared that the Chinese did not have his own best interests at heart, and I had clear instructions to watch their movements closely.[19]

The Chinese instructors were attached to the Bureau of African Affairs which since 1960 had co-ordinated Nkrumah's attempts to subvert other African countries and further his Pan-African ambitions.[20] One of its most important tasks was the administration of a guerrilla camp where dissidents of various African countries were trained in subversive techniques. Originally this had been staffed by Russian instructors, but they had proved lax and unpopular and the Chinese were called in to stiffen discipline.[21]

In an attempt to clear the way for better relations with its neighbours the post-Nkrumah government published[22] details of the organization of the camp, from which we learn that on the recommendation of the Chinese leader, Colonel Yen Leng, the camp was moved from its original site at Half-Assimi (which he considered too near the Ivory Coast border for explosives training) to Obenamasi. The Chinese asked for a Land Rover, so they could spend their weekends with the Chinese embassy staff in Accra; they also asked for a batman and a new cook, since the one they had was 'irresponsible' (presumably the same one whose wife the Russians had found so delectable). Other requests were more relevant to the business in hand: they requested certain chemicals so that explosives techniques could be taught immediately, and they asked for the students to be divided into language groups.

Over two hundred students from such countries as the Ivory Coast, Niger, Dahomey, the Congo and Cameroon attended the first course. Basic training consisted of the fundamentals of guerrilla warfare, strategy and tactics, explosives, weapons, telecommunications and first aid. Some of the students complained that they had not learned about explosives, but the Chinese explained that only those with some scientific background could be taught about explosives – the 'illiterate and unintelligent' could receive only training in weapon handling.

Correct political thinking, as an essential part of Chinese guerrilla strategy, was also taught. It was not very wideranging. As a Cameroonian student admitted when the camp was discovered by the army after the coup: 'We learned about Mao Tse-tung. We did not hear anything about Marx or Lenin.'

THE COUP

At the beginning of 1966 Nkrumah left Ghana to visit North Korea and China. Banners, life-size portraits and large crowds greeted him in Peking, and on the night of 24 February a banquet was given for him in the Great Hall of the People. In his welcoming speech Liu Shao-chi said that although most African countries had won independence, the revolutionary struggle against imperialism was by no means completed. Further victories had yet to be won.

The irony was not lost on commentators – earlier that day a group of soldiers had seized power in Accra, and deposed the absent President.[23] Throughout the five-day visit the Chinese press refrained from mentioning the coup, and the official programme went ahead as planned. But during the time Nkrumah was in Peking Ghanaian soldiers beat-up four Chinese experts, and on the day he left the new government demanded the immediate withdrawal of all Chinese technical experts and the reduction of the embassy staff to eighteen.

Although China was indignant at the beating-up of the experts, reaction to the request for the withdrawal of technical personnel and later to the revelations about the training camp was surprisingly formal and mild. The Chinese side pointed out that construction of the Integrated Cotton Textile and Knitwear factory at Juapong and the pencil factory at Kumasi was in 'full swing'. 7 000 tons of equipment for the former and 1000 tons for the latter had arrived in Ghana, and China had already paid for the local costs of construction. Before handing over the equipment China demanded a receipt.

Referring to the training camp, a Chinese note of 19 March said, . . . 'the military experts as well as the economic and technical experts sent by the Chinese government to work in Ghana were dispatched at the request of the government of the people of Ghana in pursuance of the relevant agreements signed by the two countries. They always worked in accordance with the arrangements made by the Ghanaian government.'

Nevertheless, diplomatic relations were suspended on 20 October, and the embassy staff recalled home. As in the notes protesting against the breaking of relations by the Central African Republic and Dahomey, China blamed imperialist machinations, but asserted that nothing could destroy the profound friendship between the two peoples.[24]

SUMMARY

Nkrumah's overthrow while he was in Peking seemed to epitomize in dramatic fashion the failure of China's disruptive policies. It was the 'peg' on which commentators could hang all the diplomatic reverses China had suffered in Africa over the previous three years.

But, as I hope this country by country examination has shown, China was not simply a trouble-maker doggedly and persistently pursuing her aims of world revolution in Africa and elsewhere. There was no coherent plan to 'subvert the continent' as Western commentators supposed; China was in fact feeling her way, taking decisions pragmatically, and usually cautiously. She was surprisingly sparing in her support for revolution, stressing rather the need for revolutionary self-reliance; when she did actually intervene, as in the Congo, she was anxious to keep her involvement secret, for fear of frightening moderate states with whom she hoped to maintain or establish government-to-government relations. The total of her disruptive activities was in fact surprisingly small, but was made to seem larger partly through her own extravagant propaganda, partly through hostile exaggeration of the extent of her activities. In some cases the publicity surrounding a diplomatic setback was out of all proportion to the actual cause – for example in Dahomey and CAR, where China had behaved blamelessly. In one case (Ghana) China was simply responding to a request made by the government, just as the US might respond, for example, to a Brazilian request for military advisers. Only in the Congo, Burundi and Kenya was any substantiated evidence produced of Chinese subversion – and even that amounted to very little.

Nevertheless, the publicity, exaggerated or not, did undoubtedly harm China's image in African eyes. Criticism, naturally, was loudest amongst Ghana's neighbours who thought of themselves as targets for Chinese subversion. Under the vigorous lead of Houphouet-Boigny, Francophone leaders in West Africa issued a stream of anti-Chinese statements. At a meeting of the Presidents of the Ivory Coast, Niger and Upper Volta in January 1965, Houphouet-Boigny warned his colleagues of the dangers of communism allied to peoples with a population problem: 'Against this peril let us safeguard our unity as the apple of our eye.' President Yameogo rather mysteriously warned those 'who by their silence are promoting the Chinese invasion of the continent'. President Hamani Diori of Niger accused China of giving guerrilla training (in Nanking) and finance to members of the outlawed Niger Sawaba party, based in Accra. On his re-election in October 1965, he expressed the hope that relations with certain East European countries would improve but there was no question of recognizing China which 'gives ideological and military training to nationals of other countries, and assists them financially to create subversion in their countries' (Radio Niamey, 11 October 1965).

In East Africa criticism was more muted (except of course from Kenya), although China's activities in Kenya drew an unfavourable response from President Obote, who warned foreign powers against interfering in Uganda's internal affairs. Later, in 1967, he terminated the contracts of Chinese military instructors because of their attempts at political indoctrination. President Kaunda's initial, possibly Christian-based, fear of the Chinese was responsible for Zambia refusing to allow the Chinese railway surveyors into the country to make a preliminary report on the Tanzam railway.

It would be a mistake, however, to believe that China necessarily regarded as a failure of policy what in the West were called reverses or setbacks. Visible signs of Chinese activism, such as the expulsion of a correspondent or a diplomat, drew a warm response from the extremists, and helped to polarize opinions. By now China would have adjusted to the fragility of African governments – today's dissidents could easily be tomorrow's leaders; backing for such people could easily be justified, especially if they were opposing a reactionary regime, or one heavily dependent on the West. It was also a very cheap way of publicizing China's revolutionary pretensions. The entire Chinese disruptive effort in Africa, so often characterized as 'massive' or 'pervasive', and conjuring up images of 'yellow hordes' swarming all over the continent, in all probability amounted to some thirty guerrilla instructors and about £2 million in finance. Like the constructive side of China's activities it was a very economical offensive.

However, it was remarkable how ineffective the disruptive approach proved to be. Not a single hostile government was overthrown by Chinese-aided dissidents, nor were policies even changed in an attempt to accommodate such elements. And the bad publicity surrounding such activities merely alienated governments which might otherwise have been disposed to friendship with China. African leaders, having won political independence, were by this time trying to establish their economic independence. They wanted economic aid, not political advice. It was natural that they should resent implications that they had not won 'true' political independence, and even more natural that they should resist attempts by the Chinese, or anyone else, to help opposition groups achieve that 'true' independence.

There were indications that the Chinese took these lessons to heart, as greater emphasis was put on constructive cooperation with independent African countries of whatever political hue, while disruptive activities came more and more to be confined to the 'safe' southern part of the continent.

THE ZIG-ZAGS OF REVOLUTION

But in 1966 the setbacks had to be explained – at least on a theoretical level. Chinese commentaries spoke increasingly of the 'twists and turns' of the revolution, of the 'zigzag path' to final victory and of the useful lessons to be learned 'by negative example' from upheavals and revolutionary storms. Setbacks were caused by the death-bed counter-attacks of imperialism, but, as Chairman Mao pointed out, 'Even great storms are not to be feared. It is amid great storms that human society progresses.'

Chen Yi, asked by a Japanese correspondent in January 1966 whether the postponement of the African-Asian Conference and the coup in Indonesia meant China was becoming more isolated, replied

Although some adverse currents have appeared in certain areas in Asia and Africa, the general situation in these countries is excellent ... At the same time tempestuous struggles against imperialism, colonialism and neo-colonialism headed by the United States have arisen everywhere – in Japan, South Korea, the Congo and Southern Rhodesia. The surging revolutionary struggles of the Asian and African peoples against imperialism are the main current in the situation in Asia and Africa ... Although certain individuals in Afro-Asian countries have joined the imperialists' anti-Chinese chorus because they have entered into the service of imperialism, and although the modern revisionists are also supporting the anti-Chinese hullabaloo, they are after all a small handful. (NCNA, Peking, 4 January 1966)

In an article written the day after Nkrumah left Peking, the *People's Daily* enlarged on the idea that recent reversals were the inevitable result of the sharpening of class struggle and that a great Armageddon-like battle between the revolutionary and the counter-revolutionary forces was taking place – 'World history is entering upon a phase of upheavals of unsurpassed magnitude.' Imperialism would not accept defeat lightly and in the anticipated counter-attacks the progressive forces might even meet temporary reverses. These, however, would only serve to raise still higher the people's political consciousness.

Facts have proved and will continue to prove that no force on earth can impede or check the revolutionary movement of the oppressed peoples and nations, which will continue to leap forward despite the twists and turns in the road of advance. (*People's Daily*, 1 March 1966)

A later article in the newspaper emphasized the educative nature of these 'twists and turns'. For example,

The Congolese people's struggle suffered severe setbacks a few years ago as a result of the attacks by imperialists, colonialists and neo-colonialists, the betrayal by revisionists and the lack of experience on the part of the revolutionary forces. However, having paid for their lessons with blood, the people of the Congo attained new heights of political consciousness ... Today, this struggle of the Congolese people, after traversing a tortuous path, has made much headway compared with several years ago ... While there is progress, its path has twists and turns; this is the dialectical unity and the universal law of development of revolution. (*People's Daily*, 7 March 1966)

For a time, however, the revolutionary and politically conscious forces of Africa and the rest of the world's 'countryside' were going to have to face the imperialists' counter-attacks on their own. China was about to obey this universal law and enter a bizarre twist in her own development: the cultural revolution.

Notes

1. A contrary view, however, was taken by two RAND analysts (RAND memorandum RM-4814-PR, 1965) who argued that the document was (a) mild and (b) directed at North Vietnam as a warning to the National Liberation Front not to expect Chinese military support. Another realistic assessment was put forward by John K. Fairbank, testifying to the Senate Foreign Relations Committee, who chided commentators for overreacting 'to the visionary blueprint of world revolution put out by Lin Piao'. All these American reactions are quoted by Larkin, op. cit., pp. 196–7.

2. But in Vietnam the 'paper tiger' raised a real tiger in increased US involvement. As Larkin points out, the war 'seems to rest on misunderstandings of the gap between Chinese wishes and Chinese capabilities, if not a fundamental misreading of Chinese intentions themselves. China's capabilities are exaggerated, China's control of events in Vietnam is exaggerated, but, believing China's role so large, many United States policy makers cannot tolerate accommodation to Chinese influence and involvement in Southeast Asia.'

3. *Revolution in Zanzibar*, East African Publishing House, 1967.

4. Ibid., p. 25.

5. Tung Chi-ping and Humphrey Evans, op. cit., p. 223.

6. Adoula had been shown documents implicating the Soviet embassy; they included requests from Gbenye to the embassy for weapons, tape recorders, counterfeit money, miniature pistols in the form of cigarette lighters, double-bottomed suitcases and travelling facilities to the Soviet Union for the 'young militants'.

7. Predictably, the Soviet Union was also under attack from China for her early silence on the new Congolese rebellions, as a result of which she was accused of playing the role of accomplice in the US imperialist crime of repressing the national independence movement in the Congo. However, 'advanced revolutionaries there had learned to distinguish between true and false friends'.

8. The guerrillas themselves were anxious to disclaim outside assistance –

they too regarded themselves as nationalists without outside 'affiliations'. Soumialot, for instance, denied any Chinese assistance (*New York Times*, 14 August 1964). Mobutu chuckled over Mao's assertion (made during Mobutu's 1973 trip to China) that he (Mao) had spent a lot of money and men in the Congo. But it seems likely Mao was talking more figuratively than accurately. (See also note 6, p. 173.)

9. Several reports indicated that China wanted to see the CNL hold and administer a large tract of the country before recognizing the government. She did not want to make the same mistake as she had made with Gizenga. China has in fact never recognized an African government-in-exile, the risks are obviously too great.

10. See Emmanual Hevi, *The Dragon's Embrace*, Pall Mall Press, London, 1967, p. 108.

11. See Claire Sterling, 'Chou En-lai and the Watusi', in *The Reporter*, 3 March 1964, pp. 22–3.

12. *Le Soir*, 22 September 1964.

13. *The Times*, 30 April 1964.

14. With the polarization of Kenyan society into rich and poor Odinga's 'socialism', however vague, continued to have an attraction for the less affluent, and he never lost the support of the Luo tribe. Had his party not been banned immediately before the 1969 election it would have made a strong challenge to the government. He could still be Kenyatta's successor.

15. Attwood, op. cit., p. 259.

16. Kenya claimed to have captured Chinese weapons from the shiftas, which is quite possible since the Somali government – itself a recipient of Chinese arms – probably backed the major secessionist group in the NFD, the Northern Province People's Progressive Party. But the Somalis denied there were any Chinese military instructors in the country.

17. See the *Financial Times*, 29 December 1964.

18. Victor Le Vine, writing in *Africa Report*, April 1966, p. 8.

19. Quoted in W. Scott-Thompson, *Ghana's Foreign Policy 1957–1966*, Princeton University Press, 1969.

20. For example, in May 1964 the Bureau prepared a series of 'Political Questionnaires for Activists', which listed in great detail subjects on which information was to be gathered in each country. Nkrumah was particularly anxious that his Pan-African aims should not be pre-empted by any regional grouping, such as the proposed East African Federation. Thus, under the Kenyan heading agents were asked: 'Kenyatta is ageing – there is a scramble for successor. Find out whether Murumbi, Tom Mboya and Oginga Odinga have, any of them, plans for a takeover bid of the government.' Elsewhere the activists were asked: 'Has Ghana to do some lobbying in Sierra Leone for choice of leadership?'

21. A report on the instructors during the 1962–1964 courses stated: 'The Russian instructors themselves proved to be a problem. They were given a car, a cook, a houseboy, an unlimited supply of food and alcoholic drinks. They had a patronizing air towards the members of the Bureau who were serving as translators. . . .' The head of the camp was doubtless glad to see the Russians replaced; he had written a long report as far back

as 1962 detailing complaints against them. According to him they had wasted food and drink, had behaved arrogantly and on one occasion 'one of the instructors even tried to seduce the wife of the cook after getting the cook drunk'.

22. *Nkrumah's Subversion in Africa*, published by Ghana Ministry of Information, May 1966.

23. When told about the coup on his arrival at Peking airport Nkrumah affected, according to his Foreign Minister, an air of 'stubborn nonchalance'.

24. The new Ghanaian government believed that China was trying to help Nkrumah regain power, alleging on one occasion (see *Ghana Times*, 23 February 1967) that China had given him £500000 for that purpose. This seems unlikely – China would have realized the hopelessness of Nkrumah's situation, but she might have provided him with a 'pension' during his exile in Guinea.

10

THE CULTURAL REVOLUTION

'As worthless as a heap of dog's dung'
Red Guard description of Chen Yi.

FOR over three years Chinese domestic and foreign policy was distorted and disrupted by the extravagant event known as the 'great proletarian cultural revolution'. During its violent and unpredictable course her head of state was dismissed and her foreign minister denounced and downgraded. Abroad, even some of China's most uncritical friends were alienated, both by events within China and by the activities of her 'revolutionary' diplomatic service.

Superficially, and as presented to the outside world, the cultural revolution was Mao's instrument for safeguarding the purity of the revolution. For those who were too young to have experienced the real communist revolution, an artificial revolution was created in which they could relive some of the rigour and excitement of the first revolution, as well as take stock of its achievements. Wrong tendencies were to be pointed out and corrected, and those of the old guard who were found lacking in revolutionary zeal and purity were to be routed out. The Red Guards were Mao's defenders of the faith.

But that is to take Mao's own interpretation of the cultural revolution at face value. Another explanation is given by studying the roots of the movement. Certain Chinese experts[1] now take as their starting point for the cultural revolution a central committee meeting held in Lushan in 1959, at which a broad range of Mao's radical domestic and foreign policies were attacked by the then Minister of National Defence, Peng Teh-huai. He argued for increased Soviet military, economic and technical assistance, and appeared to have the support of a number of the top leadership, including, it must be apparent in retrospect, Liu Shao-chi.

Mao's reaction to this challenge to the wisdom of his policies was to press ahead more vigorously with his radical programme – with the creation of people's communes, the revival of the militia movement and above all with the Great Leap Forward, under its slogan 'let politics take command'. The failure of all these policies, and the concomitant economic crisis, led to widespread criticism of Mao's leadership. Fearful that he was losing support in his own party, Mao once again went on the offensive, and in September 1962 at the Tenth Plenum initiated the 'socialist education' campaign, designed to eradicate opposition and win mass support for his radical policies. This too, it appears, failed to silence the critics or mobilize mass support for Mao. Just as he was pondering the next step he was persuaded that a play by Wu Han, *Hai Jui's Dismissal*, constituted a defence of Peng Teh-huai and was therefore a personal attack on him. He felt he had to take extreme action. At the end of 1965, therefore, he merged the socialist education campaign into the far more militant cultural revolution. Both movements had the same objective, the elimination of opposition to Mao, but whereas the first used mainly persuasion, the cultural revolution used coercion and violence. Mao's support in his hour of need came from the People's Liberation Army, its leader, Lin Piao, Mao's close comrade-in-arms, and from young fanatics whose admiration for Mao probably blinded them to the real issues. The fact that the cultural revolution was born a violent revolution had important repercussions in the conduct of China's foreign affairs during the period 1966–1969.

THE FOREIGN MINISTRY DURING THE CULTURAL REVOLUTION

The Foreign Ministry and its personnel came in for virulent criticism during the cultural revolution. At one time the building was totally occupied by Red Guards and China's foreign affairs were in the hands of a 'red diplomat fighter', Yao Teng-shan, a chargé who had been expelled from Indonesia for interfering in that country's internal affairs. Chen Yi was under constant attack for his 'rightist tendencies' and in August 1967 the Red Guard slogan of 'Overthrow Liu (Shaochi), Teng (Hsiao-ping, the CCP Secretary-General) and Tao (Chu – head of the Propaganda Department)' was temporarily replaced by 'Overthrow Liu, Teng and Chen.'

Chen Yi had particularly earned the hatred of the radicals by his employment of 'work teams'[2] to resist the intrusion of Red Guards into the Foreign Ministry and affiliated institutions. He was also one of the few leaders brave enough to speak out against the excesses of the cultural revolution, saying the Red Guards could only speak of the weaknesses of others and on one occasion that they had 'gone mad'.

For over a year the battle between Chen Yi, seeking desperately to protect the Foreign Ministry professionals, and the Red Guards ebbed and flowed. At times it seemed as if Mao completely removed his protection from the Foreign Minister, during which Chen would have to make humiliating 'self-criticisms' in front of mass rallies. At the apogee of the anti-Chen movement, in the first half of 1967, the Red Guards were allowed to set up a Criticize Chen Yi Liaison Station in the Foreign Ministry to oversee its work. Pamphlets were published with such titles as *What Poison this Chen Yi Is* (written by the Capital Congress of Red Representatives, People's University Three-Red Seize Chen Yi Regiment) and in August thousands of people attended a 'Thoroughly Criticize Chen Yi Rally'.

Chen was accused by his opponents of sympathizing with Liu's supposed foreign policy line of 'three surrenders, one extinction': surrender to US imperialism, to Soviet revisionism and to reactionaries, and extinction of the flames of revolutionary warfare throughout the world. Amongst his other crimes he had 'stubbornly executed the bourgeois reactionary line in the overseas Chinese affairs system' and had reportedly said that the thought of Mao Tse-tung, being purely Chinese, should not be exported. He had forbidden Chinese embassies to use big posters, had refused to allow students to go abroad to revolutionize embassies and by obstinately supporting Liu and opposing Mao he was 'as worthless as a heap of dog's dung'.

But Mao, possibly advised by Chou, a friend and admirer of Chen, stopped short of dismissing the minister, and during the whole time he was under attack Chen functioned as China's Foreign Minister. In May, for example, when the Red Guards under Yao were rampaging through the Foreign Ministry, beating up officials and going through secret documents, Chen Yi received delegations from Arab countries and as Foreign Minister pledged China's support for their conflict with Israel. At celebrations to mark National Day in October he was on the rostrum beside Mao. In view of Chen's later shelving (he was never dismissed altogether), it is difficult to see why Mao did not sacrifice his Foreign Minister earlier – it would certainly have been a popular move with the radicals. It may have been that Mao realized Chen commanded the loyalty of the Foreign Ministry professionals, and that his dismissal would have led to a complete collapse of their morale and possibly to the disintegration of a diplomatic service carefully built up over a long period of time.

Certainly, the bureaucrats themselves were under heavy pressure, and for many months it must have been virtually impossible to have carried out the normal functions of a Foreign Ministry. The radicals criticized the work and ideological suitability of the Peking staff, but more particularly they attacked China's overseas diplomats.

ATTACK ON DIPLOMATS

The published attacks on diplomats reveal a less high-minded side of the cultural revolution: jealousy of China's ruling class by less successful and probably less able compatriots, who also possibly had less opportunities. The Red Guards singled out for their severest criticism career diplomats, who were accused of living a decadent, bourgeois life abroad. The nub of the radicals' complaints against the Foreign Ministry comes in a *Red Flag* tabloid of June 1967, called 'Thoroughly Smash the Foreign Affairs Ministry's Privileged Stratum'. Foreign diplomats are accused of visiting night clubs, going to Western films 'depicting nude women', driving around in Cadillacs – and even commanding subordinates to massage them. An ambassador's salary of 480 Yuan a month is 'scandalous'. While this privileged stratum lives extravagantly abroad 'drinking to their heart's content' their working-class compatriots at home 'brave the rigours of the elements to create social wealth'. The emissaries are 'afraid of waging struggle and making revolution [and are] . . . so scared that they dare not spread the thought of Mao Tse-tung and distribute the revolutionary booklet *Quotations from Chairman Mao*. They also 'establish connections with the ruling groups of the countries in which they are stationed, flattering them and applauding them as much as they can.'

Clearly these people should be brought to task and at the beginning of 1967 all of China's ambassadors abroad, with the solitary exception of Huang Hua in Cairo,[3] were recalled to Peking for ideological revision.

The withdrawal of the ambassadors and other senior embassy officials left China's embassies abroad staffed by subordinates of varying degrees of seniority. In Africa counsellors took over the embassies in Guinea and Congo-Brazzaville, first secretaries in Zambia and Mauritania, a second secretary in Kenya, a commercial counsellor in Mali; in Tanzania, Algeria and Uganda the embassies were run by officials who had had no known previous post. In the absence of any other guidance these relatively inexperienced men, and others throughout the world, took their cue from events within China. To prove their revolutionary zeal they tried to propagate the cultural revolution and the Mao cult in the countries to which they were assigned. To give the lie to Red Guard accusations that theirs was a life of luxury they led a deliberately spartan existence. To parallel the violence of the Red Guards they used provocative, violent language, in some cases actually perpetrating violence themselves.

For much of 1967 embassies received minimal direction from Peking, and some of the severe diplomatic setbacks that China suffered in this period are accounted for by headstrong action initiated by junior embassy staff anxious to demonstrate their loyalty to Mao and to the Red revolution. For a brief time in August they would have received instructions from Yao, who, according to a Red Guard newspaper of October, actually sent cables (presumably very 'red') to foreign embassies without consulting either Mao or Chou. This is reported to have enraged Chou, who had overall responsibility for foreign affairs and who regarded this as a direct affront to his authority. Rudderless, the officials made one diplomatic blunder after another, even in those countries with which China had previously enjoyed excellent relations. Excessive zeal in promoting the cultural revolution earned sharp rebukes from Nepal and Burma. In Cambodia, even such a long time friend as Prince Sihanouk was forced to take retaliatory action against the embassy's excesses by closing down Chinese-run schools and deporting several Chinese nationals.

This hiatus in Chinese foreign policy did not last long, but it would be foolish to pretend that it did not have harmful consequences. Moderate leaders wondered seriously if China's leadership was still sane, while even China's most uncritical friends had moments of doubt. Apart from those countries which actually ruptured diplomatic relations as a direct result of cultural revolutionary excesses, many others eyed China and her diplomats with considerable suspicion for many years afterwards – and some still do.

CONTINUITY OF POLICY

But it is the continuity of foreign policy through the cultural revolution which is perhaps more striking. Where excessive zeal or language were used it was generally in countries, like Kenya or Tunisia, where it did not matter all that much, and where China's real state interests did not lie. What little evidence there is suggests that the Foreign Ministry bureaucrats were in the saddle again remarkably quickly after the first flush of the revolution, and that in those countries which they considered important to China's interests they were busy immediately mending diplomatic fences.

On the personnel side, for example, it was generally assumed that the recalled ambassadors were in some form of disgrace (it was widely rumoured amongst diplomats in Dar es Salaam that the former ambassador to Tanzania, Ho Ying, was working as an agricultural labourer on a commune. If so, it did him no harm because he emerged after the cultural revolution as a Vice Foreign Minister). But an examination of the guest-list at banquets given for visiting foreign delegations during the cultural revolution is revealing. For example, Chin Li-chen, the ambassador recalled from Zambia, attended all the major functions during President Kaunda's visit to Peking in June 1967. Similarly, in August the recalled Malian ambassador, Ma Tzu-ching, escorted a Malian government delegation, and in October the Mauritanian ambassador, Lu Chih-hsien, was present at the functions held during President Daddah's visit. Although impossible to state categorically, this would seem to indicate that the recalled diplomats were at least keeping tabs on their areas, and might even have been directing operations in their former countries at the Foreign Ministry. A further indication of continuity in the foreign service was given in 1969 when of the seventeen ambassadors sent to overseas posts (seven to African countries) thirteen had held similar positions prior to the cultural revolution and the other four were top Foreign Ministry officials.

In subtler ways too it is apparent that despite all the revolutionary shouting, the management of China's foreign affairs during the cultural revolution was in the hands of competent officials who were aware of long-term goals. For example, at the time of Kaunda's visit in 1967 the Chinese were almost as anxious to build the Tanzam railway as the Tanzanians and Zambians were to have it built, and were therefore eager to impress him. They must have been aware of his distaste for the excesses of the cultural revolution (the Zambians had clamped down on cultural revolution propaganda), as well as his general suspicions of communism. Thus, at the very height of the cultural revolution the Zambian-Chinese communiqué at the end of his visit is a study of moderation, with only a single sentence devoted to the cultural revolution, and written in non-polemical language. It could only have been drafted by Foreign Ministry professionals who knew their man and their job.

Yet only two months later, during the visit of the radical Brazzaville Prime Minister, Ambroise Noumazalay, Chou made a highly militant speech, full of propagandist references to the cultural revolution and to the brilliance of Mao Tse-tung thought. It is tempting to assume that the experts knew that this sort of language would be quite acceptable to Noumazalay, who in fact returned it in full measure in his speeches (Kaunda did not mention the cultural revolution at all in his major speech).

A striking piece of evidence that the cultural revolution did not interfere with long-term foreign policy objectives was the final commitment to go ahead with the Tanzam railway, made in September 1967.

In practical terms the cultural revolution effected a contraction of China's interest in Africa, and with the outside world in general. For three years most senior officials and policy-makers were preoccupied with internal developments, and with their own survival. Relations with foreign countries were on the whole important only insofar as they bore on developments within China. For much of the time China's diplomats abroad were concerned, not with day-to-day inter-state business, but with propagating the Mao cult and with ensuring that their revolutionary zeal did not go unnoticed either by their hosts or by their masters in Peking.

This slackening of activity can be measured quantitatively by the sharp drop of aid commitments made during the period (with the notable exception of the Tanzam railway) and by the decrease in the number of African visitors to Peking, and of Chinese visitors to Africa. In 1967 fifty-three African delegations visited Peking, and in 1968 the number dropped further to an all-time low of just twelve. Chinese delegations to African countries numbered seventeen in 1967, and fourteen in 1968.

Aid agreements illustrate the most noteworthy feature of the cultural revolutionary period: a polarization of relationships. The vast bulk of Chinese aid went to friendly, radical countries. There were simply not the resources, nor the political will, to help countries whose relationship with China was lukewarm. Aid was used as a means of rewarding old friends, not, by and large, for winning new ones or for trying to persuade recalcitrant states to change their minds about China. The countries which benefited most from Chinese aid during the cultural revolution were thus Congo-Brazzaville, Guinea, Tanzania (and 'by extension' Zambia), Mauritania, Mali and to a lesser extent Somalia.

What leaders of all these countries had in common was that while they were not unreservedly enthusiastic about the cultural revolution – especially its more extravagant manifestations in their own countries – they did at least refrain from public criticism. And on visits to Peking they or their ministers were prepared to pay glowing tributes to the success of the cultural revolution and to the brilliance of Mao Tse-tung's thought.

Aid was withheld, or at best implemented slowly, in countries which openly criticized the cultural revolution or which too publicly condemned, or banned importation of, revolutionary propaganda. Egypt, for example, which was very lukewarm to the cultural revolution, did not receive the industrial machinery which China had said it would supply between 1965 and 1968. Nor was it able to draw on the Chinese loan of £28 million pledged in 1964. Algeria was severely critical of the cultural revolution, especially after about sixty Chinese attacked a Soviet diplomat's car in Algiers in February 1967, apparently in reprisal for the beating-up of Chinese students in Moscow. Algeria too, therefore, found it difficult to persuade China to fulfil aid commitments made in 1963, although work did start on a large exhibition hall in Algiers during the cultural revolution. In May 1968 Moroccan dockers refused to unload a Chinese freighter carrying cultural revolution propaganda (this was linked to a protest against the alleged persecution of Moslems in China during the cultural revolution). Morocco, never a large recipient of Chinese aid, received none at all during the cultural revolution. The special cases of Kenya and Tunisia are discussed below.

Amongst the larger aid projects started or completed during the cultural revolution were, in Guinea, the Kinkon hydroelectric power station, the Macenta tea factory, the groundnut oil factory at Dabola and the prestigious 2500-seat People's Palace; in Mali, the Bamako match factory and the Segou textile mill; in Congo-Brazzaville, a radio station, the Kinsoundi textile mill and a small shipyard; in Somalia a national theatre; in Tanzania, the Friendship textile mill, the Ubongo farm implements factory, and in Zanzibar a shoe factory and a sports stadium. China also agreed to build a railway linking Guinea and Mali, and the survey team had completed its work when President Keita was overthrown in November 1968, and the plans were temporarily shelved.[4] In addition, the highly successful Chinese medical and agricultural teams were dispatched to all these countries, and occasional Red Cross donations for the relief of drought or for some other natural disaster were made.

As with political relations and with foreign service personnel, therefore, it is possible with aid to trace a thread of continuity through the cultural revolution. The aid programme was limited; but the well-publicized arrival of Chinese medical teams, or water surveyors, or the opening of a new factory, or the laying of a foundation stone, all continued to remind Africans of the ongoing constructive side of their relationship with China.

NEED FOR APPROVAL

China's most insistent demand from her African, and other friends was for public endorsement of the aims of the cultural revolution and for verbal tribute to the brilliance and superiority of Mao Tse-tung's thought. To be really effective this tribute had to be phrased in revolutionary jargon. It was astonishing how many African leaders were prepared to abandon 'normal' speech in order to please the Chinese, often in fact outdoing their hosts in gobbledegook. In official communiqués the influence of the Chinese is particularly obvious, with African delegations agreeing that they had been inspired and impressed by China's great cultural revolution and asserting in propagandist terms the primacy of Mao Tse-tung's thought.[5]

These endorsements were widely publicized in the Chinese press, and it seems certain they were elicited mainly for internal consumption. Enemies might say China was isolated, but how could that be true when 'great' and 'revolutionary' leaders from Albania, from Congo-Brazzaville, from Guinea, freedom fighters from all over Africa and friends everywhere so unreservedly praised China's revolutionary achievements? As a PLA soldier wrote in an article:

The Chinese people are never afraid of encirclement by anybody. How is it possible to encircle the 700 million people who are armed with Mao Tse-tung's thought and have friends all over the world? (*People's Daily*, 21 September 1968)

The credentials of the foreign admirers was hardly likely to be questioned, for who in China was to know that the South West African National Union was a political movement only in the minds of its few officials in a Cairo suburb, or that the Pan-Africanist Congress was an impotent separatist group, or even that the voices of such 'powerful' friends as Mali, Albania and Brazzaville did not really count for very much in the outside world?

Leaders with a certain amount of self-respect, such as Presidents Nyerere and Kaunda, were careful not to be drawn into this trap, and were very sparing in their use of Chinese jargon – they did not want to be branded as Chinese 'lackeys' either by the West, with whom they still had to deal, or by their own opposition elements. Possibly, the Chinese might now in retrospect – particularly with their emphasis on self-reliance – admire this reticence to endorse wholeheartedly an alien movement and to sacrifice national and personal pride in the service of another creed. Certainly, those who indulged in frantic sychophancy were not regarded at the time, and even less so now, with great favour by their more level-headed colleagues. I remember listening with ever-increasing amazement to a Chinese-programmed speech delivered at Dar es Salaam University by a member of the Pan-Africanist Congress; amongst the first to leave in protest and in boredom were other freedom fighters, from movements like FRELIMO and SWAPO, who told me they had been 'nauseated' by the performance.

But at the time the Chinese were seeking approval quite indiscriminately. NCNA correspondents shamelessly reported such spontaneous ejaculations as 'I will love Chairman Mao forever', 'I shall read Mao Tse-tung's thought every day' and 'I am very happy to see Chairman Mao in such good health' (the Chinese were rather sensitive to Western press reports that Mao was either ill or dead). A selection of African comments on the cultural revolution gives an idea of how far some Africans were prepared to go in order to please the Chinese.

Mao Tse-tung is the greatest revolutionary leader of our times . . . On the banner of Mao Tse-tung is written with golden letters the following slogan: Everything for the Revolution, while on the black banner of the revisionist pirates is painted in the most captious colour the following slogan: Everything for survival at any price . . . Long live Mao Tse-tung, our great guide and comrade-in-arms. (Viriato Dacruz, Angola, at the June 1966 emergency meeting of the Afro-Asian Writers' Organization)

Mao tse-tung's thought is the living soul of the African revolution. Without the guidance of Mao Tse-tung's thought, the revolution in Africa is hopeless. I believe that Mao Tse-tung's thought is the saviour of all oppressed peoples. By studying Mao Tse-tung's thought we know how better to conduct the revolution. (NCNA, Algiers, 11 August 1966, quoting a meeting of the Pan-Africanist Congress)

Mao Tse-tung's thought is the torch of world revolution. [China's achievements] were won by the Chinese people themselves after the Soviet experts had withdrawn . . . All the Chinese people love Chairman Mao. Chairman Mao is always with the people. (NCNA, Cairo, 31 May 1966, quoting Sithole of COREMO)

I saw with my own eyes that workers, peasants and soldiers are studying Chairman Mao's works with great eagerness, trying to apply his ideas in their daily life . . . The Chinese people, under the guidance of Mao Tse-tung's thought, will build a revolutionary and socialist country. (Mohamed Dahan, a writer from French Somaliland, who said that wherever he went he had to give vent to his feelings by shouting, 'Long live Chairman Mao.')

The determination of the Chinese people never to lay down their arms is in conformity with Chairman Mao's theory of armed struggle . . . The only road for the people of Zimbabwe is to arm themselves with Mao's thought and launch an armed struggle. (G. Savanhu, a member of ZANU at the Afro-Asian Writers' meeting)

Other delegates at the Afro-Asian Writers' meeting talked of Mao Tse-tung's thought as 'the acme of Marxism-Leninism in our time', 'the sunshine that illuminates the path of revolution', 'the spiritual atom bomb', and 'the inextinguishable torch and red sun for all revolutionaries of the world'. A Niger delegate was moved to recite a poem in praise of Mao Tse-tung – 'our beacon which illuminates . . . the darkest, farthest horizons.'

Every event turned on the cultural revolution and Mao Tse-tung's thought. The successful launching of a nuclear guided missile in October 1966, was hailed as a triumph for Mao's thought, while, according to NCNA, foreign businessmen at the

Kwangchow Export Commodity Fair ascribed the range of goods on display to the 'powerful impetus generated by the current great proletarian cultural revolution'.

In Africa, surgical feats performed by the medical teams were the result of diligent study of *The Quotations of Mao Tse-tung*. At receptions to mark China's National Day, huge illuminated portraits of Mao Tse-tung were hung in embassy courtyards, and such films as *Chairman Mao with a Million Members of the Cultural Revolutionary Army* were shown. Propaganda booklets were sold or given away, Mao badges were on sale everywhere.

Naturally, much of this activity was resented, even by friendly countries. Almost every country with which China had relations at some stage either severely limited or banned outright the distribution of propaganda – even Tanzania was forced to prohibit the wearing of Mao badges, while more moderate countries, like Kenya and Malawi, banned absolutely the importation of all Chinese publications.

VISITS

If verbal tributes to the cultural revolution, diligently collected by NCNA correspondents all over Africa and at meetings of pro-Peking organizations, constituted support for China, visits to China by African leaders and their subordinates did so even more.

A political leader took a deliberate risk visiting China during the cultural revolution. However unfairly, he was bound to be branded 'red' by his critics, internal as well as external, and there is no doubt that China was extremely grateful to the three African heads of state (Nyerere, Kaunda and Daddah) and the Prime Minister (Ambroise Noumazalay of Congo-Brazzaville) who visited China during this time. The reception given to the visitors, and the enormous press coverage given to their every movement, was overwhelming. During the whole period of the cultural revolution only heads of state from Africa seemed prepared to brave the obvious risks. In 1968 Nyerere was the only guest of any distinction to visit China. As Chou En-lai told him at a welcoming banquet.

At a time when China's great proletarian cultural revolution has entered the stage for the seizure of all-round victory, His Excellency President Nyerere has made light of travelling thousands of miles and come to our country for a friendly visit. This is a great support and encouragement to the Chinese people. (NCNA, Peking, 18 June 1968)

And when Nyerere left, Chou said,

The support given by the people of Tanzania and the rest of Africa and the revolutionary people of the whole world to our great proletarian cultural revolution constitutes a tremendous encouragement to the Chinese people. (NCNA, Peking, 21 June 1968)

In his own speech Nyerere was more circumspect about Tanzania's 'support' for the cultural revolution, but he did say

. . . if you found it necessary to begin a cultural revolution, in order to make sure that the new generation would carry forward the banner of your revolution, then certainly we need one . . . Today, after the cultural revolution, the spirit of China is even greater than before. (NCNA, Peking, 21 June 1968)

THE CULTURAL REVOLUTION AS A MODEL

Although militant Chinese embassy officials did their best to 'export' the cultural revolution, few African countries were prepared to import it, or even imitate it. However, in four countries – Guinea, Tanzania, Congo-Brazzaville and Mali – certain features of the cultural revolution, notably the emphasis on youth movements and people's militias, were adopted for local use. In two cases these adoptions led indirectly to coups: in Mali, Keita's institution of a People's Army was seen by the traditional army as a threat to its pre-eminence and Keita was ousted by a military coup (but relations with China continued on a friendly basis); in Congo-Brazzaville Massemba-Debat, after reshuffling his cabinet in January 1968 to give it a more moderate appearance (he was worried about Chinese influence, particularly on the Prime Minister, Noumazalay, and thought the youth movement – based on the Red Guards – appeared to be 'confused') was forced to resign in September, following an army coup in August, provoked by the army's fear that the Defense Civile, the militant arm of the Jeunesse, trained by Cuban and Chinese instructors, was challenging its traditional authority. As in Mali, the Chinese had no reason to regret this coup: at the end of 1969 the new head of state, 'Chairman' Marien Ngouabi, declared Brazzaville to be Africa's first People's Republic, attempting, under the Congolese Party of Labour, to implement scientific socialism on the theoretical basis of Marxism-Leninism. Chinese influence remains strong in Brazzaville, despite good relations between the PCT and the CPSU and a weakening in the position of the youth movement because of its ties with extreme left opponents of Ngouabi.

In Guinea, Sekou Touré, dressed in a Mao suit, launched the country's own cultural revolution. A people's militia – 'the true pioneers of the economic and cultural revolution' – composed of some 10000 members was formed. It is also recorded that the Minister for National Education had to undergo a session of 'self-criticism' before his cabinet colleagues because he had written in the party newspaper that certain party members had misappropriated funds.

TANZANIA'S 'CULTURAL REVOLUTION'

But it was in Tanzania, where Nyerere had said a cultural revolution was needed, that China's inner turmoil was reflected most accurately. Tanzania's militant Youth Leaguers, known as 'Green Guards', roamed around correcting 'erroneous tendencies', such as the wearing of mini-skirts, the listening to 'decadent' Western music, the reading of decadent Western literature (*Playboy* was first cut, then banned) and the use by Tanzanian girls of skin-whitening cream (a common practice in all African countries, where white is generally regarded as beautiful). A People's Militia was formed, and for a time Nyerere badges were worn. Tanzania's ambassadors were temporarily recalled, and Chinese revolutionary jargon was employed widely in the party newspaper, *The Nationalist*.

Although on the surface these appear rather feeble attempts to copy China's example, the real purpose of 'Operation Vijaana', as Tanzania's 'cultural revolution' was known, like China's, was probably internal. Nyerere is a master at balancing different forces within Tanzania – one year he gives primacy to the party, another year he gives more authority to the army; he is constantly 'bringing up' or 'sending down' different

6

sections of the community. I suspect that in 1968–1969 he felt it was time to give youth its head, and the formation of the Green Guards and other somewhat spurious youth organizations was one method of allowing young people (many of whom were frustrated by lack of job opportunities) to let off steam – certainly the semi-official removal of mini-skirts owed more to youthful exuberance than ideological conviction. But the movement went too far, and was reined in before it could do too much damage. Nyerere may have been thinking of the cultural revolutionary events when he warned students at the inauguration of Dar es Salaam University in 1970 not to 'become intellectual apes whether of the Right or of the Left'.

But neither in Tanzania nor anywhere else in Africa did the cultural revolution become a major influence, or turn into anything very much more than a slightly fashionable student movement based on the capital city. It never became a mass movement, and as a model it was totally unsuitable to African conditions.

VIOLENCE

Violence, of thought, language and deed were hallmarks of the cultural revolution in China, and violence was a feature of Chinese attempts to get its ideology accepted in African countries. Unfriendly leaders were attacked in the most virulent terms – Mobutu, for example, was variously called an American lackey, butcher and 'running dog'. A *People's Daily* article of 15 April 1967 ranted,

Mobutu, the degenerate betrayer of the Congolese people and murderer of Lumumba, has now, as if by magic, made himself up to look like a different man, waving the banner of the Congolese national hero Lumumba. Isn't this fantastic?

Violent actions were encouraged and applauded. When a Tanzanian youth smashed a portrait of Queen Elizabeth in a Morogoro 'colonialists' club' and replaced it with one of Nyerere, the *People's Daily* commented in an article entitled 'A Good Sweep of the Iron Broom':

We warmly hail: It's very fine! This revolutionary action of Tanzanian youth . . . There is no construction without destruction.

In Zambia the Chinese embassy organized students to stage a mass demonstration against the government-owned *Zambian Mail* after its (European) editor had written an article criticizing the intellectual élite at the university. The embassy staff provocatively cultivated the student nephew of Simon Kapwepwe, the Home Minister, a youth who had been involved in a brawl with another minister, in celebration of which the Chinese threw a beer party for him and his friends. Kaunda reacted by banning the distribution of Chinese propaganda and by restricting contacts between all diplomats and students. He also appointed a European security officer to keep an eye on Chinese activities, just as Nkrumah had earlier done in Ghana.

Violence was particularly apparent in China's dealings with Tunisia and Kenya. With neither country had she been on good terms prior to the cultural revolution, and it is probably correct to assume that if the Foreign Ministry professionals decided to allow the radicals to let off steam in areas in which China's vital interests were not at stake, Tunisia and Kenya would have been two such places.

TUNISIA

Diplomatic relations had been established with Tunisia after Chou's visit (see p. 63) and had never been particularly warm. Bourguiba was probably the most outspoken of all the leaders of African countries with which China had diplomatic relations, and the loss of Tunisian friendship would not have been felt very acutely in Peking. Shortly after his blunt farewell speech to Chou he labelled China's African and Asian policies as 'colonialism camouflaged as ideology' and said Africans were allergic to them. And after China's third nuclear explosion in May 1966 the party newspaper *L'Action* had some gratuitous advice for China's leaders: 'It is deplorable that after almost fifteen years of revolution, the grim struggle of China against population pressure and under-development should be made two-fold by a competition which is as crushing as it is vain.'

But it was Tunisia's advocacy of a 'two Chinas' solution to the question of UN membership that provoked Chinese wrath and made a rupture of relations inevitable. In the first half of 1967 the actions of the Chinese embassy, led by a militant chargé after the recall of the ambassador in January, seemed indeed designed to provoke such a break. Disorders at Tunis University in March were said later by the ruling Destour Party to have been partly financed by the Chinese embassy with the aim of subverting the police and the army. After the June Arab-Israeli war the Tunisian government also saw the hand of the Chinese embassy behind various demonstrations throughout the country, and therefore placed travel restrictions on Chinese diplomats. In August China accused Bourguiba of 'slandering' Chairman Mao, and in protest withdrew four coaches sent to Tunisia under a physical culture agreement. Tunisia countered by detaining a Chinese table-tennis coach and a member of the embassy staff.

In September, when the Foreign Ministry in Peking was still under Red Guard occupation and the anti-Chen movement was at its height, China issued a note which could only have led to a break in relations. It accused Tunisia of siding with US imperialism thereby splitting the Arab anti-imperialist front and

In trying to use its opposition to China to divert the attention of its people and cover up its own crime of entering further into the service of US imperialism and Soviet revisionism and selling out the interests of the Tunisian and other Arab people, the Tunisian government will certainly come to no good end. (NCNA, Peking, 16 September 1967)

Tunisia demanded an apology by a certain date. The embassy refused, and on 27 September the entire Chinese staff left for Peking, where a rousing welcome, suitable for 'fighting red diplomats' awaited them.

Commenting on this episode in December, Feng Piao, Director of the Information Department of the *People's Daily*, wrote

. . . severance of relations can do us no harm. We have no diplomatic relationship with the US, but we carry on just the same. Severence of relations will only make a mess of things politically and economically for a given country, since we can then support the people of that country to make a revolution . . .

It seems reasonable to assume that this inflammatory language was a reflection of the disruption going on in China, and in particular in the Foreign Ministry, at the time. But it is also true that the continuance or severance of relations with Tunisia was not of vital importance to China in any case, and that the bureaucrats, probably Chou himself, calculated that no great harm would be done to Chinese interests in Africa by throwing the crumb of management of relations with Tunisia to the radicals, especially if it left them with the impression they were 'revolutionizing' China's foreign policies.

KENYA

Disruptive activity, as we saw in Chapter Nine, had been countenanced in Kenya well before the onset of the cultural revolution, and it is therefore not surprising to find that a lot of revolutionary 'steam' was let off there too during the cultural revolution. The virulence of the 'diplomatic' language would almost certainly have provoked any other leader to have broken off relations, but, as noted earlier, Kenyatta was convinced it was better to have potential enemies where he could see them, rather than risk the possibility of his country being subverted from outside. Kenya's handling of the Chinese embassy during the cultural revolution was clever, and indicated the degree of political sophistication which Kenya had attained. The actions of the Chinese were made to resemble those of petulant schoolboys caught breaking bounds, overreacting to provoke expulsion only to find that instead they were merely kept in class after lessons.

Relations between China and Kenya started to deteriorate badly in the first half of 1967, as the cultural revolution got under way. Following the recall to Peking of the ambassador earlier in the year, Li Chieh, the chargé, was expelled in June, leaving the embassy affairs in the hands of a militant second secretary.

Li's expulsion came about as a result of a letter written by the Chinese embassy and published in two Kenyan newspapers, in which the Kenyan Minister for Economic Planning, Tom Mboya, was attacked for 'helping US imperialism out of its difficulties' in a speech to the Kenyan National Assembly. The letter continued,

He even venomously places US imperialism that is aggressive in nature on a par with the People's Republic of China that has been persistently opposing imperialism and uttered the nonsense that not only the Americans of the CIA had to be watched, but also the Chinese.

Mr Mboya's intention is very obvious, that is, to divert the attention of the Kenyan people from their anti-US struggle and to sow discord in and sabotage the friendship between the Kenya peoples (and China).

Mr Mboya's fabrications and slanders can only result in dropping on his own feet the rock he has lifted. (*East African Standard*, 27 June 1967)

The official protest note against Li's expulsion issued by the Chinese Foreign Ministry justified the letter, and continued in similar vein, complaining of Mboya's 'vicious slandering' of China and accusing the Kenyan government of doing 'a lot of bad things to sabotage the relations between the two countries in the last two years.' In wall-poster language it went on:

Certain ministers in the Kenyan government have time and again openly opposed China by viciously attacking the domestic and foreign policies of the Chinese government and even indulged in personal attacks on the Chinese premier . . .

By taking the present step to seriously sabotage the relations between the two countries, the Kenyan government caters to the very needs of imperialism and modern revisionism, goes against the interests of the people of Kenya and elsewhere in Africa and undermines the Afro-Asian peoples' solidarity against imperialism. (NCNA, Peking, 1 July 1967)

In retaliation Kenya's chargé in Peking was given forty-eight hours to leave China, and in August Red Guards smashed the windows of the Kenyan embassy – which was partly a tit-for-tat for the smashing of the information windows outside the Chinese embassy in Nairobi in January.

The distribution of Chinese propaganda material was banned in Kenya,[6] but otherwise the Kenyan government reacted very mildly. As late as November 1968 the Chinese seemed determined to provoke a break in relations when a diplomatic note complained of Kenyan press coverage of Taiwan's National Day and repeated the assertion that the Kenyan government was 'working in the service of US imperialism'. Kenya rejected the note for its 'insulting tone and baseless insinuations', but did nothing more than increase surveillance of the embassy behind its 'Chinese wall'.

As in the case of Tunisia, the antagonization of the Kenyan

government was of no great matter and may have been useful in dissipating youthful revolutionary fervour in an area where important interests were not at stake. Nevertheless, these excesses naturally soured relations – and to some extent still do – between Kenya and China. More importantly, they were read about in neighbouring Tanzania – and therefore showed Tanzanians a side of Chinese activities with which they themselves were not familiar. In that respect the cultural revolutionary aberrations in Kenya were probably later regretted by China more than those in Tunisia.

CHINA AND THE REST OF THE WORLD

The period of cultural revolution coincided with outside events of quite crucial importance for China, events which would have made Africa of only secondary importance in foreign policy considerations even if the cultural revolution had not made that inevitable in any case. The first was the escalation of America's involvement in Vietnam, so that for the first time since the Korean War China felt seriously physically threatened by the old enemy; the second was the border confrontation with the Soviet Union in early 1969, which appeared to convince the Chinese that the Soviet Union intended to expand her empire at China's expense, and thirdly was the fear that the two super powers were about to reach a détente and enter into collusion against China.[7]

Against this three-pronged threat China could offer very little, although the explosion of a hydrogen bomb in June 1967, and the successful launching of a nuclear missile indicated that she was striving to find a military answer.

In the absence of a convincing deterrent the best China could do, especially for internal consumption, was to assert that she had the support of all the world's revolutionary peoples, that imperialism and revisionism were in their death throes and that ultimate victory would go, in the words of Lin Piao's thesis, to the world's countryside over the 'towns' of the developed world. There was thus an unprecedented amount of propaganda devoted to the 'revolutionary storms' sweeping Africa, Asia and Latin America, to the 'imminent total collapse of imperialism' and to the 'excellent world situation'. Foreign visitors to China were asked to endorse the heroic stand of the South Vietnamese people, to applaud the revolutionary struggles of Afro-Americans and, if they could be persuaded, to condemn the crimes of the 'new Tsars'. The impression received by a reader of the *People's Daily* would be of near worldwide support for China and of continuing victories in those few places where imperialism and revisionism stubbornly resisted.

This bolstering was of great psychological importance – that the situations described did not exist or were grossly exaggerated did not matter. The ignorance of Chinese about the outside world greatly helped the propagandists: few Chinese, for example, would have seen the joke in the assertion made in NCNA's year-end review of the world situation on 29 December 1967 that, '. . . the Darjeeling people's armed struggle, like a clap of spring thunder, has shaken the earth of India.'

In Africa great emphasis was placed on the just-beginning struggles of liberation movements fighting in the non-independent territories, and on the supposed 'victories' gained by freedom fighters in the Congo, which continued to absorb a great deal of Chinese attention. A communiqué issued at the end of the eleventh plenary session of the eighth Central Committee (the meeting which formally launched the cultural revolution) described the revolutionary situation thus:

The blazing fires of anti-imperialist armed struggle are raging over wide areas of Africa. The brilliant thesis of Chairman Mao that 'political power grows out of the barrel of a gun' and that imperialism can be defeated through people's war is blazing the path of the oppressed African people towards victory. This year, Africa has witnessed new fires of armed struggle sparked off by the peoples of 'Spanish' Equatorial Guinea and Zimbabwe (Southern Rhodesia). In the heartland of Africa, the armed struggle of the Congolese (Leopoldville) people against US imperialism and its lackeys has entered its third year. In 'Portuguese' Guinea in west Africa, Mozambique in east Africa and Angola in central Africa, the flames of armed struggle against the US-supported Portuguese colonialists are burning more intensely than ever and shaking the very foundation of Portuguese colonial rule. The patriotic armed forces of 'Portuguese' Guinea are in control of half of their country. Mozambican guerrillas are active on the vast land in five out of the nine provinces of the country. Manuel Mahluza, Education Secretary of the Mozambique Revolutionary Committee, declared recently: 'By arming ourselves with Chairman Mao's great thesis on people's war, we can defeat the Portuguese colonialists who are nothing but paper tigers.'

In other African countries which are not yet independent, the people are launching national independence movements. The people in 'French' Somaliland recently raised their strong voice for immediate independence. In southern Africa, British imperialism was forced to accept the independence of Bechuanaland and Basutoland within this year, thanks to the strong impact of the people's struggle for independence. The African people throughout the continent are also launching powerful movements to condemn the British government for conniving with and shielding the white colonial regime in Southern Rhodesia and to demand an end to the colonial rule of the South African racist regime over South-West Africa. (NCNA, 29 September 1966)

The independent African countries have shaken off their colonial shackles, and are striking further blows at the colonial forces. They are maintaining high vigilance and waging a tit-for-tat struggle against all sorts of sabotage and subversive plots of imperialism headed by the United States. In July this year, the courageous Congolese (Brazzaville) people crushed in time another large-scale subversive plot, the fifth engineered by imperialism since the August revolution of Congo in 1963.

The governments and people of Tanzania and Uganda adopted measures in May this year which have exposed and hit at US and British imperialism for their neo-colonialist activities and subversive plots. (NCNA, 29 September 1966)

As an objective piece of reporting this did not bear much relation to the actual situation, or at least suffered from exaggeration and optimism. As an encouragement to the Chinese people, surrounded by enemies on all sides, it served its purpose very well.

THE CULTURAL REVOLUTION AND REVOLUTIONARY SUPPORT

While American action in Vietnam and supposed worldwide US-Soviet collusion created the need of revolutionary support *for* China, preoccupation with the cultural revolution inhibited Chinese support *to* these revolutionary groups. In fact, very rarely did Chinese support go beyond verbal encouragement, partly because of logistic difficulties, partly because of the poor state of the Chinese economy. China's material support for the African liberation groups is discussed in Chapter Fourteen. During the cultural revolution this assistance was severely circumscribed, and probably only amounted to token donations and the provision in China of guerrilla training to selected numbers.

Other than in the non-independent countries, two other revolutionary situations flared up in Africa during the cultural revolution. The first was the Arab-Israeli War in June 1967, and the other was the Nigerian civil war.

CHINA AND THE SIX-DAY WAR

Chou En-lai's message to Nasser of 6 June spoke of the Chinese people 'standing firmly by the UAR people', but there was no mention of China offering any material assistance, and certainly not a repetition of the offer made at the time of Suez (see p. 16) to send Chinese volunteers. There was, however, a mass demonstration of 1·2 million people in Peking in support of the Arab cause.

The fact that Egypt relied so heavily on the Soviet Union for economic and military support did not inhibit the Chinese from severely criticizing the Soviets and suggesting that their actions were in fact 'sham support but real betrayal'. Just as in Vietnam, the Soviet Union and the United States were improbably portrayed as acting in collusion in the Middle East. On 7 June NCNA said the two super powers had acted in league at the UN Security Council, thereby 'putting out the conflagration' (which China presumably welcomed as a diversion away from Vietnam – but it was hardly a diplomatic thing to say). There was no mention in the Chinese press of any material support for Egypt, but *Al Ahram* reported that China had offered a gift of £3·5 million and 150000 tons of wheat. It is known (from an official of the Australian Wheat Broad, which has good commercial relations with China) that at least 50000 tons of wheat were diverted to Egypt. But the gift of money never materialized.

CHINA AND BIAFRA

If China was preoccupied with Vietnam and US-Soviet collusion,

Africa was no less preoccupied during the three years of the cultural revolution with the Nigerian civil war. The attempted secession of the Ibo people from the rest of Nigeria proved a divisive issue on a continent-wide basis, with four African states – Gabon, Ivory Coast, Zambia and Tanzania – supporting 'Biafra' and the rest of Africa backing the Federal government or remaining neutral.

Quite apart from the introspection caused by the cultural revolution and a corresponding unwillingness to embark on any new foreign adventures, China was in a quandary over what to do about Biafra. Although the Nigerian civil war was 'revolutionary' in the sense that it was disruptive, the Biafran leadership could hardly be called politically radical. Indiscriminate Chinese support for Biafra would too obviously be opportunism, and for a long time China remained silent on the war.

The Federal side was equally uncertain what to do about recognition of China, which it felt might pre-empt possible Chinese support for Biafra. But a senior Nigerian diplomat has revealed in conversation[8] that the decision not to seek diplomatic relations with China was taken on the grounds first, that this might antagonize the US, from whom support was confidently – but mistakenly – expected, and secondly, that such a move would confirm the beliefs of private elements in the US – who were already aiding Biafra – that the war was one 'against communism', with Biafra defending the purity of the West against the Soviet-aided Federals. The Biafrans themselves encouraged this version of the war, in their propaganda accusing Lagos of being a communist 'beach-head'.

But even within Biafra there was, from an early stage, a pro-Chinese lobby, headed by a long-time communist, Professor Chike Obi, and Professor Kalu Ezera, a special political adviser to the Biafran leader, Colonel Ojukwu; late in 1967 these two visited China, but on their return Obi was jailed. Ezera disappeared after the war, and is presumed dead.

The position of the Chinese lobby was complicated by the presence of a more numerous pro-American group, and even further by a pro-Soviet group, composed of a conglomeration of university lecturers, like Ikena Nzimiro and Chimire Ikoku, and trade unionists like Ikoro of the Dock Workers' Union and

Ifedira of the Electricity Workers' Union, who had been cultivated in Lagos by the Soviets before the war. For a long time the pro-American group, which included such men as Pius Okigbo, Biafra's top economist, and Francis Nwokedi, Ojukwu's foreign affairs adviser, held out hopes that the US would eventually come out in favour of Biafran secession; they therefore discouraged an approach to China in case it should inhibit such support. The pro-Soviet group were similarly opposed to approaching China, but their position was complicated by the fact that the Soviet Union was one of the main arms suppliers to the Federal government; this did not prevent a delegation, led by Ezera, from visiting Moscow to see if this support could be switched.[9]

By the middle of 1968 Biafra's position was becoming desperate. Her territory was shrinking daily and it was clear that without considerable military assistance the army would have to surrender. Ojukwu was persuaded that China represented his last chance of keeping alive the Biafran dream. Approaches were made and the harvest reaped when in September, sixteen months after the outbreak of war, China broke her silence, coming out – somewhat indirectly – in favour of Biafra in a speech made by Chen Yi at a banquet for the visiting Foreign Minister of Southern Yemen:

In Africa, Soviet revisionism, in league with US and British imperialism, is even openly supporting the military government of Federal Nigeria in massacring the Biafran people in a vain attempt to squeeze into Nigeria and enjoy an equal share with imperialism there. (NCNA, Peking, 20 September 1968)

A few days later NCNA, in similar vein, condemned

... the crimes of US and British imperialism and Soviet revisionism in supporting the Federal Nigerian military government's massacre of the Biafran people. [This had] aroused the indignation of the Biafran people and the people of Tanzania, Zambia and other African countries ... The tragedy brought about in Nigeria and Biafra by the US and British imperialists and Soviet revisionists in their collusion to redivide the sphere of influence in Africa has provided a further lesson to the people and the rest of the world, who will strengthen their solidarity and resolutely resist the intervention by US and British imperialism and Soviet revisionism.

In a letter to Mao, Ojukwu expressed Biafra's deep gratitude for China's 'increasing sympathy and understanding' and said the Biafran people were deeply touched by the NCNA article 'as well as the other manifestations of your growing appreciation of the real issues involved in the conflict'. A sign of Biafra's desperation was given when Ojukwu, a Western-educated capitalist, referred in the letter to 'Anglo-American intrigues backed by Soviet revisionism' and to 'the progressive social ideal which inspired the birth of our republic'. For good measure he added that Biafrans were consoled by the knowledge of 'the shining example of the Chinese people's struggle under your able leadership against American imperialism and later against Soviet revisionism'.

This doubletalk did Ojukwu little good, for China did not comment at length again on the Biafran war until June of the next year. But neither did China's statement do *her* any good, coming as it did only two days after an OAU meeting which confirmed the OAU's support for Nigerian territorial integrity and opposition to secession. Nigeria herself reacted mildly, reducing, but not banning, imports of Chinese goods and. abstaining – for the first time – on the substantive resolution on Chinese representation at the UN, which she had previously supported.

However, the implication of the phrase 'other manifestations of your growing appreciation of the real issues involved' was of course that China was giving Biafra material support, an interpretation given some credence by allegations by both Chief Anthony Enaharo, the Federal Information Commissioner, and by Colonel Benjamin Adekunle, a divisional commander, that Chinese 'mercenaries' were fighting for Biafra and by the capture of Chinese weapons from Biafran soldiers.[10] There was, however, no evidence whatsoever produced to substantiate the first charge and the capture of Chinese weapons does not necessarily prove a direct link between Biafra and China.

Most journalists covering the Nigerian war did, however, assume that Tanzania played an intermediary role, and I know from my own investigations in Dar es Salaam that every fortnight, for most of 1969, a Constellation, loaded in complete secrecy in the government hangar at Dar es Salaam airport, and then flew on to Libreville, the capital of Gabon, the main entrepôt for goods destined for Biafra. A widely believed rumour, that Tanzania shipped to Biafra Chinese weapons properly destined either for her own army or for liberation groups based in Tanzania, was constantly denied by government spokesmen. I do know that Tanzania sent maize and beans to Biafra, which could theoretically account for the Constellation's cargo. But given Tanzania's firm support for Biafra, and the need to explain the presence of Chinese weapons there, I am inclined to believe that Tanzania did supply Chinese arms to the secessionists.

China's very limited support for Biafra illustrated two trends in Chinese foreign policy during the cultural revolution. The first was unwillingness to endorse *all* groups engaged in warfare, quite regardless of their ideology,[11] (and – in Biafra's case – despite the fact that it was opposed by British imperialism and Soviet revisionism.) The second was China's complete inability, for economic and logistical reasons, to furnish, even to real and revolutionary friends, anything more than token aid. After the cultural revolution was over, and China sought to legitimize her relations with African countries, these considerations continued to constrain her support for revolution.

Notes

1. See, for example, 'Mao's "Cultural Revolution": Origin and Development' by Philip Bridgham in the *China Quarterly*, No. 29, 1967 – on which I have drawn for this summary.

2. Work teams were armed groups formed by the moderates to protect their interests against the radicals, and were first used in the spring of 1966 to quell campus violence. At one time Chen commanded fifteen work teams, which even included some of his vice-ministers, and they protected such institutions under Foreign Ministry jurisdiction as the Commission for Cultural Relations with Foreign Countries, the Overseas Chinese Affairs Commission and the Peking Foreign Languages Institute. When Mao took over direction of the cultural revolution after the 11th Plenum he ordered the recall of the work teams, an order which Chen initially disobeyed and for which he had to publicly apologize later.

3. During the cultural revolution Huang was also used as a roving ambassador. Apart from assignments in the Middle East he attended independence celebrations in Mauritius in April 1968, after which the two countries agreed in principle to establish diplomatic relations. In August he was at Congo-Brazzaville's Revolution Day.

4. Although China could hardly have known the ideological leanings of the new military leaders she was quick to assure them of recognition and of her continued friendship, in contrast to her actions after Nkrumah's overthrow. China again offered to build the railway in 1973.

5. For example, the communiqué issued at the end of a visit by a delegation from Mauritania (a conservative, Moslem country) affirmed that 'The Mauritanian delegation is firmly convinced that the unprecedented great proletarian cultural revolution initiated by the great Chairman Mao Tse-tung in China with a population of 700 million is of extremely profound and far-reaching international significance.' (NCNA, Peking, 17 February 1967).

6. It still is – as late as 1971 two Rhodesian refugees were given eighteen-month sentences for being in possession of the *Little Red Book* and other Chinese publications.

7. Soviet–US collusion was even supposed to be occurring in Vietnam, where the bombing of Hanoi and Haiphong was seen as 'a product of the filthy political bargaining between the United States and the Soviet Union' (Kuo Mo-jo, the chairman, in his final speech to the June 1966 Afro-Asian Writers' emergency meeting in Peking).

8. Ogunsanwo, op. cit., p. 311.

9. I am grateful to Godwin Ironkwe, who was Reuters correspondent in Biafra during the course of the civil war, for the information contained in the above two paragraphs.

10. As a Reuters correspondent I accompanied the international team of observers to the war front in late 1969. Federal soldiers showed us a selection of arms captured from retreating Biafran forces, which included Chinese anti-tank mines and AK-47 automatic rifles made in China.

11. At the end of 1969, in a last desperate attempt to attract Chinese support, Ojukwu issued the Aharia Declaration, a manifesto outlining the political creed of a future independent Ibo state. It contained plans for the state ownership of all property and other socialist suggestions. Biafra collapsed before China had time to react to the declaration.

II
THE NEW CHINA

'Let the West serve China'
MAO TSE-TUNG

THE border clashes between Chinese and Soviet troops in February 1969 awoke China's leaders from their three-year introspection and focused their attention sharply on external dangers to the security of the state. Modern revisionism was clearly becoming a greater threat than old imperialism. Allies would have to be sought everywhere against the 'New Tsars'. A slight rapprochement with the United States might even prove necessary.

Reactions to Czechoslovakia

The Chinese must have been encouraged in this search for friends by the extreme reactions around the world to the previous year's invasion of Czechoslovakia by the Soviet Union. Africans in particular had always been uneasy about the Soviet Union's Eastern European 'empire', and her efforts to retain it by force were virulently criticized throughout the continent. If it can be taken that silence implied disapproval, only Mali, somewhat surprisingly, positively approved the invasion; even Egypt, the recipient of so much Soviet aid, was ambivalent in her attitude, explaining that the Soviet Union had not wanted to send in troops, but had been forced to do so 'because of the part played by world Zionism', according to Radio Cairo. Positive approval did, however, come from the Afro-Asian Solidarity Committee of Nigeria, which together with the National Trade Union Council congratulated the Czechoslovakian government for its 'wise request for aid from the

Warsaw Pact allies'. Almost alone of national communist parties throughout the world, the sycophantically pro-Soviet Communist Party of South Africa also praised the Soviet Union's actions.

Elsewhere in Africa, President Kaunda's hope 'that God will help the Czechoslovakian people to fight against Russian imperialism' was echoed in radio and newspaper comment, government statements and demonstrations. In Tanzania, TANU party youths demonstrated outside the Soviet embassy and broke its windows; in Nairobi, where the government radio called the invasion 'a naked and brutal manifestation of the worst form of imperialism', students carried banners proclaiming 'Russians murdered Dubček' and 'Czechoslovakia, a lesson for Africa'. Radio Kinshasa proclaimed that '. . . Muscovite communism has once again degraded itself in the eyes of the world', Ghana referred to 'unjustified aggression',[1] the *New Nigerian* newspaper to 'a shameful and inexcusable act'. An official Tanzanian government statement expressed 'profound shock' and added that Tanzania opposed colonialism of all kinds, whether old or new, in Africa, in Europe or elsewhere.[2] Expressions of revulsion and shock were also made by Senegal, Uganda, Tunisia and others.

Although still preoccupied with the cultural revolution, China had naturally joined the anti-Soviet chorus. It was a good opportunity for some cheap propaganda. But the intensity of feeling against the Soviet Union, and the distrust felt for her by almost all African countries, must also have been noted by policy makers in Peking. They may well have calculated that the Soviet Union's actions had created something of a vacuum in Africa; leaders, unwilling to rely on the former colonialists, disappointed by the United States and now disillusioned with the Soviet Union, might be casting around for a new 'big power' friend. If the hypothesis is correct, it would explain the eagerness of African countries to recognize China once the cultural revolution was over, as well as China's generous aid commitments made during the 'diplomatic offensive' – given to demonstrate China's big power capabilities.

THE END OF THE CULTURAL REVOLUTION

Even without the border clashes, and the consequent need for

China to go out into the world in search of support, it seems likely that the cultural revolution would have been drawing to a close in 1969. Its main objectives – a shaking-up of the old order and the removal of Mao's principal rivals – had been achieved. At the ninth congress of the CCP in May, the cultural revolution was officially declared over.

For well over a year afterwards foreign policy initiatives were very limited, and very cautious. It was a difficult time for the Foreign Ministry bureaucrats, doubtless still nervous after the momentous events of the preceding three years, and, after the relegation of Chen Yi at the ninth congress, without constant leadership. Chou once again took foreign affairs under his personal wing, but until internal conditions had completely settled he was unable to devote as much time to the Ministry as he would doubtless have liked.

The most obvious outward sign of a gradual return to normality was the dispatch, in mid-year, of ambassadors. The first to go, in May, was the ambassador to France, followed by the ambassador to Pakistan. In June, the ambassadors to Tanzania, Guinea, Zambia and Congo-Brazzaville left Peking, followed in subsequent months by those to Mauritania and Algeria. They were all experienced career diplomats; Wang Yu-tien, for example, the ambassador sent to Brazzaville, had previously been ambassador in the Sudan and Kenya and had been Director of the West Asian and African Affairs Department. Chin Li-chen was re-assigned to his former post in Lusaka.

The 'thaw', as it inevitably came to be known, was gradual. Violent language was moderated and the revolutionary image firmly played down. Stories carried in three English-owned East African newspapers in July that China had issued a set of eight stamps featuring revolutionary figures in the Third World, including Babu and Odinga, were labelled 'sheer fabrications' and their supposed 'reproduction' in a further newspaper, the Nairobi *Daily Nation*, a 'despicable forgery'.

The only people who did not benefit from this more benign outlook were, of course, the Russians. Film shows, featuring documentaries with such titles as *Down with the new Tsars* and *New Tsars' anti-China atrocities*, were shown in China's embassies, without eliciting, at least from governments, much sympathy. China continued to talk of US-Soviet collusion, especially in

Vietnam and in the Congo where the two 'openly collaborate
... in fostering the reactionary forces and frantically suppressing the people's struggle for national liberation.' But somehow
the fire seemed to have gone out of the invective. The Chinese
chargé in England attended the Royal Ascot race meeting,
and everywhere people started talking of the 'new China'.

If 1969 was the year of the 'de-freeze', 1970 saw the beginnings of the real thaw. Friendship, cultural, technical and
governmental delegations to and from Africa increased, and
for the first time China emerged as by far the largest communist
donor of foreign aid. Her total aid of £180 million committed
during the year exceeded by over £100 million the combined
aid commitments of the Soviet Union and the Eastern European
countries. Tanzania and Zambia received £81 million each
for the construction of the railway, which exceeded by over
£30 million the credit granted by the Soviet Union to Egypt
for the construction of the Aswan Dam, and marked China out
in African eyes as a major new aid-giving power. The political
impact of the Tanzam agreement in East Africa was almost
matched in West Africa by a Chinese gift to Guinea of £4·1
million in the wake of an abortive Portuguese-inspired invasion,
and by the subsequent dispatch to Guinea of a team of Chinese
doctors skilled in treating war wounds.

The year also saw the beginning of the 'diplomatic offensive'
which was to gain China her seat in the United Nations.
Canada's recognition in October sparked off a chain reaction,
and in Africa, Equatorial Guinea and Ethiopia had established
relations before the year was out. The next year there was a
virtual rush to recognize China with Nigeria,[3] Cameroon,[4]
Sierra Leone, Togo, Senegal, Rwanda, Burundi and Tunisia
either establishing or resuming relations with Peking.

October was a momentous month for Sino-African relations,
with the African vote at the United Nations just tipping the
scales in Peking's favour[5] and the first ever visit by a foreign
emperor to China in her long history, in the shape of Emperor
Haile Selassie of Ethiopia.

The diplomatic offensive by no means stopped with China's
admission to the United Nations. In February 1972 Ghana
resumed the relations which had been broken off so peremp-
torily six years previously; other nations followed – Chad,

Mauritius, Madagascar and Dahomey. In November China could really claim to have gained respectability: legitimate government-to-government relations were finally established with the old enemy, Zaire – as the Congo had by then become. In January 1973, General Mobutu, whom, according to ancient Chinese propaganda was an imperialist 'running dog' and murderer of Lumumba, went to Peking.[6] The hand-clasp between the Zairois President and the eighty-year-old Mao Tse-tung was as historic as the one between Chou En-lai and Nasser which only eighteen years previously at Bandung had initiated China's modern interest in Africa.

End of the 'united front from below'

This vast expansion of China's legitimate relations with African governments of every political hue was gained at the expense of revolutionary dogmatism. No longer could Chou or any other Chinese minister tell an African leader that his continent was ripe for revolution, still less that his own regime did not meet with approval in Peking and that it was China's internationalist duty to help the opposition overthrow it. The price of respectability was the abandonment of subversion and the 'united front from below', and their replacement by a correct, 'normal' relationship.

In some cases the African government made these normal relations conditional on China's undertaking to cease support for opposition groups either within or outside the country. For example, an unpublicized clause was written into the agreement whereby China and Ethiopia established diplomatic relations stating that China would cease supplying materials to the Eritrean Liberation Front, the Moslem separatist group which she had backed, through Syria and South Yemen, since about 1965.[7] Confirmation that this was so came in November 1971 from an ELF spokesman who said that Peking, 'which had previously supported us as part of the international revolution', no longer did so because of China's policy of widening her international relations. It seems probable that by mid-1973 China was not supporting any dissident group within any African country with which she maintained normal relations. Possibly certain individuals, either potential leaders within the government apparatus or in open or covert opposition, benefited from a small amount of largesse. But it was no longer really necessary: China was no longer interested in fomenting revolution for its own sake or in trying to replace existing governments. She was prepared to deal with any *de facto* government, whether it was headed by a soldier, an emperor or a revolutionary. Even with General Amin.

Expansion of aid

A more material price was also exacted for the normalization of relations, for in almost every case, China marked the establishment or renewal of diplomatic relations with a generous aid commitment. Although these aid agreements only indicated China's willingness to supply Chinese goods and services to a certain value over a certain period of time, their size made a considerable psychological impact – £28 million to Sudan, £42 million to Ethiopia, £8 million to Burundi, £13 million to Mauritius, £17 million to Tunisia, £42 million to Zaire and £36 million to Cameroon. In mid-1973 China was either actively engaged on or was making feasibility studies of a number of major new prestige projects; these included the Tanzam railway, which was at least a year ahead of schedule by this time and entered Zambia in August; the Guinea-Mali railway; a hydro-electric dam on the River Bouenza in Congo-Brazzaville; a 1800-acre rice scheme in Uganda, including provision of a dam and irrigation system; a new airport in Mauritius; a 50000 capacity stadium in Sierra Leone, a 30000 capacity stadium in Somalia and a huge scheme to build a fifty-mile canal from Ghana's Lake Volta to the Accra plains. There were important road projects in Sudan, Somalia, Rwanda, Zambia and elsewhere; Chinese medical teams continued to provide services to remote rural areas. Communications between China and Africa also began to improve, with a telecommunications link established at the end of 1972 by the East African Posts and Telecommunications Corporation, and with Ethiopian Airline's inaugural flight to Shanghai in February 1973.

This huge effort was made possible partly by the ending of the Vietnam war, and the release for aid purposes of the estimated £150 million a year Chinese subsidy to North Vietnam. But aid also came to be seen as much more part of an aid-trade package, and China's trade with Africa, which had been only 3 per cent of its total world trade in 1956 had by 1972 grown to over double that amount. Chinese consumer goods and unsophisticated manufactured products were on sale throughout Africa. In turn China was buying considerable quantities of raw materials – cotton from Kenya, Uganda, Tanzania, Egypt and Sudan; sisal from Tanzania and Kenya; copper from Zambia, and it seems certain that China's interest in Zaire stems partly from her huge reserves of minerals. Probably China's African trade was just about financing her African aid, and from China's point of view that was good business (for further details see Chapter Thirteen).

(for further details see Chapter Thirteen).

SINO-SOVIET DISPUTE

The 'new China' may have been prepared to forget past differences with Zaire, and even with the United States. It could not do so with the Soviet Union. But even in this most bitter of disputes the line changed perceptibly. China disclaimed any ambitions to 'big power' status, and against what she termed the 'hegemonic' practices of the super powers, she posed the combined force of the smaller, poorer nations, armed only with their self-reliance. China became the champion of the poor (the Third World) against the rich (the West, but including the Soviet Union).

The Soviet Union has been somewhat puzzled by this development, but has decided to brazen it out, taking the line that, yes, she may be rich, but that shows the success of her system and her method of development, and also means she is more capable of helping the less well-off. Soviet propaganda has therefore concentrated on the paucity of China's aid efforts, on her inability to build large industrial projects and on the unprofitable nature of the projects she has already completed. A typical example would be this comment by Moscow Radio made in August 1972:

China's low degree of technological progress and its economic backwardness make it impossible to build the great enterprises which might be the foundations of the economies of the Afro-

Asian countries. Chinese industry cannot supply equipment up to modern standards. Many factories built with Chinese assistance are not economic and prove a heavy burden on national budgets.

Moscow opposes the idea of self-reliance with continued reliance on support from friendly socialist countries. For example, Radio Peace and Progress took issue with the Chinese UN delegate, Huang Hua, for advising people struggling against oppression to rely on their own strength. In an obvious distortion of his meaning, the Radio said,

This appeal is nothing but another provocation against the national liberation movement. Applied to the existing conditions in Africa it signifies that Peking, in order to serve its own selfish interests, wants to isolate the struggling peoples of Angola, Guinea-Bissau, Mozambique, Zimbabwe and the African South from their friends, the people of the socialists countries, from all anti-imperialist forces, and this means that they would be left without arms to face the racist colonialist regimes which are receiving large-scale military, economic and political aid from the Western imperialists.

Soviet ideology, limping along behind events, has had to make some painful adjustments to changing conditions in Africa. But on a theoretical level the academicians have now invented the concept of 'non-capitalist development'. In Africa, usually singled out as being on this road are Egypt, Algeria, Guinea, Congo-Brazzaville, Tanzania and Somalia. The road, of course, has many 'twists and turns' in it. Professor R. A. Ul'yanovskiy, for example, found that

Non-capitalist development is a very complicated process, presupposing an extremely prolonged co-existence of contradictory tendencies. Some of them are not only not consistently socialist, but sometimes even contradict the principles of socialism. But here of course is the distinction between it and the direct socialist path! For it is a question of leading towards socialism the productive forces and people's masses of backward countries which for objective reasons are not yet prepared for the immediate construction of socialism. There is simply no way of overcoming the existing contradictions other than by preparing and training the popular masses and leading them towards socialism, *given their present level today.*

Against this tortuous reasoning, the Chinese message of self-reliance seems crystal clear.

As far as possible China has tried to sweep along her African allies in the 'anti-hegemony club'. The *People's Daily* editorial on Africa Day said that

... the unity among the African countries and among the African people has grown stronger constantly in the struggle against aggression, subversion, control, interference and bullying by imperialism, social-imperialism, colonialism and neo-colonialism ... The African people are our good friends ... We are comrades-in-arms, trusting and relying upon each other in the fight against ... the power politics and hegemonic practices of the superpowers. (*People's Daily*, 25 May 1972)

The movement has obviously touched a chord, especially in the United Nations where a 'China group' of third-world nations is growing. It even received an endorsement from General Mobutu, whose final communiqué after his visit to China stated that 'Both sides affirm that China and Zaire will work together with the other countries of the Third World in combating the power politics and hegemonism of big powers.'

The general encouragement of regional groupings, such as the EEC, and 'independent-minded' countries like Yugoslavia and Rumania, as counter-balances to big power hegemony, has also been pursued in Africa. China has been particularly eager to promote a Mediterranean grouping, which is the main reason behind renewed good relations with Algeria, which has herself canvassed the idea.

During a visit to Peking in August 1971 (which he regarded as 'a new starting point in the relations between Algeria and China'), Algerian Foreign Minister, Abdelaziz Bouteflika, said numerous imperialist bases and foreign fleets had 'created a foul atmosphere in the Mediterranean'; a sentiment praised by his host, Vice-Premier Li Hsien-nien, as a 'clear cut stand' against imperialism and colonialism. It was a stand which earned rewards, for in the subsequent two years Chinese aid once more began to flow to Algeria (or more accurately the Algerians were able to utilize the commitments made in 1963).

Tunisia also joined the club when Foreign Minister Mohammed Masmoudi used a Peking banquet in September 1972 to attack the Soviet Union and the US for using the Mediterranean as an area for their rivalry. Seven Eastern bloc diplomats walked out.

Earlier, in March, the *People's Daily* had compiled a list of the countries fighting to make the Mediterranean 'a sea of Mediterraneans', including Algeria, Albania, Libya, Morocco, Tunisia, Italy, Malta and Yugoslavia. Notably absent was Egypt, whose independence was presumably circumscribed by the Soviet military presence.

Just as in Europe, where the two countries which have received Chinese praise for their 'independence' have been the two which have most embarrassed the Soviet Union – Yugoslavia and Rumania – so in Africa accolades have gone to Sudan and Egypt, both of whom have had differences with Moscow, a fact which has given China an opportunity to make serious challenges in areas where the Soviets must have thought they were irreplaceable.

China had been on relatively good terms with Sudan for some time, following General Numeiry's visit to Peking in August 1970, and two subsequent and considerable Chinese aid packages. But the Soviets had been entrenched for a long time, having written Sudan's five-year plan, and given considerable economic and military assistance to the Khartoum government. In July 1971, however, their fortunes tumbled when a coup against Numeiry, engineered by the Sudanese Communist Party, temporarily succeeded, received clear endorsement from the Soviet Union and was then defeated by pro-Numeiry forces. The Soviet Union further blotted her record when she protested strongly at the subsequent execution of the coup's ringleaders, and amid bitter accusations of unfair barter deals the Soviet Union withdrew her aid personnel.[8] China meanwhile had said nothing, but was quick to congratulate Numeiry once he had re-established his position. This silence (an 'eloquent silence', according to Moscow Radio) proved golden, as was shown by the praise heaped on China by Major-General Khalid Abbas, the head of the Sudanese armed forces, when he visited Peking at the end of the year:

Our people and our revolution once suffered from a perfidious conspiracy which was carried out by certain elements under 'leftist' slogans, in close collusion with certain people in countries in the socialist camp who claimed to be friendly with us ... Dear friends, I must mention here that our people and our revolutionary leaders will for ever be proud of the brave stand taken by the Chinese people and their militant leader Mao Tse-tung and their great party in firmly standing by our people and our revolution when the traitorous conspiracy took place and in the ensuing days. (NCNA, Peking, 17 December 1971)

China was quick to take advantage of the Soviets' discomfiture, and promptly offered to help in the training of the armed forces and the supply of military equipment, an offer which was gratefully accepted.[9]

Opportunism was also evident in China's sudden interest in September 1972, in finding ways of helping Egypt to utilize some of the £28 million credit extended as long ago as 1964 – just two months after the Soviet Union had been asked to reduce her military presence in Egypt. China might even have sown some of the seeds of discontent with the Soviet Union, because for some years Chinese propaganda and pro-Chinese Arab publications had conducted a campaign against Soviet aid to Egypt, claiming that the Aswan Dam had been badly conceived and badly built, and 'revealing' serious flaws in Soviet tanks and aircraft supplied to the Egyptian armed forces. The Soviets' position was much stronger, and more firmly established in Egypt than it was in Sudan, and continuing Egyptian reliance on the Soviet Union seems likely for a long time, certainly as long as the Middle East crisis lasts. However, just as after Suez and the Arab-Israeli War, China had shown that she was prepared to be 'a friend indeed' to Egypt, and good Sino-Egyptian relations, based in part on an expanding trade (China is now Egypt's fourth largest cotton customer), seem assured.

Notes

1. Ghana's head of state, Lt-Col Ankrah, said the invasion reminded him of the Chinese professor who refused to endorse the cultural revolution and chose instead to remain silent. When he was castigated for this by his militant son, he said: 'What is the world coming to now? We have lost our freedom of speech and now we have even lost the freedom of silence.'
2. Nyerere often referred back to the Czechoslovakian experience. I

remember at one press conference he was asked when was an invasion not an invasion? The answer – 'When it is an invitation.'

3. Although China insisted on the diplomatic formula that states seeking relations should recognize the CPR as the legal government representing all the Chinese people, the African governments also exacted some tribute. In the Nigerian communiqué, for example, China was pointedly made to recognize the sovereignty and territorial integrity of African countries.

4. The execution in January 1971 of the last remaining UPC leader, Ernest Ouandie, effectively ended the rebellion and cleared the path for relations with China.

5. African countries voting for were: Algeria, Botswana, Burundi, Cameroon, Congo-Brazzaville, Egypt, Equatorial Guinea, Ethiopia, Ghana, Guinea, Kenya, Libya, Mali, Mauritania, Morocco, Nigeria, Rwanda, Senegal, Sierra Leone, Somalia, Sudan, Togo, Tunisia, Uganda, Tanzania and Zambia. Against were: Central African Republic, Chad, Dahomey, Gabon, Gambia, Ivory Coast, Lesotho, Liberia, Madagascar, Malawi, Niger, South Africa, Swaziland, Upper Volta and Zaire. (Twenty-six for, fifteen against.)

6. On his return he said Mao had admitted to him that he had expended a great deal of money and men on the Congo. By now, early Chinese revolutionary activity had become almost a subject of nostalgia, discussed over an evening fire in the same way that an English cabinet minister might joke with Kenyatta about the Mau Mau.

7. From a private conversation with a senior Ethiopian official.

8. A Sudanese official who had dealings with the Russians told me that in 1970 the Soviet Union was due to give Sudan arms, tractors, fertilizers and jute bags in exchange for two-thirds of the cotton crop. The arms were second-hand, the tractors broke down on the way from the docks to the growing area and the fertilizer and the jute bags never materialized. The same official said the Russian attempts to impose central planning on the economy were 'disastrous'.

9. Numeiry told the Lebanese magazine *Al Hawadess* (1 June 1972) that Mao had told him that a Chinese offer of eight Mig-17s and enough modern tanks to equip a division were 'a present from the Chinese people. We do not sell arms used to fight imperialism. China is not an arms merchant.' Numeiry recalled that he said with a smile: 'If I had known your policy on arms deliveries, we would have saved the foreign exchange we had to pay the Russians.'

PART TWO

PART TWO

12

PERSONAL RELATIONS

Being yellow doesn't help them much . . .
ANONYMOUS AFRICAN

THE reaction between China and any given African state can be measured in a number of quantitative ways: by the amount of trade conducted between the two countries; by the amount of aid received; by UN voting patterns; by the number of visits exchanged, and at what level; by the signing of friendship, cultural and military agreements; by statements of support or hostility and by the establishment or rupture of diplomatic relations. By using all these criteria we can say with certainty, for example, that the interaction, or friendship, between China and Tanzania is very great, as measured by the volume of aid and trade, the frequency of high-level visits and the number of cooperative agreements. Impossible to measure, but a factor nevertheless in the continuance of good relations, is the way in which Chinese and African people react to each other. Do they like each other, do they understand each other, can they – or how do they – communicate? In general studies of relations between states this aspect has almost always been neglected, firstly because the importance of personal relations between individuals is clearly less great than political factors, secondly because the information is difficult to collect and general conclusions hard to draw. But there seems little doubt that relations between the Soviet Union and Egypt, for example, have been exacerbated by the dull, humourless behaviour of the Russian technicians,[1] in the same way as the image of the arrogant, free-spending *Yanqui* has affected relations between the United States and Latin American countries. These personal relations are a kind of undertow to political relations between states, exerting an unseen influence which is difficult to measure; this chapter is a tentative attempt to evaluate how Chinese and Africans get on together and how important this might be for inter-state relations.

BEGINNINGS

When China first began to interest herself in the African continent a few years after the communist revolution the almost total ignorance of Chinese of Africans, and vice versa, ensured that the two peoples approached each other with few prejudices. In political terms the Chinese were regarded with favour by Africans, for China had never been associated with any scramble for Africa; the Chinese were non-white and non-imperialist. Equally the Chinese had never been humiliated by any African nation, and indeed the common suffering of Africa and China at the hands of white imperialists was often stressed by both sides. During his tour of African countries in 1964 Chou En-lai constantly referred to the common struggles waged by African nations and by China against imperialism – struggles, he said, which 'though separated by great distance inspired each other'.

Apart from an ignorance of Chinese history, most Africans (except for those who lived near the few places where over the centuries 'overseas' Chinese had settled, notably Madagascar and the Kenyan coast) had no idea what a Chinese looked like. Initially, this seemed to work to the advantage of the Chinese – they were foreign, but did not look like the foreigners most Africans had become accustomed to; they therefore enjoyed considerable curiosity value. The South African journalist, Pieter Lessing, described the respective arrivals of Russian and Chinese visitors to the Congo in 1962:

I was in the Kivu province of the Congo when the first batch of about 100 Russians arrived there. For days excited minor Congolese leaders had been telling me about the great event which was pending – the mysterious Russians, the supermen who were the answer to everything, were about to descend on them, to wave a magic wand and nothing would ever be the same again.

On the given day it was impossible not to feel a deep sympathy with the simple tribesmen in their shattering disillusionment; these Russians were not supermen, they were white, European, just like the Belgians. Shortly afterwards I was in Stanleyville when a Chinese diplomatic mission arrived. The African reaction was entirely different: there was nothing European about these visitors.[2]

Until they have seen a Chinese most Africans have no conception what they 'should' look like; for many of them Chinese simply denotes a nationality, and they attach no particular facial characteristics to the term. I remember that during the Nigerian war, when there were rumours that Chinese mercenaries were infiltrating into the country, two English girls were stopped by soldiers on Carter Bridge in Lagos and their car searched. When the search was completed one soldier poked his head through the window, looked piercingly at the girls and then asked them quite seriously: 'Are you Chinese?' A similar case of mistaken identity occurred when General Amin claimed his soldiers had killed a 'Chinese' colonel during border skirmishes with Obote supporters on the Tanzanian border. The body was later identified as that of a policeman of mixed Tanzanian and German parentage.

As we saw in Part One the Chinese did try initially to capitalize on what they portrayed as a common racial identity with Africans, going so far once as to emphasize the need for 'we blacks to stick together'.[3] This device to try and persuade the Africans to side with them against the white races, particularly the Russians, backfired. They were too obviously different – as one African told the English author, Anthony Sampson: 'Being yellow doesn't help them much, as far as we are concerned. They're not black, let's face it. Let's face it'.[4] The Chinese have learned their lesson: the common characteristic stressed by Chinese propaganda now is not race, but poverty. The poor races of the world, not just the black ones, must 'stick together'.

Language difficulties

If the Chinese for a time enjoyed a rather vague and insubstantial novelty – or curiosity – value they suffered from one very considerable disadvantage: language. Even today only a handful of Africans speak Chinese, and in the mid 1950s it is doubtful if there was even one African Chinese speaker. It has

7

therefore always been up to the Chinese to learn foreign languages in order to communicate with Africans.

Immediately after the revolution, and until about 1965, Russian was the main foreign language taught at Chinese schools and colleges, after which it was replaced by English. Languages other than Russian were taught at certain institutions; for example, Arabic was taught at the Eastern Languages department of Peking University and at the Institute for Moslems, and it was reported that the first Chinese ambassador to the Sudan was accompanied by an interpreter who spoke fluent Sudanese Arabic. But in general, speakers of the two main European languages spoken in Africa, English and French, were in short supply[5] and there were virtually no speakers of the main native languages, like Swahili, Hausa or Yoruba.[6]

This was clearly a fundamental barrier to communication between, say, a Chinese-speaking agronomist and a Malian peasant, but even experienced linguists had their problems, as is shown by a story told to me by Godfrey Morrison, who was the Reuters correspondent covering Chou's stop in Mogadiscu at the end of his 1964 tour. Morrison had interviewed the Somali Prime Minister Ali Shermarke about his discussions with Chou, as a result of which he had sent a dispatch to London which said in part that Chou had been 'at great pains' to give China's version of the Sino-Indian border dispute. The next day at a press conference Chou prefaced his remarks by attacking the imperialist Reuters agency for saying he had been at great pains to make known China's version of the story. He had, he said, found it very easy.

Since the cultural revolution the language competence of Chinese diplomats and senior technicians seems to have improved considerably. Many Chinese experts arriving in Tanzania already speak elementary Swahili, which suggests they may have attended a course at one of the major Foreign Language Institutes at Peking or Shanghai, or a reported African language centre near Nanking. Some of them also attended a British-run Swahili course in Dar-es-Salaam. The Chinese certainly appear to have a facility for languages: two doctors in a Chinese medical team I met in Juba, southern Sudan, spoke excellent English, while most members of the team had learned the rudiments of Arabic as well as the local language, Dinka. On a more elementary level, even the Chinese workmen of the Tanzam railway seemed to have picked up a few words of English. An English journalist's car was stuck in the mud by the side of a road near a Chinese railway camp; eventually two Chinese technicians passed and pulled him out with their jeep. He thanked them profusely, and they replied with the only English they appeared to know: 'Peking jeep very good, Peking jeep very good.'

On the African side, the few students who have been to China have all been taught Chinese as part of their course, but to my knowledge no African university yet offers Chinese as a foreign language. However, Africans who come into every-day contact with Chinese manage to pick up a few words: a Japanese diplomat in Dar es Salaam told me that he had heard some Tanzanians shouting at him what sounded like 'Nippon'. He was quite flattered to be recognized, but when he got nearer he realized they thought he was Chinese and they were shouting 'Ni haó, ni haó' – Chinese for 'hello'. And Zanzibar Museum can claim a unique distinction; the signs are written in two languages – Swahili and Chinese.

THE CHINESE IN AFRICA

Chinese behaviour in Africa very much reflects Peking's current internal preoccupations; the most extreme example of this was during the cultural revolution when Chinese diplomats and technicians outdid each other to prove their revolutionary fervour. But before that, the somewhat exclusive, isolated lives led by Chinese aid personnel and diplomats reflected China's own isolation and cautious attitude towards the outside world, while the diplomatic offensive and the re-entry of China into the mainstream of international affairs has its analogue in the markedly warmer and more social attitude of Chinese personnel abroad.

Nevertheless, certain consistent traits, as observed by Africans, do seem to run through these periods. Most frequently commented on is one variously described as 'aloof', 'exclusive', 'arrogant' and 'anti-social'. That Chinese in a strange environment, in most cases speaking only their own language, should

prefer to stay in each other's company is not all that surprising
– it is a characteristic of other races too, not least the English.
In fact in some countries, particularly Moslem ones where the
fear of communist proselytizing is strong, Chinese exclusiveness is considered a good thing – it reduces the risk of the
population being 'contaminated'. In Mali, for example, a
journalist friend of mine often heard it said that the Chinese
'were doing a good job and not bothering us, and that's what
we like'. But other Africans regret that the Chinese do not
mix socially, and interpret their exclusiveness as arrogance.
A Tanzanian minister told me he was sorry they did not come
to parties as he would like to get to know them better. At a
lower level, a 'white hunter' in Tanzania said his African
workers did not like the Chinese because basically they felt that
the Chinese despised them; they felt uneasy, even a little
frightened, in their presence.

Fundamentally, the Chinese do believe themselves superior,
not only to Africans, but to all other races. They come from the
Middle Kingdom, considered by them for so long not just as
the centre of civilization but as actually delimiting civilization. Beyond its boundaries lived the barbarian people, fit
only to provide tribute to the Emperor, sometimes in the form
of black slaves. This traditional world view, with its assumption
of the innate superiority of the Chinese race, was bound to
affect the attitude of Chinese towards Africans. An expert on
China has told me: 'They do regard themselves as superior,
and they find it difficult to understand Africans. Basically
they feel Africans are an insubstantial people, always laughing;
for the Chinese life is not a constant joke.' There is a derogatory
Chinese word *heiren* corresponding roughly to 'nigger'; its
existence obviously has significance, but it would be wrong to
adduce a racial attitude solely on that evidence.

There are a few practical examples of what would appear to
be a superior attitude. The taking of petty privileges in Tanzania, discussed in detail in Chapter Fifteen, would seem to
stem in part from arrogance; 'queue jumping', for example,
indicates a fairly dismissive attitude towards the feelings of the
other queuers.[7] There was also what could be interpreted as a
'racial' incident in 1967 when a Chinese agricultural expert in
Tanzania was stung by a horde of bees. He was rushed to the

best hospital in Dar es Salaam but his friends refused to allow the African doctor to attend him, alleging he was incompetent. An Asian doctor was then called, but he too was rejected as incapable. By the time a Chinese doctor arrived from Zanzibar the patient was dead.

It would be misleading to suggest that Sino-African relations are 'bedevilled' by an assumed Chinese superiority, because they are not. Instances of disharmony are rare – and because of tight Chinese discipline probably rarer than those between other foreign personnel and Africans. Every now and then Africans comment favourably on their personal relations with Chinese. A senior (Zambian) executive working on the railway project told me he had excellent relations with his Chinese opposite number, and that 'we laugh a lot together'. Odinga told the American ambassador to Kenya: 'You Americans remind me of the Chinese. We can talk frankly together and we can laugh. But the Russians – well, they are different – they are too much like the British'.[8]

The attitude of African patients to Chinese doctors, obviously a special kind of relationship, is discussed in the next chapter. Finally, one section of the community – the business community – enjoys excellent relations with the Chinese; they invariably pay their bills on time. – And in cash.

The Chinese life style

If Africans find Chinese personally rather difficult to understand, they regard the Chinese life style as quite incomprehensible. The Chinese emphasis on discipline, hard work, simple clothes, spartan living conditions and above all, sexual asceticism, is quite alien to the African mentality. Time and again, all over Africa, I have heard Africans puzzle over how the Chinese 'manage' without women. In a continent where bigamy is the rule rather than the exception, and where sexual mores are generally fairly relaxed, this 'peculiarity' more than anything else marks the Chinese out as a race apart. It is certainly not a virtue which is admired: I once watched some Dar es Salaam prostitutes, who could be said to have a vested interest in the matter, jeering at about a dozen Chinese workers standing in the back of a lorry which was stuck in a traffic jam. They

were shouting phrases like 'You're not men' and illustrating
them with gestures which are universal in any language. The
Chinese looked highly uncomfortable. Lack of money would
be one explanation why the Chinese did not patronize the
local prostitutes, but rumour supplied another: the Chinese
were reputed to bring their own 'state' prostitutes with them,
one to every eight men, and the prostitutes were also expected
to do a day's work as well. I have no direct evidence to support
this claim. A few Chinese women, dressed in baggy pyjama
suits and with their hair cut short, do work in African countries,
but as one anonymous African told Anthony Sampson: 'We
don't think much of their girls; they look just like men –
particularly in those new uniforms.'[9] Very little, if any, sexual
fraternization goes on between Chinese men and African
women, or African men and Chinese women – and, in answer
to the question of a Member of Parliament who claimed he
had read about the subject in a 'Chinese' book, Second Vice-
President Kawawa said, 'the suggestion that 20 million Chinese
girls were available for marriage to Tanzanians was a shameful
attempt to disrupt Chinese-Tanzanian friendship.'[10]

The Chinese ethos of hard work is also regarded with a
mixture of amusement and disbelief by most Africans. Although
there is admiration for the hard work put in by Chinese technicians in the task of nation-building, a feeling also persists, as
some Tanzanian railway workers told me, that the Chinese
are in a sense trying to 'show up' the Africans. On a national
level this is probably no bad thing, and leaders like Nyerere
use the example of the Chinese to try and stimulate their own
people to work harder. On a personal level it could lead to a
certain amount of awkwardness when, as happened with
clearing the brush for the railway, two work gangs, one African
and one Chinese, started at the same time and after four hours
the Chinese team was some fifty yards ahead. The Chinese
work ethos is illustrated by a story told to me by a Sudanese
friend. He had been swimming in the Nile when he heard that
a Chinese worker, swimming in a group, had been lost. He
arranged for a professional life-saver to start looking for the man.
After about an hour the other Chinese asked him if there was
any chance that the lost man could be still alive. When told
there was not, the leader of the group replied, 'Oh, well, he is

no longer available to *work*. Thank you for your help,' and the Chinese left.

Africans also comment on the rather drab, colourless uniforms worn by both Chinese men and women, and contrast them with their own colourful clothes. Recently the Chinese have branched out a little – Yang Chi-liang, the ambassador to Nigeria, presented his credentials to General Gowon wearing a Western suit and tie, and some of the women have taken to wearing calf-length grey skirts.

Outside work hours the Chinese still tend to stick together, and although football matches have been played between the Chinese national side and African teams, Chinese recreations do not provide a common meeting ground with Africans. Based on my own observations, Chinese spend their spare time playing table tennis and badminton, fishing (in Dar es Salaam they also collected shells and coral heads), swimming and reading (during the cultural revolution there were compulsory sessions for reading aloud and together the thoughts of Chairman Mao). A report which I was unable to substantiate (but disbelieved) said that in the Tanzanian Selous game reserve the railway workers illegally shot game, some with machine-guns.

A Chinese agricultural team, working in Dodoma, central Tanzania, with which I spent a day in 1973, had caged some colourful local birds; otherwise their recreation consisted of table tennis and badminton, although they also said they walked through the district a great deal in their spare time to survey possible agricultural sites. They lived in simple corrugated-iron huts which they had built themselves and which were scrupulously clean. The main concession to their comfort was a Chinese cook and Chinese food, which they said was sent to them directly from China. They could not have been more friendly, showing me their agricultural experiments and inviting me to an excellent meal. They had obviously been shocked at the low standard of living in the area, but their relations with the local people, although a little stilted by the language barrier (most of them spoke moderate Swahili), were patently good. Water from their well was freely available to people in the vicinity, whom they referred to as the 'Tanzanian friends'.

Groups of Chinese were often seen in Tanzania taking photographs of each other, against an obviously African background. They went shopping in pairs or threes and were good customers for Swiss watches. Strangely enough they also used to buy Chinese goods that were on sale in Dar es Salaam, particularly paraffin stoves, which were apparently for export only and were status symbols in China. The speedy sale in 1973 by the Zambian State Trading Corporation of 3000 Chinese bicycles was attributed to their purchase by Chinese railway technicians. Returning Chinese could be seen walking up the gangplank of the ship that was to take them home proudly clutching Chinese-made goods which had probably been brought to Tanzania on the same ship months or years before. They would also be carrying the (Japanese) transistor radio, given as a gift by the Tanzanian government to every Chinese aid expert on his departure from the country.

Africans in China

Africans who have been to China to study have had, on the whole, unhappy experiences, alleging political indoctrination, poor facilities and racial discrimination. These were all documented by a Ghanaian student, Emmanuel Hevi, in a somewhat polemical book called *An African Student in China*. But his factual allegations have never been disproved, and were substantiated by Zambian students who underwent similar experiences ten years later, in 1972.

Hevi, who studied in China when the country was still recovering from the failure of the Great Leap Forward, complained of the quality of the teaching and said subjects were distorted to fit the realities of Chinese conditions. As an example, he said students were taught that since carbohydrates, fats and proteins were inter-convertible during the human metabolic process, the lack of fats and protein in the Chinese diet did not matter. In language classes the Africans were taught parrot-fashion to repeat phrases like 'The people's communes, like a newly risen sun, light the path of progress for the Chinese people,' but they were unable to make ordinary conversation. A practical objection to Chinese courses was that they did not offer a degree, and students therefore found it difficult to find a graduate job when they returned to their own countries.

But Hevi's most damaging charge was that Africans were discriminated against on a racial basis. He claimed that Chinese, even doctors, thought Africans had black skins because they did not wash. If an African student danced with a Chinese girl she would be quizzed immediately afterwards by Youth League activists about their conversation. Some shops and hotels refused to allow Africans to enter, and there was even discrimination when it came to student allowances – Hevi said Albanians, for example, were given 150 yuan a month, while African students had to make do with 100 yuan. Another African student, while refuting some of Hevi's conclusions, agreed that

From my own talks with some of the Africans I met in China, and also with students from Latin America, I gathered that they found it difficult to mix socially with the Chinese. This always boiled down to the difficulty of getting girl friends.[11]

These complaints led to protest demonstrations and requests to leave. The former were linked to the latter because the Chinese were unwilling to repatriate disgruntled students for fear of bad publicity, and the students had to take extreme measures in order to get expelled. Dissatisfied Somalis had to go on a hunger strike before they were given tickets home and other students resorted to violence. According to Hevi's figures – and he was Secretary-General of the African Students' Union – out of 118 African students studying at the same time as himself ninety-six left, and ten wanted to but could not. In August 1962 thirty Cameroonian students left Peking complaining of racial discrimination, claiming that they had been shunned by Chinese and denied access to shops open to white students. In the same year twenty Zanzibaris left after one of them had allegedly been beaten-up for asking for more than one packet of cigarettes at a hotel. In 1963 ten African students were injured in clashes between African and Chinese students following pressure on the former to speak up publicly for Peking in the Sino-Soviet dispute. Four Sudanese and twenty Somali students then asked to discontinue their studies.

China also evidently felt the experiment to further the education of Africans in China was a failure. If any African students did study in China during the next ten years the fact was not recorded officially. The only Africans to receive training in China in this time were either guerrilla fighters or technicians.

One such group of 'technicians' was the Tanzanian acrobatic team whose members were trained in China during the cultural revolution. They did not complain of racial discrimination, but were chagrined to find the male and female members of the team were quartered miles apart, and any extracurricular athletic activities were strictly forbidden. The release of energy on their return to Tanzania led to several of the girls becoming pregnant, and as a matter of national urgency the Family Planning Association was brought in to advise. It was presumably felt in the highest quarters that pregnancy would preclude all but the gentlest tumbling, and two years' training would thereby be wasted.

Freedom fighters in Dar es Salaam who had been to China for training also complained of the spartan sexual regime, and of attempts to make them assimilate Chinese culture – a ZANU man said his instructor in Shanghai had tried to teach him to eat with chopsticks, saying any other method of eating was primitive. Like the students, the guerrillas also resented efforts to indoctinate them, although they acknowledged the importance of correct political thinking in successful guerrilla warfare. Another ZANU trainee told a *Guardian* newspaper interviewer in April 1968: 'Later there were more lectures about how to brainwash peasants. This in effect was communism. We had been told by our officials to watch out for this. They feared that communism might make us revolt against their leadership.' The trainee added: 'I grew up being told by the white man that the communists were terrible people. Since I hate the white man I wanted to be one. I had the impression that the white man feared these people and I wanted the white man to be terrified of me.'

In May 1972 China reversed her policies towards students and accepted 100 engineering students from Tanzania and Zambia for courses in railway engineering. But on 25 December three Zambian students ran riot, smashed up portraits of Chairman Mao, beat-up Chinese policemen and damaged their hostel – all with the intention, they explained later, of securing their expulsion from China. Like previous African students in China they complained of the austere regime and the lack of entertainment, and said that instead of learning about railway engineering they were merely learning Chinese. Out of the original 100 students the Chinese had apparently drawn up a list of twenty-seven 'trouble-makers' and had reported them to their respective ambassadors. Discipline amongst the Tanzanians was said to be better after a dressing-down from the Tanzanian ambassador.[12] However, even the Tanzanians tacitly admitted that the training of the railway engineers in China was less than adequate when the Railway Authority quietly approached Britain towards the end of 1973 to see if British Rail could take on twenty railway trainees. It seemed likely this request would be turned down, since British diplomats in Dar es Salaam were convinced that the Tanzam line would be an economic disaster (reasoning based on their belief in an early Rhodesian settlement and Zambia's subsequent use of the more economical Beira line) with which Britain would not wish to be associated, however remotely. It seems unlikely that China will want to accept many more African students in the future, with their apparent inability to settle in compounded by the language difficulty and the unsolvable problem (as one already quoted candidly said) of 'getting girl friends.'

The experiences of students in China contrast strongly with the favourable impression made on short-term visitors. Delegations are usually shown a commune, factories and, depending on their interests, a military display, agricultural techniques or some other specialized aspect of Chinese life. They are given banquets, meet officials and often visit provincial centres such as Shanghai and Nanking. But for an important visitor it must be the pomp and circumstance surrounding his arrival, the almost theatrical welcome, that leaves such a lasting impression. Here, for example, is the NCNA description of the arrival in Peking of Zambia's Vice-President, Reuben Kamanga, in August 1966:

. . . During the welcoming ceremony at the airport the band played the national anthems of Zambia and China and Vice-President Kamanga reviewed a guard of honour.

The welcomers beat drums and gongs, and waved miniature national flags of the two countries . . . to welcome their distinguished guests from Zambia. There were bursts of applause and shouts of 'Long live Sino-Zambian friendship' and 'Long live Afro-Asian solidarity'.

The Zambian Vice-President and the government delegation he is leading then drove to the guest house through the festively decorated city. A huge portrait of the Vice-President stood at a major junction on the route. Strings of multi-coloured flags were hung across the main boulevard and the taller buildings were gay with long streamers suspended from roof to ground.

Singing and dancing, workers, students, government functionaries and people of other walks of life lined both sides of the street several deep to greet the Zambian guests.

Driving in two open cars (the guests) entered a narrow human lane of cheers and smiles, which led from Tienanmen Square, in the heart of the city, down to the guest house in the western sector.

Waving garlands, flowers and streamers, the crowds cheered heartily and rhythmically shouted 'Welcome, welcome' to greet the distinguished guests as they drove past at walking pace. Myriads of colourful balloons were released over Tienanmen Square, which was a sea of colours, flowers, garlands and banners. Huge balloons trailed slogans of welcome and friendship.

Several thousand amateur artists in full costume performed a variety of dances, turning Tienanmen Square into a huge open stage. (NCNA, Peking, 19 August 1966)

The obvious stage-managing of such a welcome as this would hardly be likely to bother the centre of so much attention, nor would he question the description of himself in the Chinese press as an important figure on the world stage. Subsequent meetings with Chinese leaders, often with Chairman Mao himself, would convince such African visitors of their own importance. But on some occasions a genuine spirit of camaraderie seems discernible; at a banquet held during Kaunda's June 1967 visit to China, the Zambian President conducted the Zambian guests singing 'Our Land is Good', after which Chou diplomatically rose and conducted the Chinese in singing 'Sailing the Seas Depends on the Helmsman'.

Such apparent warmth between Chinese and Africans is comparatively rare. Close personal relationships would in any case be constrained by linguistic and cultural differences, but these are compounded by what would appear to be a formal restraint placed on the Chinese against socializing with local people, a restraint which is by no means limited to Chinese working in Africa, since the phenomenon has been noted elsewhere in the world. This remoteness almost certainly adds to the mystique which they enjoy as a result of their 'strange' appearance, and for a long time the Chinese were held in awe by Africans, and were endowed by them with more intelligence – or more cunning, depending on the speaker – than they actually possessed. Kanyama Chiume, one of the ministers dismissed by Banda for allegedly associating too closely with the Chinese, told the Malawian parliament: 'We tend to give the Chinese more credit than they deserve. They are not always as intelligent as all that.'

After nearly twenty years in Africa the Chinese are now beginning to lose some of that mystique, and as China's international policies become more relaxed so, recently, has the attitude of her personnel in Africa towards the local populations. To Western questioning about their relations with the Chinese, Africans still remain highly defensive, perhaps not surprisingly in light of the interpretations put by the press on these relations in the past. They suspect an unseen trap; Joe Appia, Ghana's roving ambassador, was very evasive when I questioned him in London in 1973 about a trip he had recently made to China. He felt, I believe, that any Western journalist was bound to be hostile to China and in answer to a question whether he thought China was still engaged in any subversive activities in Africa, replied: 'It's amazing how people assume other people are doing what they themselves are doing – they build up other people in their own image.' On personal relations he merely said the delegation had been treated hospitably, but the fact that he could remember only the name of Chou En-lai of the Chinese to whom he had spoken indicates more than linguistic difficulties. To most Africans Chinese still are anonymous faces, not personalities in their own right.

Notes

1. When I visited the Aswan Dam in 1964 the Egyptian taxi driver pointed out the swarms of Russian technicians, tapped his head, looked at the sky and told me, 'They have no fantasia, no fantasia.' The British, he assured me, had plenty of 'fantasia'.

2. *Sunday Telegraph*, 15 March 1962.

3. This theme was stressed by a Chinese acting troupe, seen performing in the early 1960s in Rwanda by a British diplomat. A tableau depicted a black man sitting on a throne; a Chinese actor with a white face mask then entered and knocked him off (groans from crowd). A Chinese with no mask entered, knocks the 'white man' in turn off the throne, picks up the African from the ground and helps him back on to the throne (cheers from crowd).

4. Halpern, op. cit., p. 390.

5. Tung Chi-ping told Bruce Larkin (op. cit., p. 238) that although his political reliability was in doubt, he was chosen to go to Burundi simply because he could speak French, and French-speakers were rare.

6. Although a few may have been trained at the centre in Mogadiscu (see p. 91).

7. However, according to one source (Emmanuel Hevi, *An African Student in China*) foreigners in Peking have an unwritten right to go to the head of queues – perhaps Chinese in Africa feel they have a similar right.

8. Attwood, op. cit., p. 242.

9. Halpern, op. cit., p. 390.

10. Reuters dispatch from Dar es Salaam, 24 June 1968.

11. Kojo Amoo-Gottfried, *Race*, April 1964.

12. Further trouble between students – and even diplomats – and their Chinese hosts was reported at the end of 1974. The *Sunday Times* (27 October 1974) said there had been unpleasant scenes between African diplomats and their Chinese drivers, who complained of overwork. Two envoys also quarrelled with the Chinese because aid teams going to their countries refused to fill in visa forms completely. African students put up a poster at their institute complaining they were spat on by Chinese students after a rowdy football match, and some 'feigned madness and organized brawls in order to be sent home'.

13
TRADE AND AID

'Peking is wooing many Asian and African countries'
Soviet propaganda

TRADE

CHINA has published no official statistical reports on her economy since 1960 and issued no data on her international trade since 1958. Figures for the latter therefore have to be estimated from the import and export returns of China's trading partners, figures which are sometimes incomplete and at times even deliberately misleading. Statistics for China's own economy can only be guessed at, or inferred from Chinese purchases in the world market, although occasionally a top official will quote what appears to be an accurate production figure – Chou En-lai, for example, has freely given details of China's total oil production.

But even allowing for fairly large margins of error in the statistics available, discernible patterns are evident in China's international trade. The first is a determination to balance imports and exports, or if possible achieve a surplus in China's favour. Except for a few exceptional years, when heavy quantities of foodstuffs had to be imported due to adverse weather conditions in China, this balance, within a margin of about 5 per cent has been struck. With trade balanced, 'invisible' expenditures – on such items as debt servicing, freight, insurance etc – have been met by the remittances to China of Chinese living overseas, which have averaged some £80 million annually. Since Chinese imports, mainly of machinery and capital goods, from the developed countries have inevitably

China's trade with her main African trading partners (£ millions)

IMPORTS

Country	1958	1959	1960	1961	1962	1963	1964	1965	1966	1967	1968	1969	1970	1971
Egypt	12·5	11·8	16·7	5·2	6·9	5·9	6·4	16·1	11·6	6·8	6·0	6·8	6·5	8·1
Morocco	1·1	2·2	2·4	1·3	1·1	2·2	5·0	3·3	3·2	3·0	2·6	2·7	3·0	7·2
Nigeria	—	—	0·4	1·4	—	0·4	0·6	0·7	Neg	0·9	0·2	0·2	0·5	0·2
Sudan	0·7	1·0	3·4	1·4	3·3	4·5	1·7	5·5	4·0	2·7	3·5	7·6	7·1	13·2
Tanzania	0·2	0·1	0·3	Neg	—	3·7	2·3	4·3	3·4	2·8	2·7	4·5	3·4	4·9
Uganda	—	Neg	1·8	3·3	—	4·0	3·2	6·2	1·2	1·4	1·7	0·5	0·6	0·6
Kenya	0·2	0·2	0·3	Neg	0·2	0·4	0·4	0·6	0·9	1·1	0·4	0·5	0·6	0·9
Zambia							1·2					6·1	5·6	

EXPORTS

Country	1958	1959	1960	1961	1962	1963	1964	1965	1966	1967	1968	1969	1970	1971
Egypt	9·0	8·3	7·4	6·7	6·9	7·1	6·4	13·1	14·4	8·3	8·0	5·3	7·5	3·7
Morocco	5·7	2·6	2·5	3·1	3·1	2·5	4·3	4·3	6·3	4·7	4·4	5·4	4·5	5·0
Nigeria	1·4	1·9	1·8	2·3	1·6	1·6	3·1	4·9	5·0	6·3	3·7	6·4	8·2	11·8
Sudan	0·5	0·9	0·8	1·7	1·4	1·1	2·4	2·3	4·5	6·1	3·4	5·8	4·8	9·6
Tanzanzia	—	Neg	Neg	Neg	Neg	Neg	0·3	1·7	3·7	3·1	4·3	4·7	15·4	35·0
Uganda	—	Neg	Neg	Neg	Neg	0·3	0·3	1·0	1·7	0·8	1·0	1·0	0·9	0·8
Kenya	Neg	Neg	Neg	Neg	Neg	Neg	0·7	0·9	1·9	0·8	1·6	1·3	1·4	0·8
Libya	—	—	0·1	0·2	0·3	0·7	0·5	1·7	2·8	3·6	4·4	6·2	4·4	1·3
Zambia														—

	1958	1959	1960	1961	1962	1963	1964	1965	1966	1967	1968	1969	1970	1971
China's estimated Balance of Trade with all African Countries	+2·4	+1·3	−12·2	+5·7	+6·1	+0·5	+3·1	+3·4	+31·8	+41·2	+35·0	+22·8		

Sources: (a) African countries' trade returns.
(b) UN Economic Commission for Africa, *Foreign Trade Statistics of Africa.*
(c) US Department of State Research Study: *Communist States and Developing Countries – Aid and Trade in 1971.*

1 January–May figures.
– = Nothing.
Neg. = less than £10 000.

NOTE: Some African countries with which China trades, like Mali, Guinea and Congo-Brazzaville do not give sufficient details for meaningful figures to be deduced. Others, like Algeria and Ghana, give one figure for their trade with *all* communist countries, including China, the Soviet Union and East Europe.

exceeded the value of her exports to them, China has relied on her exports to the developing world to achieve the desired balance, and her trade with Africa, in surplus every year but for one since she started trading with the continent, has made an increasingly important contribution to this goal (see table).

This desire to 'balance the books' has been parallelled by an equally puritanical distrust of the mechanisms of credit, occasioned mainly by the treatment China suffered at the hands of the Soviets, on whose credits China had to pay interest charges alone of 120·8 million roubles in the period 1950–1964 – an experience which has led her to offer her own loans interest-free. With her impeccable commercial reputation (she often pays debts *before* their scheduled repayment) China would have no difficulty in obtaining long-term credits from international bankers; with a continuing need to import both foodstuffs and capital goods there seems a possibility now that China will relax her self-imposed ban on accepting credit, especially if she can be persuaded that it implies no 'unequal relationship' with the creditor country. Certainly, bankers have been amongst the most assiduous visitors to Peking since former President Nixon's visit and the trade possibilities it opened up.

Another feature of China's foreign trade has been its pragmatism illustrated principally by the fact that trade with the Soviet Union – although on a reduced level – has been conducted throughout the period of the Sino-Soviet dispute. Trade with the old enemy, Japan, has also been carried on. In Africa, throughout the 1960s one of China's main export markets was Nigeria, a country with which she did not have diplomatic relations and with which throughout the civil war she was on bad terms.[1] Trade with Egypt has also survived political vicissitudes. Early on in China's relations with Africa Chan Hiang-kang, the commercial attaché in Cairo, had initiated trade with such unlikely partners as Ethiopia, Tunisia and Libya, while a Chinese trade delegation even had the gall to visit Cameroon, albeit without result, at a time when China's support for the illegal UPC was being widely publicized.

Trade with South Africa

A consistent theme of Soviet propaganda against China, and

one taken up occasionally by African governments as well, is that China has continued to trade with Rhodesia and South Africa. In a commentary on Moscow Radio in December 1971, for example, Vasiliy Stepanov alleged that

For twenty-five years now China has been trading with South Africa. Reports issued in several countries indicate that trade between the two has increased almost to £10 million in the past few years. China supplies Pretoria with oil in exchange for copper, diamonds, lead and zinc. In Rhodesia, China buys chrome, while Chinese exports to the Portuguese colonies run up to £13 million. (Moscow Radio, 11 December 1971)

Radio Peace and Progress repeated the charge, quoting the *Times of Zambia* as saying that Chinese trade with South Africa had grown to 20 million rand a year, and adding that 'The Peking leaders skilfully used the trade fair of the Republic of South Africa in Hong Kong in the autumn of 1964 to sign a secret ten year trade agreement with the republic!' (Radio Peace and Progress, 8 May 1972).

Earlier, in January 1964, the *Times of India* reported that the China National Cereals, Oils and Fats Import-Export Corporation was maintaining trade links with South Africa through the French firm, *Louis Dreyfus*. It said that in 1962 China's trade with South Africa consisted of exports of pharmaceuticals, textiles and light machinery and imports of food grains, the two-way trade being worth about £1 million. In 1963 the South Africa Foundation, a non-political body giving facts about the South African economy, said South Africa's exports to China, mainly maize, had increased considerably and were worth £2·25 million in the first two months of the year.

China's reaction to these earlier allegations was to deny them completely and to state that China had not traded with South Africa since July 1960. However, sharp-eyed observers noted that the phrase used was that the 'Government of the PRC' had not carried on trade with South Africa, a semantic formula which did not exclude the possibility that a government agency, like the Cereals Corporation, might be continuing to deal with the Republic. The denial did not carry much weight in any case because until March 1963, when South Africa ceased to publish separate figures for her trade with

China, details of Chinese-South African trade were readily available in the Republic's trade returns. Also, a South African trade commissioner was reported in Peking in 1963, and in November of that year Prime Minister Verwoerd's office sent a booklet to China's state buying agencies explaining the benefits of trade with South Africa.

Similar blanket denials have been issued to the later charges. In January 1972 the Foreign Ministry wrote to the UN Secretary-General affirming that all trade connections with Rhodesia had been severed long ago, while a *People's Daily* article denied a Soviet claim that a Rhodesian delegation had visited Peking and signed a trade treaty increasing Rhodesian exports to China, adding 'This vile rumour-mongering of the Soviet revisionists shows how far they have gone in their degeneration and how desperately they are seized with want of heart and with apprehension.' (*People's Daily*, 2 March 1972).

In the absence of hard evidence either way neither China nor her accusers can expect much credibility to be attached either to the allegations or to the denials. However, some highly placed trade sources in Zambia have assured me they have evidence that China has continued to import Rhodesian tobacco, possibly via West Germany, while officials in the mining trade in Sudan told me they knew China had imported Rhodesian chrome as late as 1972. Given China's pragmatic trading policies these claims do not seem improbable.

TRADE AND POLITICS

Although pragmatic, Chinese trade does not operate entirely in a political vacuum; favourable trading agreements are concluded with states that China wishes to reward for political favours, either received or expected, while contracts are sometimes withheld from countries with whose policies China is not satisfied.[2] An early example of the former was China's willingness to buy Egyptian cotton in 1955 at a time when Western buyers were refusing to pay a reasonable price, and when China was particularly anxious for good political relations with Egypt. China took 15 000 tons, thus bolstering the Egyptian economy which was dependent on cotton sales for 80 per cent of its foreign exchange needs. This was not, however, simply an altruistic measure – China was at that time desperate for cotton, more or less at any price. A political, or non-commercial, gesture was made to Sudan in 1964 when Sudanese economists became alarmed at the very high sugar bill, then running at £8 million yearly. China delivered 500 000 tons of refined sugar at £51 per ton, compared with an average c.i.f. value of £80 per ton declared by traditional exporters like Taiwan and France. In 1965 China made a similar gesture towards Tanzania, which had three million pounds of surplus tobacco for sale and which she had been unable to dispose amongst her normal purchasers. China stepped in to save the situation and bought two million pounds, earning considerable goodwill. Smaller purchases of items useful, but not essential to China, such as incense from Somalia or sea cucumbers from Zanzibar, can also be regarded as political gestures – to show that China is making every effort to be a willing trade partner, even though the items are not strictly what she requires.

On a few occasions China has run the risk of jeopardizing smooth inter-state relations by insisting on the terms of a contract to the letter. The most notable example was in 1969 when Zambia, after a good harvest the previous year, had contracted to supply China with maize; in fact the 1969 harvest was poor, China insisted on sticking to the deal and Zambia was forced to spend over £500 000 of hard currency on buying Canadian maize to make up the shortfall. It was also reported that China asked Zambia to foot the bill for the air transport of radio transmitters, supplied under an aid agreement, from Dar es Salaam to Lusaka.

I have heard of several instances in Tanzania in which Chinese representatives pushed a hard business bargain to unacceptable limits. From trade sources I learned that in 1972 China offered to buy the entire Tanzanian cotton crop, but was told that half had already been sold. The Chinese immediately offered to buy the remaining half, but at 15 per cent below the world price then ruling. They were told to come back the next day. This they did, and announced that they were prepared to pay the world price – but only if they could buy the entire crop. Once again, they were shown the door. I also understand that in March 1973, the Chinese charged well over the world price for a shipment of rice to Zanzibar, and that this was taken hardly by President Jumbe, who had committed himself to eradicating the food shortages experienced on the island under Karume. It was also rumoured that the Chinese were re-selling (at a profit) copper purchased from Zambia – but since they paid cash and themselves took the risks this has the appearance of straightforward commercial speculation. These examples tend to support the general impression given by trade circles in Africa and elsewhere that the Chinese are tough businessmen, not averse to turning the screws a little if the commercial circumstances are right.

Early Chinese trade

The majority of China's early trade was conducted with the countries of North Africa, whose economies were more developed than those of sub-Saharan Africa and whose inhabitants had more sophisticated tastes – Chinese green tea, for example, had for long been popular in Morocco. Another feature of early trading was that in general it was conducted with countries which did not benefit from Chinese aid. This was partly for coincidental political reasons – consistently throughout the 1960s China's main African trading partners were Egypt, Morocco, Nigeria and Sudan, countries in which limited amounts of Chinese aid would in any case have made little impact – but also because Chinese 'exports' to such countries as Mali, Congo-Brazzaville, Guinea and Tanzania in fact served as aid; aid, in other words, consisted of credit with which to buy Chinese goods.

But a barrier to the speedy expansion of Sino-African trade was the non-complementary nature of their respective economies. Both China and the African countries were importers of manufactured and capital goods; both were exporters of unsophisticated finished products and raw materials – there was no fundamental basis for a major commercial relationship. It was partly for this reason, as we saw in Part One, that in the mid-1960s China increasingly turned her attention away from West Africa and towards the commercially more promising markets of East Africa.

In recent years both sides of the trade equation have

improved. China has now become the major importer of cotton from Sudan, Tanzania, Uganda, Kenya, and also imports from Egypt and even Morocco; she buys sisal from Tanzania and Kenya and copper from Zambia. On the African side traditional trading ties with the former colonial power, especially among the Francophone states, have been deliberately weakened, while there is a growing appreciation of the cheapness and increasing quality of Chinese goods. Initially there was considerable sales resistance to Chinese products, based on the belief that 'British (or French) is Best'. In many former British colonies Hercules was a synonym for bicycle. 'Sheffield steel' described any steel article of quality and there was a great snob element in owning anything British-made, particularly clothes. But this attitude is changing, partly perforce as governments direct where imports will come from, partly because China, as a senior official in the Tanzanian State Trading Corporation told me, has studied the African market and refined and improved her products to suit it. A representative of the oldest established trading company in Zambia has written to me that there is still

. . . an element of prejudice against Chinese bicycles and bias in favour of British makes. However, Chinese bicycles are well thought of by our own people in Zambia, as are the other goods which they have purchased for the parastatal companies which include corned beef, knitwear, china, glass, clothing, kitchenware and batteries. Our people in Zambia pay regular visits to the Canton Trade Fair and have found the Chinese very efficient to deal with and increasingly relaxed.

The cheapness of Chinese goods is certainly a major factor in their favour in the African market. At the luxury end of the market, expatriates in Dar es Salaam used to buy Chinese silk dressing-gowns for less than £5 and a 210-unit dining service for under £10. A 'panga' (a sort of scything instrument) cost about £1, but – almost certainly for my benefit – Tanzanian workers told me it only lasted a quarter as long as a good 'Sheffield-made' one.

But the main current criticism of Chinese goods is not of their quality, but the fact that their ready availability inhibits the importing country from setting up light industries to manufacture comparable goods; a more sinister interpretation would be that China is neutralizing potential competition. This aspect was stressed by a Radio Peace and Progress broadcast which commented that 'even in the field of light industry the Peking leaders have deliberately tried to smother industries whose products would compete with China's exports to Africa'. An objection to this argument is that it would not be economical for a single country to establish, for example, a factory to manufacture paper clips. And with the present poor record of African economic cooperation it is unlikely that a regional group would agree to set up a single factory to serve them all. It also ignores the fact that under aid agreements China *has* helped African countries to establish light industries, such as textile mills, match and cigarette factories, shoe factories etc, whose products will presumably eventually keep out similar Chinese exports.[3] An additional argument in favour of importing cheap Chinese consumer goods is that since China gives long-term, interest-free credit the importing country is conserving valuable foreign exchange until the loan has to be repaid. Nevertheless, the criticism does have some validity, in that the only sort of industrialization most African countries could envisage in the near future would be the manufacture of such items as tyres, building materials and other light products such as toys, office equipment, bicycles, etc. which they presently import from China. Intra-African trade in such products has already been affected – Kenya has complained that her exports to Tanzania have been reduced because of Tanzania's need to buy goods from China under the railway agreement.

Strategic materials

Early Chinese propaganda claimed that the US and other developed countries maintained an interest in Africa because their industries could not do without the continent's mineral wealth. The *Peking Review*, commenting on Western exploitation of Africa, claimed that

The amount extracted alone is startling enough. For instance, it accounts for 99 per cent of the columbite; 98 per cent of the diamonds; 80·1 per cent of the cobalt; 47·7 per cent of the antimony; 24·4 per cent of the copper and 29·4 per cent of the manganese ore. Africa's output of uranium exceeds the combined production of the US and Canada, and between 60 per cent and 80 per cent of the total output in the capitalist world is produced in the Congo alone. To a considerable extent the major imperialist countries such as the us, Britain and France depend on Africa for the raw materials in their weapons of mass destruction. (*Peking Review*, 5 July 1960)

The theme that the us was interested in the Congo only for its strategic materials was repeated in a Chinese play on the Congo situation. A Belgian character tells an American general advising the un mission: 'If not for Katanga's uranium you'd never have made your first atomic bomb.' But since China's discovery of uranium in Sinkiang she has shown less concern about the us's exploitation of it in Africa.

Of more interest has been Africa's copper wealth. Although China's production of copper has been estimated[4] at about 100000 tons annually, there is a considerable shortfall between production and consumption. An agreement was signed with Chile in 1972 for the annual purchase of 65000 tons, and with Zambia in 1971 for China to buy 1000 tons a month; during 1973 heavy Chinese buying of the metal on the London Metal Exchange was partly responsible for pushing copper's price to record levels. Following the 1973 right-wing coup against President Allende of Chile, China increased its copper purchases from Zambia, contracting to buy 24 000 tons a month throughout 1974.

The only other strategic material China has imported from Africa has been cobalt, which she has bought from Morocco. us officials reportedly warned Morocco against selling the element, which can be used in a nuclear programme, to China, but the Moroccans apparently asserted their independence and refused to comply with the request.

The possibility of expanding Sino-African trade by the export to China of oil (especially by Nigeria which has repeatedly expressed disappointment at the trade imbalance) has diminished as details of China's oil industry have come to light. In 1972 China's crude oil production amounted to 29·5 million tons, which was sufficient for her own needs and enabled her to enter an agreement with Japan to export low sulphur content oil from the Taching field, part of which would be returned in the form of refined oil.

Despite the signs that China's own mineral and energy resources are adequate for her own needs and could sustain a high level of industrialization it is difficult not to see certain recent Chinese initiatives in the light of her interest in raw materials; the most striking are good relations with all the major copper-producing countries – Chile, (even after the military coup) Peru, Zambia and Zaire. Others have included assistance to Guyana to exploit her bauxite resources and the renewed offer to build the Guinea-Mali railway (Guinea possesses huge bauxite and ore reserves); and the extremely generous aid offer to Zaire after so many years' enmity might well be linked with that country's great mineral reserves. China's need for considerable imports of cotton, which, although not a strategic material, contributes significantly to the Chinese economy through its re-export as finished textile goods, also seems well assured through good relations with the major African producers.

The future of Sino-African trade

Although it seems certain that Sino-African trade will increase in absolute terms over the next decade, it is likely that it will decline in relative terms from its present level of around 30 per cent of China's total trade with the non-communist world. As China moves away from her old philosophy of total self-reliance, and talks of the need to import foreign technology and complete plants, her trade with the industrial countries is bound to grow spectacularly. In 1972 alone she committed over £200 million to the purchase of Western aircraft, and has expressed great interest in importing more machinery, machine tools, steel, fertilizer, lorries and oil-industry equipment. In return she has envisaged exporting chemicals, farm produce such as rice, meat, silk, tea and fruit juice, textiles and animal raw materials. In that pattern there is little prospect for a greatly increased trade with Africa. It also seems likely the present trade imbalance will increase, as China tries to achieve a greater surplus in her African trade to balance the heavy imports from the industrialized countries.

Although China will play only a small role in the economies and international trade of the majority of African countries, she is capable, as she has shown in the case of Tanzania, of making a major impact. By 1971 China had become Tanzania's main supplier, replacing Britain, and was also that country's major aid donor. Her pre-eminent position in Tanzania, and increasingly in Zambia, seems assured: trading patterns, slow to change, are difficult to reverse once under way as suppliers gear themselves to new lines, learn new servicing techniques, build up spares, adapt existing machinery and as customers become accustomed to the products. With her generous credit terms China also seems likely to break into new markets, especially in those countries where there is a foreign exchange shortage or where the recipient country has signed an aid agreement tied to the provision of Chinese goods. At the beginning of 1974, for example, China and Sudan signed a trade agreement envisaging a £35 million two-way trade, with China importing Sudanese cotton, beans and sesame and exporting textiles, tea, tyres, canned goods and light manufactured products.

AID

Economic aid has been by far China's most important, and influential, instrument of foreign policy in her dealings with African countries. If it is true, as an American government report[5] baldly states, that Chinese aid merely serves China's 'political and economic self-interests', nevertheless that aid has been useful, apt, given on more generous terms than by any other donor – and has been welcomed, and praised, by nearly every African government that has received it. And in a number of cases, for example in the help given to Morocco to establish a green tea industry cited in the previous section, it has been genuinely altruistic. Numerous governments have also praised Chinese aid as being completely free of political strings.

What then are the advantages to China of giving aid to distant countries in Africa, where over half of China's total world aid has been concentrated, which cannot assist China in a conventional military sense or even be considered as ideological allies? The official Chinese view, which has already been examined, is that by helping to strengthen the economies of the recipient countries China frees them from colonial or neo-colonial control and thus strengthens the world's anti-imperialist forces – which is 'in itself a tremendous support to China'. This, broadly speaking, is true but there are more tangible benefits too. China regards her aid as a 'weapon' in her dispute with the Soviet Union and to a lesser extent in her differences with the West; she uses it to demonstrate the excellence of her developmental model, thus strengthening her position as a champion of the Third World; she cites the praise of recipients to demonstrate to her own population the esteem in which China is held, and holds up the achievements of aid personnel as models to be copied internally; finally, she uses aid to stimulate trade. It is true, therefore, that China, like all other aid donors, uses aid to serve her political and economic self-interests – but she differs from them in the generosity of her terms.

Aid as a 'weapon'

China entered the 'aid war' only with reluctance. As a developing country herself, she was not anxious to commit scarce resources to what amounted to economically non-productive ventures: shortage of foreign exchange meant that Chinese aid would have to be mainly in the form of Chinese goods and services which could be ill spared. It was, in short, a commitment to sacrifice. But the dispute with the Soviet Union, and to a lesser extent with Taiwan, which also used aid in her African diplomacy, made inevitable China's emergence as a donor. Africa was chosen as the most suitable area to enter the competition: African economies were similar to China's economy and therefore suitable to China's methods; a limited amount of well-directed aid would make a disproportionately large impact on a small, poor country; finally it was an area relatively neglected by Moscow, where China could start on a more or less level footing with her rival. (From 1954 to the end of 1971 China's aid commitments to Africa amounted to £446 million, compared with the Soviet Union's £867 million, whereas in the Near East and South Asia, the Soviet Union had given aid worth £1687 million but China only £232 million; comparative figures for East Asia were: Soviet Union £55 million and China £100 million, and for Latin America Soviet Union £104 million and China £19 million – see table, pp. 208–9).

As we saw in Chapter Five, China sought to distinguish her

aid from that of the Soviet Union even before the open acknowledgement of their dispute, and to the initiated her eight principles of aid-giving were a clear summary of China's own grievances against Soviet aid. After the dispute came into the open, aid was used by both communist powers in an attempt to win influence, and the supposed ineffectiveness of each other's aid became a regular ingredient in their propaganda warfare. The Soviet Union claimed China was not technically competent enough to extend useful aid, while China emphasized the harshness of the Soviet Union's terms. They have also questioned each other's political motives, with the Soviet Union claiming that

Peking is wooing many Asian and African countries, endeavouring to make them bases of its activity. Exploiting the difficulties in Pakistan and the complications between that country and India, it is trying to catch the Pakistani leaders in its net. Chinese emissaries are hard at work in Africa . . . The aid given to some African and Asian nations is meant to break their links with the socialist states, make them dependent on Peking and turn them into instruments of its policy. (*New Times*, July 1971)

China has counter-claimed that

In providing 'aid' Soviet revisionism aims not only at fleecing the Asian, African and Latin American people. What is more important, it wants to dominate the recipient countries politically so as to establish a colonial rule of the new Tsars. Its 'aid' is adapted to and closely co-ordinated with its counter-revolutionary global strategy. As it regards South-East Asia and the Middle East as important strategic points for its expansion abroad, it gives priority to these regions in its 'aid' programme so as to tighten its grip there. (NCNA, Peking, 21 June 1969)

China has also contrasted the hard work and dedication of her own experts with the lives of luxury led by Soviet technicians:

The people of friendly countries can also see with their own eyes that whenever the Soviet revisionist 'experts' arrive at a place, they, like the imperialist 'experts', always stretch out their hands to ask for foreign-style houses, motor-cars, electric refrigerators, various privileges and special treatment. Nobody knows how many times their wages are higher than those of local personnel . . . When they occasionally visit the sites, they assume an overbearing attitude,

Chinese, Soviet and East European Economic Aid to Africa

(£ millions to nearest million)

	1954–1971				1970				1971				1972	1973
	PRC	SU	E. Eur.	Total	PRC	SU	E. Eur.	Total	PRC	SU	E. Eur.	Total	PRC	PRC
Algeria	33	150	34	217	–	–	–	–	17	80	–	97	–	–
Burundi	–	–	–	–	–	–	30	30	–	–	–	–	8	–
Cameroon	–	3	–	3	–	–	–	–	–	–	–	–	–	36
C. Af. Rep.	11	–	–	1	–	–	–	–	–	–	–	–	–	–
Chad	–	–	–	–	–	–	–	–	–	–	–	–	–	18
Congo (B)	10	3	–	13	–	–	–	–	–	–	–	–	18	10
Dahomey	–	–	–	–	–	–	–	–	–	–	–	–	18	–
Egypt	34	428	229	691	–	–	–	–	–	–	–	–	–	–
Ethiopia	35	37	6	78	–	–	–	–	–	83	46	129	–	–
Ghana	14	32	37	83	–	–	–	–	42	–	–	42	–	–
Guinea	24	59	10	93	4	–	–	4	–	–	–	–	–	–
Kenya	7	16	–	23	–	–	–	–	–	–	–	–	–	–
Mali	19	20	9	48	–	–	–	–	–	–	–	–	–	–
Madagascar	–	–	–	–	–	–	–	–	–	–	–	–	–	4
Mauritius	–	–	–	–	–	–	–	–	–	–	–	–	13	–
Mauritania	10	1	–	11	–	–	–	–	8	–	–	88	–	–
Morocco	–	32	12	44	–	18	–	18	–	–	–	–	–	–
Nigeria	–	2	15	17	–	3	–	3	–	–	12	12	–	–
Rwanda	–	–	–	–	–	–	–	–	–	–	–	–	9	–

Senegal	—	—	—	—	—	—	—	—	—	—	—	—	—	18
S. Leone	—	10	—	10	—	—	—	—	—	—	—	—	—	—
Somalia	47	24	2	73	—	—	—	—	—	46	—	46	—	—
Sudan	29	23	44	97	14	—	4	18	15	31	—	46	—	—
Tanzania	90	7	2	99	81	—	—	81	—	—	—	—	—	—
Togo	—	—	—	—	—	—	—	—	—	—	—	—	18	—
Tunisia	—	12	25	37	—	—	—	—	—	—	—	—	17	—
Uganda	5	6	—	11	—	—	—	—	—	—	—	—	—	—
Zaire	—	—	—	—	—	—	—	—	—	—	—	—	—	42
Zambia	85	2	—	87	81	—	—	81	—	—	—	—	—	—
African Total	446	867	425	1738	180	21	34	235	128	163	89	384	83	128

Near East and South Asia	232	1687	502	2421
East Asia	100	55	109	264
Lat. America	19	104	168	291
World total	797	2713	1204	4714

— = Nothing or less than £1 million.

Sources: (a) African countries' published economic data.
(b) US Department of State Research Study: *Communist States and Developing Countries – Aid and Trade in 1971.*
(c) *African Research Bulletin.*

NOTE: These figures are intended only as a guide for comparative purposes, and have therefore been rounded for convenience. The amounts represent aid *committed* – it has not in all cases been fully drawn.

only talking and making gestures without doing anything. (*People's Daily*, 26 September 1969)

Potentially damaging though the political accusations are, they are probably ignored by recipient governments as simple shots exchanged in the continuing polemical warfare. More damaging, because closer to the truth, are the accusations of technical incompetence and economic exploitation. In an article clearly referring to the Soviet aid record in Somalia, the *People's Daily*, after the customary glancing blow about the comfort of the Soviet technicians being the paramount consideration, wrote that the Soviets had agreed to supply a milk factory, a meat and fish-processing plant and three state farms. But the milk factory produced expensive items, like butter and cheese, which were consumed not by the local population but by the wealthy European population, while the Soviets demanded immediate payment for the meat factory, which took four years to build; since the recipient had no money the Soviets took processed meat in repayment –

In other words this meant that the Soviet revisionists moved the plant to Africa for its own production, utilizing cheap African material and labour. The three farms also came to nothing. Is this 'aid' or is this 'plunder'? (*People's Daily*, 15 November 1967)

While the Soviet Union's accusations about the level of China's technical competence and ability to provide large-scale aid have been made to look a bit sour by the Tanzam railway, there is a certain edge to the claim that '. . . the main purpose of Chinese credits is to ensure the widening of exports of Chinese goods to the Asian and African markets.' (Moscow Radio, 26 June 1971).

Although the Soviet Union's aid record has come in for the most vituperative attack, China has not allowed US aid policies to escape unscathed. Chinese propaganda has attacked its supposed harsh terms, including its tied nature, its commercial and political motivation and the quality of American aid experts. Under the title of 'US Imperialism Steps Up Enslavement and Plunder of Asia, Africa and Latin America through "Aid",' a lengthy NCNA article claimed that

US imperialism is stepping up its political enslavement and economic plunder of the peoples of Asia, Africa and Latin America under the cloak of 'aid'. This is one of the most important means of carrying out its neo-colonialist policy frenziedly in these regions since the end of the Second World War . . .

Numerous facts have proved that US imperialism's 'aid' is a means to interfere flagrantly in the internal affairs of the recipient countries and areas and to carry out undisguised political bribery. Through its 'aid', US imperialism blatantly forces the recipients to join the aggressive military blocs it has rigged up, to supply it with military bases or to dispatch mercenary troops to take part in its war of aggression . . .

A report of the US House Committee on Foreign Affairs in 1957 has made it clear that the 'most important reason' of providing economic 'aid' abroad is to provide the United States itself with 'an opportunity to direct [the recipients'] development along lines that will best serve our interests'.

First of all, US imperialism takes advantage of its 'aid' to step up the plunder of raw materials and mineral resources in Asia, Africa and Latin America. The very first US foreign 'aid' bill stipulates that the recipient countries and areas are obliged to provide the United States with the raw materials it needs. The so-called 'Food for Peace' programme and later the 'Food for Freedom' programme, both of which are aimed at dumping surplus American farm products, also stipulate the use of US 'surplus' agricultural products in direct exchange for the raw materials of the recipient countries and areas.

Secondly, US imperialism also uses 'aid' to open up markets abroad for dumping US commodities. According to stipulations made by the US government, 90 per cent of the US foreign 'aid' funds must be used to buy US goods. The US press revealed that export financed by 'foreign aid programmes' has a very large share in the total volume of exports of many US industries. For example, nearly 40 per cent of the export of American steel products, 30·4 per cent of chemical fertilizer exports, and 29·5 per cent of the export of railroad transportation equipment were purchased by the recipients with US 'aid' funds. Moreover, the recipient countries and areas often have to buy US goods at prices on the average 40 per cent higher than those of the international market. (NCNA, Peking, 8 September 1969)

The article goes on to detail how aid paves the way for rapacious private investment, expresses horror at the high rates of interest charged and concludes that US aid is 'nothing but a poisonous bait and a trap.'

8

In her aid programme China has also been anxious to prove Western experts wrong. Thus in Somalia

The colonialists who had ruthlessly exploited the Somali people for nearly a century used to assert, evidently with ulterior motives, that 'it doesn't pay to grow rice in Somali', and that 'tobacco grown in Somali wouldn't burn', etc. Therefore, Somali had to import rice and cigarettes year after year. (NCNA, Mogadiscu, 12 April 1968)

Chinese agro-technicians, however, 'ignoring the assertions advanced by the colonialist authorities ... travelled 6000 kilometres under the tropical sun or in torrential rains', found the ideal spot for growing both rice and tobacco and established successful schemes. Similarly, Chinese experts 'exploded the malignant lie spread by the colonialists' that sugar-cane and tea could not be grown in Mali, wheat in Zanzibar or rice in Guinea. Undoubtedly these successes have greatly enhanced the prestige of the Chinese amongst the local populations, giving them, as it were, magical powers superior to those of the white man.

The Chinese model

The second function of Chinese aid is to demonstrate the excellence of China's developmental model, and its relevance for African countries. The fourth of China's eight principles of aid-giving commits her to helping the recipient country to embark on the road to self-reliance, the virtue which China had thrust on her when the Soviet Union withdrew her aid personnel so precipitously. In this context China often quotes the proverb of the man who is given a fish, which will give him food for a day; but the man who is given a fishing-rod will have food for life. Chinese aid therefore stresses 'on-job' training of local people and the Chinese have built factories which process local raw materials – textile mills, match, shoe, cigarette and farm implements factories, sugar refineries, cement works, etc.

China's own solution to the problems of her great population, and the potential unemployment danger, has been to encourage the construction of numerous labour-intensive, cottage-industry type projects, sited all over the country, a solution which she also recommends to African countries.

Chinese-aided projects are invariably simple and stress labour rather than machinery; in two important cases, the textile mills in Dar es Salaam and Brazzaville, Chinese projects have contributed significantly to alleviating urban unemployment. Indeed, the Friendship mill in Dar es Salaam, with an initial labour force of 3000, immediately became the largest employer of labour, in the manufacturing sector, in the whole of East Africa; at the beginning of 1974 a further 2000 workers were recruited.

My own observations convince me that the Chinese are scrupulous in honouring their undertaking to train local personnel. Contrary to local rumour that 'the Chinese are taking our jobs' there were no Chinese operators or managers in the Chinese-built shoe factory on Zanzibar, which I visited at the end of 1973; at the Friendship mill, four years after its opening, there remained a team of twelve Chinese advisers, and they were about to leave. At the Ubungo farm implements factory, also in Dar es Salaam, a small team of three Chinese advisers was at the factory three years after its opening. But there, and at several other Chinese-built factories in Zanzibar and in Tanzania, the management was entirely in local hands.

In all the Chinese-built enterprises that I have seen, and I imagine in most of the ones that I have not, there are visible reminders of the builders: Chinese calendars, pictures – sometimes of Chairman Mao – usually a small plaque in the local language and in Chinese, and at the larger factories a model of the building, again annotated both in Chinese and in the local language. In Tanzania the continued Chinese 'presence' is emphasized by the near-universal use in offices and factories of Chinese equipment, imported under the Tanzam agreement, and including such items as files, paper clips, pencils and other sundry office paraphernalia.

In all their aid activities the Chinese seem anxious to *demonstrate* the efficacy of their methods, as if they were saying to the Africans: there, that is the way we do things, and we think it works – now you try. There is no attempt to *insist* that the Chinese way is the best way, although that naturally is the implication. Nowhere is this attitude of demonstration more apparent than in agricultural aid. I watched a Chinese agricultural expert in Dodoma, central Tanzania, smile broadly when it was explained to him that the local people, the Wagogo, worshipped their cattle and considered it punishment for them to be harnessed into a plough. He said in a businesslike way that the Wagogo should learn to use their resources properly, and arranged demonstrations to try and prove that oxen, firstly, were not harmed by ploughing and secondly, how much more efficient than a hoe was an ox-drawn plough. His team was also demonstrating water conservancy (by building mud walls around fields) and new higher-yielding strains of wheat and sorghum.

It is perhaps too early to say how effective China's aid to Africa has been as a model. Leaders would undoubtedly like to believe that their people have been inspired to work harder by the Chinese example, but the evidence I have seen and heard suggests that Africans are more amazed – in a pacific way – than inspired by tales of Chinese hard work. The Wagogo living near the agricultural team cited above had even convinced themselves that the Chinese worked at night – to hide the 'magic' powers which enabled them to get so much done. Although there is admiration, and gratitude, for the hard work done by Chinese experts there is also a feeling that the Chinese are in some ways rather peculiar for undertaking it in the first place.

Whatever impact abstract models, such as hard work, frugality and discipline may, or may not have, on African audiences there has been little attempt made yet by African governments to copy specifically Chinese *institutions*. Tanzania has gone further than any other African country in appreciating the usefulness of certain Chinese institutions. Her adaptation of elements of Chinese schooling methods, particularly the emphasis on practical training, of aspects of communal life, of the People's Militia system, of adult education and of decentralization policies are discussed more fully in Chapter 15. But it can be argued, and *is* argued by independent-minded Africans, that the similar circumstances existing in China and in Africa would in any case throw up similar solutions and to a certain extent, similar institutions. After the failure in most African countries of such Western institutions as parliamentary democracy and European legal systems, independent African countries are loth to accept institutional models from so distant, strange and in many ways so irrelevant a place as China. In the post-independence era 'African solutions to African problems' has become an increasingly popular cry, and any leader who dared suggest adopting outright peculiarly Chinese institutions risks being charged with neo-colonialist tendencies. However, the relevance of certain Chinese institutions to present African conditions is so blindingly obvious that they will surely eventually be copied; pride can be salvaged by semantics. For example, the solution to Africa's urgent need for more medical personnel surely lies in the creation of a service modelled on China's 'barefoot doctors'. The Chinese model can be played down by calling them 'Zambian medical auxiliaries', or whatever. Similarly, one of the answers to every African country's dilemma of increasingly overcrowded cities, is to establish village industries – along the lines of China's village steel industry. Again, there is no 'disgrace' in copying China's model, and certain African leaders are prepared to learn as much as possible from the Chinese experience. A party of twenty-five Ujamaa villagers from Tanzania, for example, visited China in 1973 to study commune life. But until the language barrier is more fully overcome this type of experiment has little more than novelty value.

The core of the Chinese model is self-reliance, and Chinese emphasis on its virtues have undoubtedly touched a chord in Africa. The message has been preached, by African leaders, in African and in international forums. Yet, in many ways, African countries have seemed more prepared to accept the theory than the practice: production of African foodstuffs has steadily declined throughout the 1970s, and in 1973 Black Africa actually became a net importer of meat. At the same time there has been an increasing reliance on external aid, in practically every Black African country, for development projects. Paradoxically, an increasing amount of this aid has come from China, whose practice, in this case, would seem to conflict with her own ideology.

By implication self-reliance cannot be taught, and Chinese theory often stresses that Chinese solutions to Chinese problems should not be copied wholesale – there are no universal prescriptions, only particular solutions to particular problems. However, example can help, and Chinese technicians have shown considerable ingenuity in evolving extemporaneous solutions to problems they have encountered during aid activities. For example, Chinese workers constructing the Kisoundi Textile Mill in Brazzaville found that

. . . 4·2 million red bricks were needed, which was beyond the capacity of the local kiln. The Chinese engineering and technical personnel decided to make cement bricks themselves and immediately built sheds and moulds for this purpose . . . they worked side by side with the Congolese workers and made more than 2·5 million cement bricks as a substitute. This ensured the needs of construction and saved building expenses.

As the shortage of bricks was overcome, another difficulty cropped up. Steel girders and beams and reinforced concrete prefabricated parts had to be transported by a flatbed trailer which was lacking on the work-site. After putting their heads together, the Chinese personnel built a simple flatbed trailer by using the wheels of concrete mixers and steel tubes . . . To save expenses, the Chinese personnel built with their own hands windows and doors of more than 3000 square metres, which, according to the original plan, were to be processed somewhere else. Furthermore, they built a workers' club and canteen by making use of waste materials. (NCNA, Brazzaville, 24 August 1969)

In Guinea, Chinese experts building a tea processing plant

. . . made a habit of collecting old nails and small pieces of boards and corrugated roofing in their spare time and used them to build some auxiliary workshops, warehouses, store-rooms for fertilizer and insecticide, and two bathrooms for the Guinean workers. (NCNA, Conakry, 31 March 1968)

Many examples of Chinese ingenuity and self-reliance have cropped up during the building of the Tanzam railway. Whether African workers have absorbed the lessons and as a result are now more self-reliant themselves is impossible to tell, although, according to NCNA dispatches, Africans say that 'Our Chinese friends . . . pass on to us the revolutionary spirit of self-reliance and working hard with great vigour. This spirit is the most precious treasure.' (NCNA, Brazzaville, 24 August 1969).

Aid-giving for internal reasons

Praise for Chinese aid from recipient countries is useful to

China not only for external propaganda reasons, but also helps to boost domestic morale and enhance the reputation of the CCP. Additionally, the exploits of aid experts, cited frequently in the Chinese press, are held up to the Chinese population as models of selfless behaviour to be emulated at home. NCNA reports from African countries speak of Chinese personnel 'sweating under the equatorial sun', 'ignoring the blisters in their hands and physical exhaustion', 'walking thousands of kilometres in all weathers' and 'defying all difficulties'. The articles talk admiringly of the self-reliance and the 'utter devotion to others without any thought of self' of the experts. It is, admittedly, only their internationalist duty – but their selflessness is also a model of behaviour for their compatriots at home. During the cultural revolution the exploits of aid personnel served the subsidiary purpose of enhancing Mao's personal image: they, and, according to NCNA, the African recipients, attributed all successes to the study and application of Mao Tse-tung thought.

Chinese aid personnel are conscripts, not volunteers, chosen, I have been told by Chinese sources, primarily for their ideological commitment. They must believe it is their internationalist duty to help African countries, an attitude which goes a long way to explaining the exemplary behaviour of Chinese aid experts. The Tanzam railway workers were on a two-year contract, and were paid at the rate of 180 shillings (about £10) a month; they were not allowed to bring their families with them.

Western, and particularly South African, propaganda has made much of the fact that the railway workers are drawn from the PLA railway pioneers, and has deduced from this that a Chinese 'army' is swarming over the Tanzanian and Zambian countryside. While it is true that the pioneers have virtually monopolized railway building in China, there is also a civilian corps – and some of their members have been seconded to the Tanzam railway. Nor, contrary to propaganda, are the railway workers armed – except with spades. A secret American report has established that the Tanzam force was drawn more or less at random from units all over China, which may suggest that the Chinese wanted to give foreign experience to as broad a range as possible of their people.

Aid experts work hard, not only out of self-esteem, but because they would not like to take a chance that another factory-building, agricultural or medical team was doing better, either in their vicinity or in the rest of Africa. This competitive aspect of aid activity was pointed out to me by a Chinese medical team working in southern Sudan; they appeared to know what other aid teams in Africa were doing, both from magazine articles and from the radio. They obviously took pride in hearing their own achievements spelled out.

Chinese can refuse to serve in Africa, once chosen, but they have to have a compelling reason. In exceptional cases, their wives, but not their children, can join them. Once in Africa, defections are few; but I know that several Tanzam workers sought political asylum in the Swedish embassy in Dar es Salaam – and it was, quietly, granted.

Aid and trade

The fourth function of Chinese aid, as a stimulator of trade, was discussed in the previous section. In recent years aid and trade agreements have increasingly been linked together, and there is little doubt of China's anxiety to at least finance the aid programme through increased trade. Chinese trade is served both by the direct export of Chinese goods on long-term credit and by arrangements under which local costs of aid projects are offset by the recipient's purchase of Chinese goods – under the Tanzam agreement, for example, Tanzania and Zambia are each committed to importing about £4 million worth of Chinese goods a year.

The African viewpoint

African leaders have formed a highly favourable opinion of Chinese aid, and have said so publicly on numerous occasions. Nyerere found it freer of political strings than any other foreign aid, as did Numeiry, Kaunda, Sekou Touré, Ngouabi, Keita and other leaders. The hard work and dedication of Chinese experts has been frequently commented on. 'They have been working for Somalia heart and soul,' Ali Alio Mohamed, the Minister of Public Works, said of Chinese agricultural workers. 'Tanzanians have now become accustomed to the excellent hard work, dedication, high skills and selflessness of the Chinese expert technicians and workers,' according to Tanzanian ambassador in Peking Paul Mwaluko, while in a speech during his 1968 visit to Peking Nyerere said, '. . . the thing which most impresses Tanzanians about the Chinese workers who are now in our country is their enthusiastic hard work.'

Chinese aid has also brought some unexpected economic dividends for certain African countries. We saw earlier that in Ghana, the Soviet Union was obliged to re-schedule the payments of her experts as a result of the low salaries paid to Chinese aid personnel. The Russians were put in a similar position in Zanzibar, where China requested the government to reduce the salaries of all Chinese experts to £23 per month – in order to comply with Mao's teachings on 'plain living and hard struggle'. Shortly afterwards a Russian working on Zanzibar complained to an interviewer: 'The Zanzibaris are coming to expect us to live in conditions like the local people, earn similar wages, and generally behave like the Chinese. It's ridiculous.' (*The Guardian*, 13 May 1971)

A few countries, notably Mali, Guinea and Somalia could claim to have benefited from aid competition between China and the Soviet Union; equally Tanzania and Zambia could say the Soviets reduced their commitments because of the overwhelming quantity of Chinese aid. On the other hand, Western fears about Chinese 'influence' in those two countries led directly to a £5·4 million us loan to Tanzania for reconstruction of the Tanzania-Zambia highway and a Canadian £1 million offer to reorganize Zambian Railways in preparation for the Tanzam link. It is also possible, but incapable of proof, that other donors may have softened the terms of their loans, or made some other concessions, in the light of China's aid terms, and the expressed admiration of Africans for Chinese aid. Africans certainly feel that Western donors should take a leaf out of China's book: in July 1971 the Ghanaian newspaper the *Daily Graphic* contrasted Britain's attitude to the problem of Ghana's debts with the generosity of China towards Tanzania and Zambia, whose railway loan was 'virtually a free gift'.

Character of aid

Over 40 per cent of Chinese aid to Africa has been devoted to the communications sector – railways, roads and transmitting equipment – a fact seen by some commentators as significant. They talk of a Chinese communications network criss-crossing the continent, a view which ignores the fact that local personnel man the Chinese-built radio stations in Tanzania, Zambia, Mali, Congo-Brazzaville, Somalia and elsewhere and which does not examine deeply what strategic importance a road in Zambia, Somalia or Sudan could have for China. There are undoubtedly marginal advantages in becoming involved in the communications sector – as a form of aid, roads can be built by Chinese labour and therefore do not drain foreign exchange resources; the building of roads or railways is a long-term project, unlikely to be interrupted by a change of government and therefore guarantees a Chinese presence for several years ahead; roads and railways (which locally are bound to be known as the 'Chinese road' or 'Chinese railway') are used by many people all the time and serve to remind them of Chinese assistance, and finally, their construction gives the Chinese access to previously unknown regions, usually distant from central authority (which was an advantage, for example, during the cultural revolution when Chinese personnel – in some cases illegally, as in Zambia – were distributing propaganda to local populations). But the theory that they will eventually be useful in some grand Chinese strategic design seems far-fetched.

About 15 per cent of Chinese aid has been committed to the agricultural sector – to rice, tobacco and tea schemes; to dam and irrigation projects and to state farms. 10 per cent has been in the form of commodity credits. Of the remaining 35 per cent about 20 per cent has been devoted to light industrial projects, almost always processing local raw materials, 10 per cent to such projects as sports stadiums, theatres, cinemas, conference halls and hospitals and the final 5 per cent has been given in the form of hard currency grants, usually to help balance budgets or for the immediate relief of disaster.

In Africa, one of the most successful forms of Chinese aid has been the provision of rural medical teams, sent sometimes to deal with an emergency but more often simply to take rudimentary medical care into remote rural areas where as often as not local doctors have never ventured. Like their engineering colleagues, the 'barefoot doctors' have shown considerable ingenuity in adapting themselves to local conditions, rigging up temporary operating theatres, 'inventing' surgical implements when none were available and quickly learning about specifically African diseases. Once again, NCNA regularly carries reports about the activities of the medical teams, often giving quite technical details of the problems they have to face. A random selection includes a difficult Caesarean birth in a makeshift operating-room, removal of cataracts, an operation for removing stones in the bladder, cure of a very sick Mauritanian child (whose father renamed him 'Chinois' in gratitude) and this gripping account of a case in Mali:

One Saturday the hospital received an urgent case and the Chinese medical personnel at once plunged themselves into the battle to save the life of the patient. It was a serious case of strangulated hernia. The patient was in a very critical condition because part of the intestine had fallen into the hernia sac and turned dead as a result of strangulation by the mouth of the sac. The Chinese medical personnel operated on him at once. In the course of the operation the patient developed a shock. Blood pressure fell to zero, his pulse could not be felt and his heart beat feebly. However, the operation was successfully performed after painstaking efforts. But as his condition was still critical and the slightest jolt might endanger his life, the patient had to be left in the operating-room with the Chinese medical personnel staying at his side for two days and nights, until he was found fit to be moved back to his ward. (NCNA, Bamako, 2 November 1968)

I myself spent a day with one of the teams in Juba, southern Sudan, where they were working immediately after the conclusion of the civil war in early 1972. The area had not had proper medical attention for over fifteen years and health and sanitary conditions were appalling. The team, which consisted of nine men and two women, worked flat out from 7 a.m. until dusk.[6] In the morning they performed an operation for constriction of some sort, in the afternoon they conducted a clinic attended by literally hundreds of patients.

One room was devoted to acupuncture, the Chinese needle treatment which has aroused a great deal of interest throughout

Africa. The Juba team did not make extravagant claims on its behalf, although they said it was useful in the treatment of sciatica, lumbago and other muscular complaints and could certainly alleviate pain for short periods. I watched one of the doctors insert ten needles in the left side and leg of a boy aged about twelve who had polio. His mother had brought him along after his sister, who had polio in the shoulder, had responded very well to acupuncture treatment. In Tanzania and Zambia acupuncture treatment was popular for a while until the patients realized there was no 'dawa' (medicine) in the needles – from missionary work they associated good health with injections, and felt cheated when they realized the acupuncture needles were, as they put it, 'dry'.[7]

In Mauritania it was reported[8] that an important chieftain approached an official in the French embassy in Nouakchott with a request for Western-style propaganda with which to oppose 'Chinese medical influence'. But in Zanzibar Chinese acupuncture and other Chinese medical treatment is held in such high esteem that islanders with a bad temper are told to take it along to the Chinese – 'they even have a cure for that.'

THE TANZAM RAILWAY

All of China's other aid projects, in Africa and elsewhere, have been dwarfed by the prestigious Tanzania-Zambia railway, whose cost of some £160 million is equal to nearly one-half of China's total aid commitments to all African countries in the period 1954–1971. The importance of this 'flagship project' to China can be gauged by the fact that various preliminary stages were implemented smoothly throughout the cultural revolution (see also p. 140). This 'step by step' approach to the project has been one of its more noteworthy features: in the five years from China's first offer to finance the railway in 1965 to the signing of the final protocol in 1970, work proceeded in definite stages – the preliminary survey, engineering survey, design, final feasibility report. At each stage any one of the three partners could have withdrawn without causing loss of face to the others. But in fact China's desire to build a prestige project, and the African countries' need for the railway, made more acute by Rhodesia's UDI in late 1965, ensured its final construction in the absence of any major economic or political snags.

The railway, referred to locally as the 'Uhuru' (freedom) line, will link Dar es Salaam to the central Zambian town of Kapiri Mposhi, 1150 miles away. The single-track line will use the 1.067 metres-wide Zambian gauge which would create surmountable difficulties if it was ever planned to link it in with the one metre East African Railways system. The railway travels through some of the most rugged country in central Africa, which has necessitated the construction of no less than 2500 bridges and viaducts and nineteen tunnels, eighteen of them on the ninety-four-mile stretch from Mlimba to Makambaku in the rocky Tanzanian Southern Highlands.

But if the logistical and engineering difficulties are impressive enough, even more impressive has been the speed at which the approximately 15000 Chinese and 36000 African, mainly Tanzanian, workforce has built the line. Construction began in 1970 when it was estimated the finishing date would be mid-1976, but after two years of almost frenzied activity it was clear the line would be completed well before schedule, possibly even being fully operational by the end of 1974. This was particularly welcome for Zambia which, after border incidents at the beginning of 1973, decided not to use traditional routes through Rhodesia for her exports. Construction has been carried on in a precise, military sort of way, with two eight-hour shifts every twenty-four hours, which, as one senior Chinese official told a journalist, meant: 'Six 12·5-yard lengths of line every five minutes twenty seconds (two miles a day)'. 'On-job' training has been given to the Africans, both on the line and at the railway workshop in Dar es Salaam. Instruction is also given at the main base camp at Mangula, central Tanzania, whose factory turns out 3600 concrete sleepers a day. Two hundred railway students from Tanzania and Zambia have gone to China for further training (amongst them the Zambian students who were expelled).

The Chinese workers have proved popular with the villagers alongside the line as they have hived off some of their electricity to the villages, and also dug wells. They are willing to give lifts to local people in their vehicles. One of the few sour notes was struck when railway workers complained bitterly of

the food supplied – the fish was bad and there were too many
beans; a compromise was reached under which the Chinese
brought in supplies and re-sold them to the workers, who then
cooked their own food. In their comments on the railway the
Chinese have stressed the joint nature of the project – it is always the Tanzanians, Zambians and Chinese – 'working shoulder
to shoulder' – who have made progress, a spirit of cooperation
symbolized by the Sino-Tanzanian Friendship Banana Tree:
two trees, representing Tanzania and China, were planted
side by side near the railway line; gradually the leaves began
to intertwine until the two trees became one.

The economics of the line have been argued endlessly, but,
give the favourable conditions of the Chinese loan, there is
little doubt of its economic viability.[9] The interest-free loan
has to be repaid over a period of thirty years, beginning in
1981 – which means that each African country will have to
find about £2·7 million per year. But by 1983, with the line
operating at its full capacity of 3·5 million tons a year in each
direction, hauled by seventeen pairs of trains daily, the railway
should easily be paying for itself and producing enough surplus
profit to repay the loan. The main staple will of course be
Zambian exports of copper and virtually all her imports, but
other hoped-for 'spin-offs' include the agricultural development
of Tanzania's potentially rich south-west, with produce going
along the line in each direction, and the development of known
deposits of coal and iron ore in southern Tanzania; at the
beginning of 1974 the Chinese gave Tanzania a loan of £31
million to build a 150-mile branch line to the deposits and to
help in their exploitation.

For China, the enormous project involved considerable
economic sacrifice. Although just over half the loan was in the
form of local costs, to be offset by Tanzanian and Zambian
purchases of Chinese goods, much of the other half involved the
Chinese in expenditure of foreign exchange – for the purchase
of earth-moving and other equipment (mostly from Japan with
some lorries from Sweden) – possibly for the purchase of steel
for the rails and of rolling-stock. The project also in effect
deprived China of over 1000 miles of railway, a considerable
sacrifice in the context of the mere 10000 miles of line built
by the government since 1949.

Clearly, the political advantages of building the railway outweighed economic considerations. From the outset China was seen to be a friend indeed to two African countries sorely in need of help: the West's refusal, and China's willingness, to construct the railway underscored political alignments in southern Africa; the offer therefore won friends not just in the two countries most directly benefiting from the railway, but amongst all independent African nations opposed to white supremicist rule. The project showed China to be technically capable of building a major industrial project, important particularly in the context of the Sino-Soviet dispute. As noted earlier, construction of the railway also ensured the Chinese presence in eastern Africa for the foreseeable future. Finally, China may also have calculated that the railway would eventually yield trading gains. The defrayment of local costs by the purchase of Chinese goods has significantly altered Tanzania's traditional trading pattern, and will also have an increasing impact on the composition of Zambia's imports. When I asked a senior Zambian official of the railway authority why China was building the railway he replied in one word: 'Trade.'

Notes

1. But there is evidence (see Ogunsanwo, op. cit., p. 313) that Nigeria deliberately reduced imports from China as a protest against China's public sympathy for Biafra.

2. This has been particularly marked with the valuable Chinese wheat contracts. Discussing the reduction in China's imports in 1971 one report (*Economist Intelligence Unit Report on China*, No. 2, 1972, p. 9) observed that 'the distribution of the required cutback in Chinese imports seems to have been strongly influenced by political factors. This is not particularly surprising; although Peking has often displayed a reluctance to allow politics to disrupt its foreign trade objectives, it has also shown a tendency, especially when the cost of not doing so was not particularly heavy in economic terms, to use trade to promote its foreign policy objectives. Clearly this is what happened in the case of Australia, whose poor performance (in securing wheat contracts) is explained by Peking's decision to concentrate its grain purchases in Canada, where the government has been pursuing a more "positive" Chinese policy.'

3. With admirable altruism China has also helped Morocco set up a green tea industry, thus adversely affecting Chinese exports.

4. By the *Economist Intelligence Unit* – see their annual review of China for 1972.

5. Department of State Research Study: *Communist States and Developing Countries – Aid and Trade in 1971*, 15 May 1972.

6. The interpreter, Dr Huang, was a most impressive man. When I mentioned he had the same name (which means 'Yellow') as the former Chinese ambassador in Cairo he concisely outlined Huang Hua's diplomatic career. (I wonder how many Britons, or Americans, would know even the name of their ambassador in Cairo?) He also displayed a sense of humour, smiling broadly when I told him I found it necessary to travel to Africa often because it was changing so fast – 'you know, permanent revolution'.

7. Zambian students in London went a stage further. In August 1972 they wrote a pamphlet for distribution in the Copperbelt, affirming that 'We must learn a lesson from Tanzania, which is almost a Chinese colony now, before it is too late', and warning their compatriots against accepting acupuncture treatment, which 'changes a person's brains'.

8. *Africa Confidential*, 1 October 1971, Vol. 12, No. 20.

9. But see p. 300 for the economic implications for the railway of the April 1974 Portuguese coup.

9. The special relationship between China and Tanzania has been described by President Nyerere (right, greeting Chou En-lai) as a "friendship between most unequal equals".

10. Tanzania has particularly appreciated Chinese assistance in agricultural projects, implemented with machinery appropriate to the country's low level of technology.

11. Africans often complain that Chinese technicians do not mix with them socially. There appear few barriers at this ceremony to mark the crossing of the Tanzam railway into Zambia.

12. Freedom fighters of the Mozambique Liberation Front (FRELIMO) hold Chinese made AK-47 rifles. But Chinese material assistance to the freedom movements has been more limited than their opponents—South Africa, Rhodesia and Portugal—claim in their propaganda.

13. A street tradesman in Khartoum selling Chinese-made toys. A big trade push has been the feature of the most recent Chinese initiatives in Africa.

14. Aid has been China's most effective instrument of foreign policy in Africa. Here a doctor belonging to a Chinese medical team examines a Dinka woman in Juba Hospital, southern Sudan.

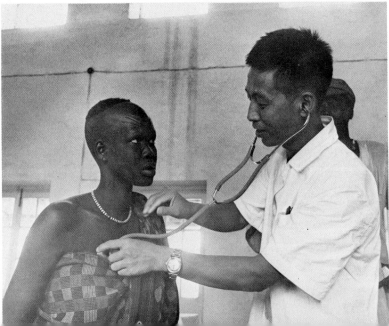

15. and 16. The £160 million Tanzam railway is China's greatest overseas aid project. In August 1973, well before schedule, the railway crossed the Tanzania/Zambia border. (above) The track-laying machine in operation during the crossing ceremony. (below) Zambian children welcoming the line with their own posters.

14

CHINA AND THE
LIBERATION
MOVEMENTS

'Enemy tires, we attack'

MAO TSE-TUNG

THE contemporary efforts by nationalist liberation groups to gain their independence from minority regimes in South Africa and Rhodesia and from the Portuguese central government* represent China's last chance in Africa of proving the value of her guerrilla techniques and the post-revolutionary value of a prolonged and violent struggle for independence. With legitimate relations established with the majority of independent countries in the continent, and with the apparent abandonment of attempts to subvert hostile regimes, these struggles also represent China's only way of asserting her revolutionary commitment and of challenging the Soviet Union as a supporter of 'just' wars.

But China's reputation, in the West at least, as a major backer of these movements has been gained in face of the facts. Her support has been sparing, often conditional and always given more in the context of the Sino-Soviet dispute than in respect of the actual merits of the recipients or in the true interests of a united nationalist movement.

The exaggerated revolutionary image stems partly from the interest of Portugal and the southern African governments in portraying the liberation movements as 'communist', or better – particularly for American consumption – as Moscow or Peking-controlled, and partly from the strident nature of

* See p. 300 for the implications of the April 1974 Portuguese coup.

China's own propaganda, which presents a misleading picture of the extent of Chinese involvement. Emphasis on the supposed communism of the movements and on massive Soviet and Chinese support is essential for both Portugal and for South Africa. For Portugal it strengthens the ideological motive for her continued hold on an African empire – the supposed 'Christian civilizing mission' – as well as reassuring the United States, her arms supplier and partner in NATO, that her African wars are part of the worldwide fight against communism. During a visit to South Africa in 1973 Portuguese Foreign Minister, Rui Patricio, told his hosts that Portugal could continue her African wars indefinitely. How long the wars continued depended on Chou En-lai and Presidents Nyerere and Kaunda – 'once they ended their support for the terrorists, fighting would be over in a few weeks'. The need to reassure American, and other, investors that South Africa is a firm 'bulwark against communism' is evident from South African propaganda,[1] which also has the subsidiary purpose of persuading the African population that the 'freedom fighters' throughout Africa are not true nationalists at all, but discredited agents of a foreign power. These needs lead to inaccurate and inflated claims of communist involvement, whereas Western *support* for the liberation movements is played down. For example, in an interview with the conservative British newspaper the *Daily Telegraph*, General Kaulza de Arriaga, the commander-in-chief of Portugal's Mozambican army, made the patently absurd claim that Chinese influence accounted for 90 per cent of the activity and equipment of the Mozambique Liberation Front (FRELIMO) South Africa and Rhodesia have made equally unlikely claims: South African Prime Minister John Vorster, for instance, told an interviewer that

The greatest single threat to Africa is that the Communist Chinese have established a bridgehead in Tanzania, and the possibility that they might, through the construction of the Tanzam railway, infiltrate farther into the heart of Africa and establish themselves on a permanent basis in Tanzania and Zambia. Like President Houphouet-Boigny [who had said that South Africa's armed forces were Africa's best defence against international communism] we are working for peace in Africa . . . we are working to keep Africa free of communism[2] . . .

It is noteworthy that most of the propaganda against the liberation movements has been directed at the considerable support they are supposed to have received from China, whereas, in fact, it has been the Soviet Union which has supplied the bulk of assistance. This simply reflects the fact that China has better propaganda value than the Soviet Union. The Soviet Union has been edging towards respectability, and even towards a détente with the United States; China has always been a more credible, even a picturesque villain, so for South Africa the red menace has always been – yellow.

Whereas China has hardly felt it necessary to deny the claims made on her behalf by hostile propaganda, most of the liberation movements themselves have always been very careful to disclaim over-reliance on communist sources and to deny communist ideological commitments. These attempts at genuine non-alignment have been helped in recent years by gifts from private individuals and foundations in the West, from the World Council of Churches and from the Swedish and Danish governments, whose contributions to the liberation funds come from their national budgets.

Dr Eduardo Mondlane, the first President of FRELIMO who was also the first liberation movement leader successfully to attempt a balance between aid from the West and from communist sources, summarized the frustrations felt against Western criticism in an interview in 1967;

What are we supposed to do if, apart from the Africans, only the communists will train and arm us? It was apparently alright for the West to ally itself with the communists against the fascists, but when we are denied Western aid we are apparently expected to do without communist aid as well ... As for the suggestion that we are tele-guided by Moscow and Peking because we accept their aid, the answer is that those who know FRELIMO know that this is simply not true. Let the West offer to help us, and then they can test whether or not we are truly non-aligned.[3]

Agostinho Neto, leader of the Popular Movement for the Liberation of Angola (MPLA), echoed these sentiments:

We are a nationalist movement with people of many opinions. We mean to build a nation, but an independent one ... We are glad of Soviet aid, that is obvious. But we remain non-aligned. We hope for aid and friendship from the West as well.[4]

The self-reliant model

The discrepancy between Chinese verbal and actual support for the movements can be explained on various levels, both practical and theoretical. Just as in economic development and in international relations China has always stressed the value to developing countries of self-reliance, so has this virtue also been impressed on liberation movements. Of course, relying on oneself does not totally exclude the possibility of outside support – but this will always be of secondary importance. Linked with the concept of self-reliance is China's belief that Marxism-Leninism should be adapted to particular conditions. Mao's major contribution to communist theory was his successful adaptation of the universal truths of Marxism-Leninism to the unique conditions of China. African revolutionaries, too, must find their own way, guided only by a few universal rules and helped – but only in a limited way – by foreign sympathizers.

Naturally, China has pointed out the practical similarities between her own revolutionary experiences and the present independence struggles, and the Nationalists themselves have drawn lessons. Andreas Shipanga, a founder of the South West African People's Organization (swapo) for example, told me once:

We all read Mao, as a practical manual of guerrilla warfare, just as we read British accounts of the Malaysian campaign – to show us how the enemy thinks. We respect China's revolution, as we respect all revolutions, and can learn from it.[5]

A deputy-chief of the Mozambique Revolutionary Committee (coremo), whose comments are valid despite the obvious anti-Soviet propaganda, said,

The methods of the Eighth Route Army and the Vietnamese National Liberation Front are right for Africa. The Russian methods are wrong – they were partly afraid of the peasants and crushed and collectivized them. The Chinese had to build a National Liberation Army on solid peasant support; they taught us we had to utilize 30 million Africans in southern Africa.

However, China has never said her revolutionary theory **should be adopted wholesale.** There will always be local

differences, and differences in social – which in Africa invariably means tribal – circumstances. The correct prescription can only be written in Africa, not in Peking.

Practical obstacles to Chinese support

The theory of self-reliance mitigates the relative poverty of
China's support for the liberation movements, but the real
reasons for her limited assistance are practical ones. Firstly,
there is the logistical difficulty – which, we saw, China encountered in her support for the Congolese rebels – of supplying and maintaining a revolution 10000 miles from Chinese
territory. Another inhibiting factor is the very considerable
cost involved in supporting revolution, and until the end of the
Vietnam war all China's spare military resources were needed
to assist an effort of vital state importance for China. She
must also be aware that in an escalation of material support
to African liberation movements she would be outbidded by
the Soviet Union, and that therefore the present low level of
assistance, where the discrepancy is relatively unnoticeable, is
to her interest. A further reason for caution is China's awareness of the dangers of escalating a long-term guerrilla war
into an immediate all-out military confrontation against
superior forces. Given southern Africa's stated position on the
dangers of an aggressive China, if China were dramatically
to increase her level of assistance to the liberation groups the
white 'axis' might well take the opportunity to strike hard at
the African host countries under the pretext of countering
foreign aggression. That China has warned Tanzania and
Zambia, and possibly also Congo-Brazzaville, of the dangers
of a pre-emptive strike from the south, I know from my own
talks with senior Tanzanian officials. In 1969 China actually
warned the host governments against countenancing a level of
guerrilla activity, particularly against Rhodesia, which would
invite a military response against them. China pointed out that
they had no defence against air or ground strikes, and that it
would be suicidal to provoke them. In this context it is of
significance that China has taken over the training of the
Tanzanian armed forces and has already supplied the air force
with Mig 17s; China also has a military agreement with Congo-

Brazzaville, but not, as yet, with Zambia. China's attitude to the desirability of encouraging an escalation of the guerrilla conflict might alter, once she is satisfied that the host countries are more capable of defending themselves.

In a few cases a further practical obstacle to Chinese support for a revolutionary movement has been afforded by state considerations, and these seem likely to play an increasingly important part in China's attitudes towards even the worthy southern African movement. We have already seen that once the diplomatic offensive was under way, China withdrew support from opposition groups in countries with which she maintained diplomatic relations, notably from the Eritrean Liberation Front. Earlier, however, she had withheld support from the Moslem separatist group, the Front for the Liberation of Chad (FROLINAT), partly because it would have been difficult to supply that situation, partly because she hoped for recognition from the government. Similarly, support was withheld from the southern Sudanese Anyanya movement, fighting to separate southern Sudan from the north. Good state relations with the Khartoum government were the reasons behind this decision. But the most obvious example of state considerations outweighing revolutionary ones, was in the initial refusal to support a liberation struggle in French Somaliland, the last outpost of French colonialism in Africa. A more eligible candidate for Chinese endorsement could not be imagined, yet China's approval of de Gaulle's independent foreign policy and subsequent French recognition of China in 1964, necessitated a cautious approach. It was not until 1966, when France was beginning to cultivate closer links with Moscow, that China, somewhat begrudgingly, added French Somaliland to her official list of countries in which an anti-imperialist struggle was taking place.

THE SINO-SOVIET DISPUTE AND THE LIBERATION MOVEMENTS

All the above theoretical and practical justifications for Chinese action or inaction in regard to the liberation movements are of small significance compared with the exigencies of the Sino-Soviet dispute. With very few exceptions China's choice of movements to support, and her actions towards these and to other groups, have been dictated by the need to challenge, surpass or embarrass the Soviet Union. There is a great deal in the Radio Peace and Progress accusation that 'Peking is enlisting its supporters within the ranks of the national liberation movement in Africa according to the principles of anti-Sovietism. They are forced to sign anti-Soviet statements and to utter anti-Soviet speeches.'

The Soviet Union's links with the African liberation struggle go back further and are more firmly established than China's. Leaders of movements in South Africa and in the Portuguese territories were prominent in the Soviet front organizations from the very beginning. Although it was open to the Chinese to make their own separate contacts,[6] in practice, the fact that most of the meetings were held in Moscow and the Soviet Union was financing the organizations – often paying the fares and expenses of the delegates as well – meant that early loyalties to the Soviet Union were built up. Scholarships at Soviet universities were offered to promising students,[7] while other Africans were offered posts in the secretariats of the front organizations. Many liberation movement leaders still hold prominent positions in the fronts – Oliver Tambo, President of the African National Congress (ANC) and Agostinho Neto of MPLA are members of the WCP Presidential Committee, as was John Marks, chairman of the South African Communist Party (SACP), before his death in Moscow in 1972. Marcelino dos Santos, acting Vice-President of FRELIMO, is a council member. Other liberation movement officials hold similar positions in other front organizations.

Through SACP, which she helped to set up in 1921, the Soviet Union has had a long association with what could claim to be the continent's oldest liberation movement, the ANC, founded in 1912 as the South African Native National Congress. Relations between the SACP and the ANC have been uneven, but were not so distant that the ANC could not rely on considerable Soviet support when it was finally banned in South Africa in 1960 and set up a movement in exile, based in Tanzania.

Rhodesia

Through the ANC, the Soviets had an early entrée into the Zimbabwe African People's Union (ZAPU), which also traced its ancestry to the SANNC. A branch of the SANNC, the Bantu Congress, had been set up in Rhodesia in 1930 to combat the Land Apportionment Act; in 1934 it changed its name to the African National Congress of Southern Rhodesia. During the debates on Rhodesia's future before UDI a regalvanized ANC, composed of the rump of the old ANC, under the leadership of Joshua Nkomo, and the Youth League, led by James Chikerema and George Nyandoro, was formed in 1957 to represent African interests. In 1959 many of its leaders were detained and the ANC banned: Nkomo was in Cairo, attending the AAPSO conference, at the time. He went to London and spent a year lobbying support for Rhodesian Africans before returning to Rhodesia in 1960 to lead a new party, the National Democratic Party, which was virtually a reconstituted ANC. The following year, this too was banned by the settler regime. Immediately Nkomo formed yet another party, ZAPU. When that was also banned in September 1962, only nine months after its formation, Nkomo began to move the entire organization to Dar es Salaam, where he had earlier been offered facilities by the Tanganyikan government, and ZAPU gradually became an exiled liberation movement committed, eventually, to overthrowing the minority regime by violence.

South West Africa

The South West Africa People's Organization (SWAPO), also went through some early sea changes. The beginnings of political activism in the territory can be traced back to the activities of Namibian students in South Africa, who, in 1952, had set up the South West African Student Body. But their hopes that a truly national party could be formed were dashed by the formation in the late 1950s of several parties, all organized along tribal lines. The two most important were the South West Africa National Union (SWANU), formed by the Herero and Mbanderu people, and the Ovamboland People's Congress, founded by the Ovambos. This later became the Ovamboland

Peoples' Organization (OPO). Initially there were hopes that all the political movements could coalesce into one national party, and in fact, one of the founders of the OPO, Sam Nujoma, was elected to the SWANU executive. But tribal differences, and ideological differences about what form political activity should take and from whom outside help should be solici ed, proved too great. Leaders of the OPO determined to make theirs *the* national movement, and in 1960, it was re-christened SWAPO to wipe out the tribal connotations. For six years the organization was non-violent, trying to effect change through the United Nations and other peaceful channels. But the rejection, in 1966, by the International Court of Justice of the case that South Africa was abusing its mandate over the territory forced SWAPO to turn to violence, and it sought, and received, arms from the Soviet Union. In the previous six years its links with the Soviet Union, partly fostered by SWAPO's own close relations with ANC, had been gradually strengthened, with SWAPO students being awarded scholarships to the Soviet Union and by the participation of SWAPO delegations at conferences of many of the front organizations.

Portuguese territories

Through scholarships, visits and meetings at conferences, the Soviet Union also built up good early contacts with the three major liberation movements in the Portuguese territories of Angola, Mozambique and Guinea-Bissau – respectively MPLA, FRELIMO and the African Party for the Independence of Portuguese Guinea and the Cap Verde Islands (PAIGC). Together with the insignificant Committee for the Liberation of Sao Tome and Principe, these three movements are associated in the Conference of the Nationalist Organizations from the Portuguese Colonies (CONCP), which actively co-ordinates their external activities by arranging conferences, delegating speakers to outside organizations, distributing joint publications and so on.

Nothing less than an entire book devoted to each territory could possibly explain in sufficient detail and with enough caveats to each tentative generalization, the development of the independence movement in southern Africa and the

Portuguese territories, and its tendency to split into opposed factions. For, although positive steps have been taken very recently amongst South African, Angolan and Rhodesian groups to sink their differences and unite, or re-unite, into a common front, the early history of the liberation movements has to be written in terms of splits.

Splinter groups came into being for many reasons, but amongst the most common were tribal rivalries, personality clashes, differences about how independence should be won and ideological orientation. The earliest differences naturally concentrated on what methods should be employed to gain the principle of majority rule, or independence from Portugal. As a broad generalization, in their formative years ANC, SWAPO and ZAPU all thought that their objectives could be gained by peaceful means, by constant international lobbying, by legitimate political activity within the countries concerned, by associating with white liberal opinion and by what they hoped would be a natural evolutionary process towards a fairer society. These principles were embodied, for example, in the ANC's moderate Freedom Charter, which declared for multiracialism and peaceful change. For a time the 'Charterists' as the moderates were called, were opposed within the organization by the 'Africanists' who objected, not so much to what was included in the Charter, but to what was excluded: the doctrine of Pan-Africanism, African liberation and the omission of any reference to the principle of 'one man, one vote' – which they saw as the only guarantee of eventual African rule. The final parting came at an ANC meeting in the Transvaal in 1959 when the Africanists were led out by Potlako Leballo, to form almost immediately the Pan-Africanist Congress (PAC), under the leadership of Robert Sobukwe, which claimed amongst other things that the ANC had been captured by a 'section of the leadership of the white ruling class'.

A similar split occurred in Rhodesia, where a faction of ZAPU, headed by the Rev. Ndabaningi Sithole, dissatisfied with what it regarded as Nkomo's pseudo-diplomacy and ineffective lobbying techniques, broke away in 1963 to form the Zimbabwe African National Union (ZANU), whose initial aims and methods, however, seemed indistinguishable from ZAPU's (adding credence to the suspicion that the split was about personalities rather than principles). But later ZANU adopted a more militant line, and was the first of the two organizations to have recourse to violent methods.

In the early 1960s the relatively soft line of ANC, SWAPO and ZAPU, and the fact that guerrilla activity had not started in earnest in the Portuguese territories could not have been unwelcome to the Soviet Union, with her emphasis on peaceful co-existence. Equally, it was natural that the extremist splinter groups, who saw their only hope in armed struggle, should look to China for support.

But the temptation to divide the liberation movements into neat 'pro-Soviet' and 'pro-Chinese' camps is to be avoided, although the notion did have some validity at the height of the Sino-Soviet dispute in the late 1960s. It should be avoided firstly because it ignores the genuinely nationalistic aspirations of every liberation movement, whose leaders, as we have already seen, resent and deny implications that because they receive aid from the communist countries they are therefore 'teleguided' by either Moscow or Peking; and secondly because China has made it her business to cultivate *all* movements and alienate none. Thus, even though Soviet influence has been clearly predominant in ANC, ZAPU and SWAPO, their representatives have never been inhibited from visiting China or their members from training there. Equally, Chinese aid flowed, however intermittently and sometimes even unwillingly, to all three Portuguese movements. By contrast, the Soviets have jibed at aiding movements they regard as patently 'pro-Peking'. Worse, certainly in African eyes, they have indulged in vitriolic propaganda against them, labelling, for example, PAC a 'black chauvinist' movement and accusing the National Front for the Liberation of Angola (FNLA) of being both Maoist and in the pay of the CIA. Other extremist groups have come under similar attack, with the result that today, while some movements are definitely 'anti-Soviet' not one is 'anti-Chinese'.

However, it was not surprising that Western journalists and other commentators, confused by tribal differences, by fine ideological 'lines', by complicated personality differences and by seemingly endless separatist tendencies leading to yet another new movement and a new set of confusing initials to learn, should try and look for some coherence and seek some simple thread to lead them through a complex labyrinth.

The Khartoum conference

The division of liberation movements into pro-Soviet and pro-Chinese camps seemed an obvious solution, and one which received unexpected endorsement in 1969 when the Soviet Union, under the auspices of the World Council of Peace jointly with AAPSO, organized a liberation conference in Khartoum, to which were invited the six movements popularly characterized as Soviet-controlled – namely ANC, ZAPU, SWAPO, MPLA, PAIGC and FRELIMO. The conference had been convened partly as a forum for the Soviet Union to explain the previous year's invasion of Czechoslovakia, which had worried the liberation movements as much as it had independent African governments. The Soviets may even have calculated that they could use their assistance to the movements as a lever to exact from them some sort of endorsement for their actions. But whatever motives there may have been for calling the conference it became an attempt, clumsy even by Soviet standards, to capture the leadership of the southern African liberation movement, not only from the Chinese, but from the Africans as well.

Theoretical organizational control of all liberation movements rested, and still rests, with the OAU's Liberation Committee, set up in 1963 at the same time as the OAU itself and charged with the responsibility of collecting 'fighting fund' dues from OAU member states, distributing this aid to movements which it deems worthy (generally, but not always, limited to one movement per country), co-ordinating action (including, if possible, healing splits) and acting as a liaison and information office for all the movements. The Committee refused to attend the Khartoum Conference, which it regarded as undermining its authority. That this was a correct interpretation was shown when the Soviet Union suggested the setting-up of an African Mobilization Committee, sited in Cairo, and with a secretariat headed by As-Sibai, Secretary-General of AAPSO. AAPSO was by this time so totally under the domination of the Soviet Union, that the manœuvre was obviously designed to give her a final say in many of the decisions affecting the whole liberation movement. The Soviet Union further compounded this tactical error by designating another front organization, the International Association of Democratic Lawyers, to look after legal problems facing the movements.

For outside observers, the theory that the movements were simply pawns in the Sino-Soviet dispute seemed strengthened by a statement issued in London by four Chinese-oriented movements, PAC, ZANU, the National Union for the Total Independence of Angola (UNITA) and COREMO, claiming the conference was 'calculated to control the liberation struggles of the Portuguese colonies and southern Africa in order to further Soviet cooperation with the US for their joint domination of the world'. A *Pravda* article counter-attacked

Pursuing the same aims (as the imperialists) of undermining unity ... the Chinese dissidents are exerting every effort to undermine Africa's trust in the USSR and other countries of socialism and to discredit outstanding fighters for peace and unity of the peoples.

[Though] taking no part in the work of the conference, these Chinese dissidents sent to Khartoum a group of correspondents who, jointly with the embassy employees, carried out subversive activities and spread false documents ... [8]

The Khartoum conference was in many ways a watershed in the relations between the two communist powers and the liberation movements. After it, all the invited movements seemed particularly anxious to emphasize their non-aligned nature and stress that they did not take orders from Moscow; China, sensing this mood, either initiated, increased or renewed assistance which had fallen into abeyance during the cultural revolution. Delegations were encouraged to visit Peking, and the respective leaders of FRELIMO, PAIGC and MPLA all visited China in the next two years. The faction within ANC which had been repulsed by the invasion of Czechoslovakia and had wanted to form a united front with PAC, evidently gained the upper hand, for, on the twenty-first anniversary of the founding of the People's Republic, ANC said in a statement that links between the people of China and the people of South Africa

... would continue to grow until our common enemies and the

imperialists, in particular US imperialism, the leader of the imperialists in their global strategy, have been wiped off the face of the earth. The establishment of the People's Republic of China was a monumental and indelible achievement in the struggle for national independence and world peace. It was a great inspiration to all revolutionaries throughout the world.[9]

The Soviet Union was evidently also aware of the new mood, for in 1970 she made an effort to re-assert her authority by convening yet another WCP-AAPSO conference, this time in Rome, for the three movements fighting in Mozambique, Angola and Guinea-Bissau. The meeting attracted a good deal of attention in the world, and predictable criticism in Portugal, because the three leaders were received by the Pope. Whether by accident or design the Soviet Union maintained a low profile during the meeting, and received no mention in the final communiqué, which stressed the nationalist aspirations of the three movements and put forward a reasoned, moderate joint programme.

CHINA AND THE SEPARATIST MOVEMENTS

Although, as noted earlier, there has been a recent tendency, partly under pressure from the Liberation Committee, for the liberation movements to re-unite (the first coalition, a joint ZANU-ZAPU military front called FROLIZI was announced in October 1971; MPLA and FNLA announced at the 1972 OAU summit meeting in Rabat that they had sunk their differences, while in 1973 PAC and ANC were still exploring the possibilities of forming a united front), splits by extremists have continued to bedevil the liberation movement. Almost without exception, China has found it expedient to lend her support, however minimal, to such groups.

Theoretically, the Chinese presumably argue that since guerrilla warfare is a long process and most African guerrilla wars are still only in their preliminary stages, it is impossible to predict which movement will eventually be victorious. It is therefore prudent to back as many contenders as possible. But the practical reasons must be more compelling. Firstly, up to now and almost certainly for a long time to come, the separatists are continually moving further to the left. They

want more extreme actions; they are usually young and therefore rebelling against what they consider to be the conservatism
of the older members. For outside support they can turn only
to the Chinese. Every split, therefore, increases the quantitative
support that China appears to enjoy, a factor which has been
important internally, especially during the cultural revolution
when China was soliciting and publishing endorsements from
as many movements as possible, even from some like SWANU,
which by that stage barely existed at all. A further practical
reason to welcome separatism – despite the CCP's own experience that revolutions can only be won by encouraging a
sense of national unity – is that, almost by definition, each
succeeding separatist group becomes smaller, which in turn
means it is less onerous to support and almost certainly more
willing to be publicly beholden to China for that support.
Requests for public endorsements for China, which have been
successfully resisted by the larger groups (especially FRELIMO
which has insisted that Chinese support for the movement be
routed through the Liberation Committee) are refused with
more difficulty by small movements (in some cases literally a
handful of disgruntled dissidents) desperate for recognition
and assistance. The scope for China to win a certain amount of
cheap publicity and to appear, internally at least, in the forefront of the world's revolutionary movement, is amply demonstrated by a brief resumé of some of the separatist developments
in Mozambique. COREMO, for example, was a front formed in
1965 to unite the anti-FRELIMO movements of MANU, MANC,
UNAMI, UDENAMO and neo-UDENAMO. Internecine squabbling within COREMO led in 1966 to the formation of a splinter
group, PAPOMO. In 1968 the Deputy-President of COREMO,
Amos Sumane, left to form UNAR, while the next year yet
another new movement, ULIPAMO, was established by a
faction dissatisfied with the COREMO leadership. While China's
opportunistic support for these groups has predictably been
condemned by Moscow, the original movements – in this case
FRELIMO – have been reticent to criticize Chinese actions,
partly presumably because they feel this would jeopardize
whatever material assistance they receive from China, partly
perhaps because they do not want to be accused of becoming
embroiled in the Sino-Soviet dispute.

China has also lent her support to 'fringe' groups like MOLINACO of the Comoro Islands and even MPAIAC of the Canary Islands, movements which have so far elicited no response from Moscow.

China's revolutionary theory

While China's motives in cultivating the liberation movements are varied, the movements themselves expect from the relationship two main dividends: China's experience, and material support. China appears more generous with the former than the latter.

We have already seen that although both China and the liberation movements agree that African revolutions must be waged by African revolutionaries, evolving if possible African revolutionary prescriptions, they also both agree that China's experiences are of great value in the present independence struggles. Chinese publications equate not only the similarities of geography but also those of history, and are constantly pointing out the usefulness of Chinese experience for Africa. The PLA's Bulletin of Activities, for example, stressed the value of Chinese military theory:

No country in this world has had more experience than we. We all understand that theory is derived from practice; because we have more combat experience, we should therefore have more superior military theories ... The summing-up of our military experience is not only for ourselves but also for the benefit of other countries and nations which are still not yet liberated.[10]

Mao's *Selected Military Writings* are closely studied by the guerrilla fighters and their general lessons applied to the African situation. In essence, these are that the countryside and the rural populations must be won first, and the towns then gradually surrounded; that the enemy should never be engaged in a pitched battle; that in any military encounter the guerrilla forces must be numerically stronger; that time is on the side of the irregular force. These points are further refined into Mao's memorable epigram: 'Enemy advances, we retreat; enemy halts, we harass; enemy tires, we attack; enemy retreats, we pursue.' The enemy too understands at least some of China's lessons: Colonel Seguro, Governor of Mozambique's northern Cabo Delgado province, said in 1966: 'The side that wins the population will win the war. There is no question about that.' The Portuguese have gone about this task partly through a 'hearts and minds campaign', partly through psychological warfare designed to antagonize local populations against the guerrillas, by telling them, for instance, that all freedom fighters are cannibals. Rhodesia tries to deny the countryside to the guerrillas by a system of pliant chiefs and an information network, and by savage sentences on any African found harbouring a guerrilla. But throughout the present war zone it seems likely that protection, not principle, will guide the attitude of local populations to the participants. Only success, in other words, will be able to guarantee further success, and loyalty will be won by proven ability to provide protection. The most successful of the movements, PAIGC (now the legitimate government of Bissau following the Portuguese coup) has the loyalty of the population quite simply because it is in control; ZANU lacks a mass following within Rhodesia because it is not.

Of equal value to Mao's explicitly military and tactical writings are general Chinese theories about the inevitable triumph of guerrilla warfare, of the superiority of men over machines, of the power of subjective forces over objective ones. Revolutionaries must be patient, they must take courage from their knowledge that strategically the enemy is weak. Maoist theory gives confidence, it bolsters morale, it reassures those who 'dare to struggle' that final victory will be theirs. Take, for example, one of Mao's most famous theses:

The atom bomb is a paper tiger ... It looks terrific, but in fact it isn't. Of course the atom bomb is a weapon of mass slaughter, but the outcome of a war is decided by the people, not by one or two new types of weapon.[11]

Or Lin Piao's addenda:

The spiritual atom bomb which the revolutionary people possess is a far more powerful and useful weapon than the physical atom bomb.[12]

The Chinese proposition that struggle is valuable, in that it awakens political consciousness and – although Chinese

9

encouragement of separatist movements would seem to belie this – may even stimulate an unsuspected sense of national unity, is also being painfully but gradually understood. Eventually, tribal differences might become insignificant in face of the common enemy; meanwhile, as Basil Davidson, a sympathetic British writer, has put it:

Though harsh years must still lie ahead, the dour prospect is lightened by a conviction that only a long period of awakening political understanding and increasing ethnic unity – and it is these crucial gains that grim years of war are being made to yield – can lead to meaningful independence. 'If the Portuguese had given us independence in 1961 instead of forcing us to fight them,' observed an MPLA leader this summer, 'it would have been worse here than in the Congo.'[13]

Material Aid

Political power, runs Maoist doctrine, grows out of the barrel of a gun, and however attractive and relevant Chinese theories might be, it is Chinese guns which African revolutionaries have most need of. But China's material assistance to the groups has been as sparing as her support for splinter groups has been generous.

Before discussing the level of Chinese material help let us examine what Chinese verbal 'support' to a liberation movement means in practice. Firstly, very rarely is a liberation movement singled out by name for Chinese endorsement. Chinese publications talk in general terms of the 'people' of a particular country being engaged in a revolutionary struggle, even in a situation like Guinea-Bissau where only one movement, the PAIGC, was ever active. This obviously allows for failure and spares China the later embarrassment of having identified with an unpopular or ineffective movement; it also means China does not have to endorse a movement, like any of the CONCP group, which also receives aid from the Soviet Union. To the Western reader Chinese articles thus have a slightly unreal quality about them, with pages devoted to 'patriotic armed struggles' and 'revolutionary peoples' but rarely a mention of the groups leading them.

Generalized support for the movements is also provided by

Chinese propaganda. Widely circulated glossy magazines, like *China Pictorial, China Reconstructs, Peking Review* and *The Call*, the journal of the Afro-Asian Writers' Bureau, regularly contain illustrated articles of the liberation struggle, often without, once again, mentioning movements by name – which at least has the advantage that they can be utilized by all the movements competing in one territory. The same could be said for Radio Peking broadcasts, which in general terms exhort the oppressed populations to rise up, give them encouraging news of the successes of freedom fighters and assure them of the continuing support of the Chinese and the world's revolutionary people. News about the activities of specific movements comes in the programmes broadcast by the liberation movements from the radio transmitters, supplied by China, sited in Tanzania, Zambia and Congo-Brazzaville. No study has been made of the effect of all this propaganda on the African populations of southern Africa, but it seems reasonable to assume that it does have a reinforcing effect and that it does boost morale.

It is equally impossible to assess Chinese material support to the movements. Neither side has ever openly publicized details of material assistance, and an approximate picture has to be built up from various sources. In general terms, however, as much by omission of reference to Chinese support as by direct evidence, it is possible to infer that the level of assistance has been on the low side. Basil Davidson, in the article already referred to, commented that

[The movements] could win much less slowly, and reduce an appalling load of suffering, if they received more aid. They receive remarkably little. How little they receive is perhaps the point that has most surprised me after looking at all three (CONCP) movements in the field. Up to this summer, for instance, the Chinese had given exactly nothing to the PAIGC and MPLA (except marginally, and in spite of themselves, through the OAU); if FRELIMO has done better in respect of Chinese aid, this is only thanks to the influence in Peking of the Tanzanian government.

With the other movements there is a cart-horse situation. Is their very low level of military activity the result of the denial to them of Chinese, and other, material assistance; or does

China desist from affording them much material assistance because they are unwilling or unable to engage in significant guerrilla warfare? A reasonable formula would seem to be that Chinese assistance must keep roughly in pace with the development of a liberation movement, especially if it is also Soviet-aided. Thus, despite prior Soviet interest, Chinese assistance to the CONCP group has increased in the last few years, as the movements have become more successful. Conversely, assistance to SWANU has dried up as that movement has lost any semblance of public support. With the splinter groups China is in a delicate position, because any material aid could be construed – and is construed by Moscow – as an attempt to undermine national unity and pose a challenge to the major movement, (which in some cases is also supported by China.) Soviet propaganda, for example, has accused China of supporting FNLA (which according to Radio Peace and Progress was also in the pay of the CIA) and UNITA (subsidized, again according to the Radio, by the Portuguese) in order to disrupt MPLA. In Mozambique, the Soviets have accused China of training COREMO guerrillas to fight, not against the Portuguese, but against FRELIMO. With the South African movements, Chinese aid will presumably continue at a minimal level until they can prove themselves capable of carrying out more than token guerrilla activity.

Material assistance comes in three forms: the supply of military hardware, cash payments and military training, both in Africa and in China. There is documentary evidence of all three methods, from which it is possible to sketch a rough picture of Chinese material aid, but which is not enough to allow us to project what the total might be.

Portuguese military reports regularly referred to the capture of Chinese and Soviet weapons. Of these the most effective is the Chinese-made Kalashnikov AK–47 automatic rifle, the weapon so respectfully regarded by the Americans in Vietnam. All the active movements seem to be armed with this weapon. Other captured Chinese hardware has included rocket launchers, hand grenades and anti-tank mines. Many guerrillas also wear uniforms made in China. By contrast, Soviet hardware is often out of date. Basil Davidson writes that Soviet aid '. . . has also been very sparing. Many of the automatics of Soviet provenance that I saw in Angola this year were German Schmeissers taken in the Second World War, and even those were in very short supply.'

This corresponds with Soviet arms policies towards independent African governments, for example, Kenya's rejected consignment of old-fashioned hardware, and also with comments I heard from freedom fighters in Dar es Salaam.

Of cash payments there is, naturally, less direct evidence, although Western press reports have referred to a 'generous' member of the Politburo inner circle, Liao Cheng-chih, reputed to pay freedom fighters and others in used £5 sterling notes. The amounts in the very few reported cases have never been large. One documented case, although not directly concerned with liberation movements, gives an idea of the extent of Chinese generosity when it comes to cash payments: Christopher Olonde, a former associate of Oginga Odinga, told a press conference in Nairobi in 1970 that he had arranged for £8000 to be paid to Odinga through the Chinese embassies in Dar es Salaam and Kampala and that during a trip to China in 1968 he had been promised a further £20000, to be paid to Odinga through Dar es Salaam.[14] In a private report a PAC member revealed that the sum of $20000 was raised by PAC delegations on each of two visits to China, sums which were not deposited in the party's account.[15] It seems likely that China's own shortage of hard currency and her fear that such funds would be misused, as in the above instance, have precluded the giving of anything but token amounts of cash to the liberation movements.

Probably China's major contribution to the movements, and the one most consistent with her principle of helping revolutionaries to help themselves, has been in the form of training. Chinese instructors have taught the principles of guerrilla warfare at camps in Tanzania, Congo-Brazzaville, Algeria and, as we saw earlier, Ghana, while African 'students' have attended courses in China, usually at a training camp near Nanking. The courses do not seem to vary very much and they include all aspects of the theory and practice of guerrilla warfare, training on both Western and communist weapons, instruction on how to establish revolutionary bases in rural areas and on how to ambush. Captured Cameroonian dissidents outlined the following syllabus which they said they had followed at a camp in China during a training course in 1961: 24–27 June – correct use of explosives, how to manufacture mines and incendiary bombs; 28 June – planning a sabotage operation; 29–30 June – how to use explosives against houses, railway lines, bridges, tanks, guns, lorries, tractors, diesel engines and aeroplanes.

These students also told, as did the trainees at the Obenamasi camp in Ghana, of ideological indoctrination – in their case ten days of lectures before the guerrilla course began. For the Chinese this would have been as much of the course as the practical training, for, as Mao wrote

'Without a political goal guerrilla warfare must fail, as it must if its political objectives do not coincide with the aspirations of the people – and their sympathy, cooperation and assistance cannot be gained.'

African government and liberation movement leaders have been well aware of this aspect of military training. As President Kaunda told a *Times* interviewer in 1968:

The only people who will teach young Africans to handle dangerous weapons are in the eastern camp. How can we expect that they will learn to use these weapons without learning the ideology as well? When they come back, we can expect not only a racial war in Africa, but an ideological one as well.[16]

In another interview, quoted earlier, a ZANU guerrilla, trained in China, said,

Later there were more lectures about how to brainwash peasants. This in effect was communism. We had been told by our officials to watch out for this. They feared that communism might make us revolt against their leadership.[17]

The ANC were so frightened of their trainees being contaminated by propaganda, especially as the Sino-Soviet dispute became more intense, that those who returned from Peking were kept under strict surveillance for traces of Maoism.[18]

SUMMARY

Considering the objective circumstances of southern Africa,

an area truly ripe for revolution and where even Western commentators anticipated eventual victory for the guerrilla forces, especially in the Portuguese territories, Chinese support for the various liberation movements has been very circumscribed. The discrepancy between Chinese verbal and material support for revolutionary movements has been noted elsewhere. The following description of China's relations with such movements in Latin America is a mirror image of the same relationship in southern Africa:

In view of official pronouncements on revolutionary storms in Asia, Africa and Latin America, one would expect to see a considerable Chinese effort to support the 'revolutionary struggles' in Latin America, particularly in the form of material and organizational assistance to the leftist extremist guerrilla groups operating in several Latin American countries. In actual fact, however, Chinese support for the guerrillas has so far been largely verbal. The real Chinese effort in Latin America has been directed at a very different and far more modest goal: not against the great imperialist foe, the us, but against Soviet influence in the area. Specifically, the Chinese have attempted to wean the weak and ineffective Latin American communist parties from their allegiance to Moscow. Having failed in this, they have endeavoured to split pro-Chinese factions off from these parties. It is significant that in the few cases where they have succeeded in doing so, the new pro-Chinese parties have not attempted to set up guerrilla fronts nor have they united with existing guerrilla movements.

In Latin America as elsewhere one is thus struck by the discrepancy between the grandiloquence of Chinese ideological declamations, which give the impression of megolomania and an utterly distorted, totally unrealistic view of the world, and Peking's actual policy, which for all its errors and failures appears to have been devised with a complete awareness of China's very limited means and possibilities.[19]

The extremists must reflect ruefully that it is they who are paying the price of China's new respectability, and that Chinese support now is the reward, not for revolutionary merit, but for anti-Soviet zeal. Peking is no longer the mecca of revolution, rather it is a haven for failed revolutionaries, an epigram Mao would not care for but which has been forced on him by the 'bourgeois' considerations of state interest.

Notes

1. The intellectual level of South African propaganda can be gauged by the comment in the propaganda magazine *To The Point* (10 March 1973) that '. . . China quietly continues to ferry its thousands of little men into Dar es Salaam, like termites burrowing into the foundations of a building.

2. *Johannesburg Star*, 15 May 1971.

3. *Observer*, January 1967.

4. *Observer*, August 1970.

5. Interview with the author in Dar es Salaam, February 1971.

6. Some of the earliest African visitors to China went on to Peking after attending a meeting of one of the fronts. Walter Sisulu, Secretary-General of the ANC, visited Peking in 1953 after the World Youth Festival – and compared Chinese communism favourably with Stalinism. Viriato da Cruz, a founder of MPLA, went to China after attending an Afro-Asian Writers' Conference in Tashkent in 1958. He later tried to form a pro-Chinese faction in the movement, but when that failed he moved to Peking permanently in 1966 and has since regularly appeared as the Angolan representative at meetings of Chinese front organizations, notably the Afro-Asian Writers' Organization.

7. For example, Manuel Lopez da Silva, Secretary-General of the now virtually defunct Front for the Fight for the National Independence of Guinea (FLING), was, in 1966, a final-year medical student at Moscow's Lumumba University. Two years later he was representing the National Union of Workers at a Moscow meeting of the World Federation of Trade Unions, a Soviet front for which a number of Africans have worked, notably the veteran Nigerian trade unionist, Wahab Goodluck.

8. *Pravda*, 21 January 1969.

9. Quoted in *Tanganyika Standard*, 5 October 1970.

10. Chester-Cheng, op. cit., p. 315.

11. Mao Tse-tung, *Selected Works*, pp. 100–1.

12. Lin Piao, 'Long Live the Victory of People's War', *Peking Review*, No. 36, p. 196.

13. *New Statesman*, 'The Seed of Midwinter', 30 October 1970.

14. For further details see the *Daily Nation*, Nairobi, 3 April 1970.

15. See Larkin, op. cit., p. 190, footnote 53.

16. *The Times*, 12 March 1968.

17. *Guardian*, April 1968.

18. See *Black Dwarf*, 26 November 1969.

19. *China Quarterly*, No. 29 (January–March 1967), pp. 111–34.

15
CHINA AND TANZANIA

'Tanzania is enriched by this friendship'

PRESIDENT NYERERE

THE relationship between China and Tanzania – 'a friendship between most unequal equals', as President Nyerere put it – has been central to China's African policies. It has been a showcase for what was called in Part One the Chinese constructive approach, and has thereby brought considerable benefits to the African state. China is by far the most important foreign aid donor and has chosen Tanzania as the site for her – and the communist world's – greatest overseas aid project, the Tanzam railway. At one time, China's embassy in Dar es Salaam was her largest overseas mission, and the numerous force working on the railway has meant there are more communist Chinese in Tanzania than anywhere else in the world, outside the Chinese mainland. China has also constructed other major projects, such as the Friendship Textile Mill, a farm implements factory and a radio transmission station. The two countries jointly own a shipping line. Chinese medical teams have worked successfully in Tanzania's rural areas. Tanzanian students have been accepted in China, cultural exchanges have been arranged. Finally, China has undertaken the training and arming of Tanzania's army, navy and air forces, as well as helped in the training of the police.

Although the material advantages to Tanzania have been considerable, China would argue that the relationship has been mutually beneficial. Tanzania's support on a number of specific issues, such as the seating of China at the United Nations and her vote against the 1968 nuclear non-proliferation treaty, has been welcome, as has her general 'membership' of the anti-imperialist club, signalled particularly by Tanzania's support for the southern African liberation movements. Tanzania's firm friendship was especially important to China, firstly at the time in the mid 1960s when she was suffering reversals elsewhere in Africa, and later, during the cultural revolution, when many other friendly countries were reluctant to associate with China too closely for fear of arousing opposition at home (as we saw in Chapter Ten President Nyerere was the only foreign head of state to visit China during 1968). Finally, the adoption by Tanzania of certain Chinese models has been of value internally for China's leaders, while Tanzania's praise for the hard work and dedication of Chinese aid personnel has often been cited in the Chinese press, with the object of encouraging Chinese at home to emulate their example. It has, in every sense, been a 'special relationship'. According to the Chinese it has 'set a fine example for the unity and cooperation among Asian and African countries',[1] while Nyerere's second visit to China was hailed as 'a tremendous support and encouragement for the Chinese people'. For Nyerere, the friendship has been based on the principles of respect and equality – 'I can state quite categorically that Tanzania is enriched by this friendship.'

Early Sino-Tanzanian relations

Although diplomatic relations were established in December 1961, the month in which Tanganyika became independent, early contacts between the two countries were minimal. This was partly because at this time China was more interested in cultivating countries in North and West Africa, partly because to the Chinese, Nyerere must have seemed a moderate, rather unpromising sort of leader. Educated at Edinburgh University, surrounded by British advisers, his army and civil service staffed with British personnel, the vast majority of trade conducted with Britain and the bulk of aid coming from there, his whole orientation was 'Western'. As he himself said, 'when it comes to actual facts, this country is completely Western, in government, in business, in the schools, in everything. The influence of this country is Western.'

If he was prepared to be open-minded about establishing links with the communist states, Nyerere did however, strongly resent the imposition of the Sino-Soviet dispute on Africa. As we saw earlier he changed the venue of the third AAPSO conference, which had originally been planned to be held in Dar es Salaam, to Moshi – to remove the anticipated Sino-Soviet bickering to a safe distance from the capital. At the conference itself he had some uncomfortable words for the two communist nations: 'I wish I could honestly say that the second scramble for Africa is going to be a scramble only between the capitalist powers.'

But it was the Sino-Soviet dispute which eventually brought Tanzania and China closer together, as a result of the two communist powers' different attitudes towards the union between Tanganyika and Zanzibar. Nyerere had watched with some alarm the developments on the island in the few months immediately succeeding the January 1964 revolution, and had come to the conclusion that it might well become a Sino-Soviet ideological battleground. Both China and the Soviet Union had granted immediate recognition to the Karume government, and both moved swiftly to follow this up with aid commitments. Both had their protegés in the new government, respectively Babu, the former NCNA correspondent and new foreign minister, and Kazim Hanga, the Vice-President, who had been educated in the Soviet Union and was married to an East German. Partly as an attempt to forestall an outbreak of the Sino-Soviet dispute on his own doorstep, Nyerere proposed a union of the mainland with Zanzibar. This move was, apparently, opposed by the Soviet Union which evidently felt that her influence with the Zanzibar government was greater than China's and that therefore she had more to lose by the proposed union. Zanzibar was also the first African country to recognize East Germany, an advantage which would presumably be lost after union with the mainland, which at that time enjoyed good relations with West Germany.

Conversely China, perhaps recognizing that the Soviet Union did enjoy greater influence in Zanzibar, felt that the union would therefore be to her advantage, and ambassador Ho Ying assured Nyerere that China was in favour of the proposal. To underline this approval, China's first credit to Zanzibar in

June 1964 (there had been a small grant of just over £200000 immediately after the revolution) was routed through the mainland authorities, while the Soviet Union antagonized opinion in Dar es Salaam by continuing to assist Zanzibar directly.[2] Shortly afterwards Kawawa paid a visit to China and negotiated Tanzania's first aid package from China, initiating the period of intense Sino-Tanzanian friendship.

Tanzania's non-alignment

Like other independence leaders, Nyerere both recognized and resented the influence in his country of the former colonial power, and its often patronizing attitude that it knew what was best for the new nation. As in other newly independent countries, Tanzania's establishment of relations with the communist powers was the first step in trying to assert a more independent foreign policy and to become more truly non-aligned. In an early summing-up of his relations with the Eastern bloc, Nyerere stressed the 'apron-strings' attitude of the West:

The big communist states are as likely to indulge in attempts to infiltrate our societies as are the big capitalist states. The major difference which I see at the moment is that the Eastern powers are not used to controlling Africa and therefore they don't assume they have a right to 'give us advice' in the same way as some of the large Western powers do. On the contrary our friendship with the communist powers is still a new thing and, by and large, they are still accepting this friendship as a bonus – at least in my experience.

To Western criticism that he was 'veering leftwards' or 'selling out to the communists', Nyerere replied that, since for so long Tanzania had been in the Western orbit, she had to make gestures towards the East in order to finish up in the centre. He told journalists accompanying Robert Kennedy on a visit to Tanzania in 1966 that Tanzania was moving eastwards politically 'because we are moving towards the centre – but we are not going to Peking'. Apart from using friendship with the communist powers to establish true non-alignment, Nyerere also clearly enjoyed what one commentator described as 'the worry which relations with China inspired in other states'. A poor and weak state, Tanzania nevertheless gained a certain international notoriety for what was regarded as a 'daring' foreign policy. Confident of his ability to contain Chinese influence, Nyerere could afford to laugh at what he considered the somewhat paranoid attitude of the West. As we saw earlier, he chided English journalists for adducing that even the suits he wore were evidence of 'pernicious Chinese influence'.

A final reason for Nyerere's initial recognition of China was the common-sensical attitude, as he has often put it, that 'you cannot ignore 700 million people'. Whatever merits or demerits China had, or was supposed to have, it seemed to him, as it seemed to other African leaders, that it was quite simply foolish to try and isolate the world's most populous nation. Tanzania's friendship was a small contribution towards rectifying that basic wrong.

At the time of the union with Zanzibar and immediately afterwards, there were practical as well as ideological reasons why Tanzania sought to draw closer to China. The first was the refusal by the World Bank, and subsequently by various other Western consortia, to finance construction of a railway linking Tanzania and Zambia, a project cherished greatly by Nyerere. His determination to proceed with the railway drew a positive response from China, which offered to investigate the possibilities within seven months of the Bank's refusal. Another was worsening relations with three of Tanzania's major bilateral aid-givers: Britain, the United States and West Germany, with whose general foreign policy line – and increasingly their particular one with regard to Tanzania – Nyerere came to disagree. In January 1964 he expelled two American diplomats for allegedly interfering in Tanzania's internal affairs, and subsequently asked the US to run down her Peace Corps force. In February 1965 – immediately after his visit to China – he requested the West German government to cease all its aid activities in Tanzania, after Bonn had reneged on an agreement to help establish a Tanzanian air force and marine police unit, in retaliation for Tanzania's decision to allow East Germany to establish a consulate in Dar es Salaam. Throughout 1965 Tanzania watched with apprehension Britain's handling of the Rhodesian situation; when the Smith regime finally declared UDI Tanzania broke off diplomatic relations with Britain, forfeiting a £7·5 million British loan geared to Tanzania's second development plan. Tanzania was also becoming increasingly sensitive to hostile Western press reports about her policies; some were just plain silly, forecasting, for example, that Nyerere was to make observation of the Chinese new year obligatory in Tanzania. Other 'yellow peril' reports included the information, rigorously denied, that China was to equip Tanzania with a ground-to-air missile system.

NYERERE'S FIRST VISIT TO CHINA

Although some of these developments were still in the future, worsening relations with the West was the general background to Nyerere's first visit to China in February 1965.

At this time, however, his own attitude towards China was still equivocal, and he made it clear that he had no intention of compromising Tanzania's non-alignment by moving from one 'bloc' into another one. The disruptive activities of the Chinese delegation at the AAPSO conference in Moshi must still have been relatively fresh in his mind, and he was also highly critical of Chinese manœuvres prior to the putative holding of a 'Second Bandung' (see Chapter Seven). In a speech given at a banquet in Peking he said,

We offer the hand of friendship to China as to America, Russia, Britain and others . . . The fears of others will not affect Tanzania's friendship with China any more than our friendship with other countries will be affected by what their opponents say of them.[3]

Chinese leaders may well have taken his last remark to heart, especially if they were still lobbying his support for the exclusion of the Soviet Union from a 'Second Bandung', as seems likely. But the very fact that Nyerere was in China at all, in the same month that the Chinese mission was expelled from Tanzania's neighbour, Burundi, was support enough, and her leaders must have been heartened by his comments on his return home that

We found out for ourselves that they are a peaceful people. The Chinese leaders impressed us deeply because they have had an experience not shared by any other world leaders: they are leaders of a revolution.[4]

Nyerere was enormously impressed by what he saw in China, and his visit was the turning-point in relations between the two countries. He realized, possibly for the first time, the great relevance for a country like Tanzania of the Chinese developmental model – with its emphasis on rural cooperatives and simple, labour intensive industries. Above all, he was impressed by the organizational methods of the Chinese, by their discipline and dedication to work, by the frugality of her leaders and by the apparent good health of the population. Speaking of Chinese aid he said,

We are the more appreciative because we realize that this capital is not surplus to your requirements, nor are your technicians otherwise employed. Certainly we on our side are anxious to learn what we can about China's development, in the hope that we shall, by its adaptation to our circumstances, be able to benefit from your experiences.[5]

On his return he stressed to a press conference that

China is very economical. The main means of transport are buses and bicycles, and it is possible that Dar es Salaam alone might have more private cars than all those found in the cities of Nanking, Shanghai and Peking. We should learn from countries like China. It would be unfair to receive aid from them if we cannot be frugal.[6]

During Nyerere's visit, the two countries, 'being convinced that the strengthening of friendly cooperation between the People's Republic of China and the United Republic of Tanzania conforms to the fundamental interests of the two countries, helps promote the solidarity between them as well as among Asian and African peoples and the common struggle against imperialism, and conduces to peace in Asia, Africa and the world', signed a ten-year treaty of friendship. The joint communiqué issued at the end of the visit, as was to be expected, reflected Chinese rather than Tanzanian authorship, although naturally there was nothing in it to which the Tanzanians could take exception. Amongst other things, the two sides held that 'the present international situation is most favourable to the peoples of the world and unfavourable to imperialism and colonialism'. Both sides pledged their support to the people of Congo, and condemned outside intervention in that country;

they both opposed imperialist aggression in Vietnam, Korea and Cuba and both expressed their determination to make concerted efforts with other Asian and African countries (which in the Chinese formula excluded the Soviet Union) for the success of the Second African-Asian Conference. Finally, the Tanzanian side

reaffirmed its support for the restoration of the legitimate rights of the People's Republic of China in the United Nations, its opposition to the imperialist plots for creating 'two Chinas', and its support for the Chinese government in their just struggle to safeguard state sovereignty and territorial integrity.[7]

Impressed though he undoubtedly was by his visit, Nyerere was not so overwhelmed that he was unable to perceive China's faults. In fact, when Chou En-lai made his first visit to Tanzania just four months later, Nyerere found it necessary to inform him that 'neither our country, principles, or freedom to determine our own fate are for sale,' adding that Tanzania – 'and I hope China' – had only two duties: to build and safeguard their respective countries. It seems that once again these remarks were connected with assumed Chinese pressurizing tactics to enlist Tanzanian support for the exclusion of the Soviet Union from the African-Asian Conference. After Boumedienne's coup, Nyerere said in any case that, out of loyalty to Ben Bella, he would boycott a conference held in Algiers under the auspices of the Boumedienne government, and, as mentioned earlier, he was reportedly shocked at what he regarded as China's cynicism in recognizing Boumedienne so swiftly and so obviously for her own interests. Until the invasion of Czechoslovakia, which truly put the Soviet Union beyond the pale as far as Nyerere was concerned, the Sino-Soviet dispute continued to mar Sino-Tanzanian relations. As late as September 1966, for example, *Al Ahram* reported that Tanzania had declined to be host to a meeting of AAPSO's executive committee on the grounds that the Sino-Soviet dispute would make it unfruitful.

Another early difficulty arose over China's attitude towards the Liberation Committee, whose headquarters were sited in Dar es Salaam and whose Executive Secretary was a Tanzanian. China had taken a leading role in establishing AAPSO's 'fighting fund' for liberation movements (see p. 46) and there-fore, like the Soviets, regarded the committee in some ways as a rival. But soon after the Liberation Committee had been founded, in 1963, some AAPSO members proposed either close working relations with it, or even a merger. China objected, and immediately before the Liberation Committee held its first meeting in Dar es Salaam, the NCNA correspondent left the capital in protest. China has continued to take little interest in the activities of the committee, and when I left Tanzania in 1970 no Chinese had even set foot inside the headquarters building.

The Chinese model

Nyerere's experiences in China contributed greatly to the evolution of his political philosophy. But so, it is fair to say, did his reading of the Fabians, his knowledge of cooperative experiments in Israel and Scandinavia and his own country's tradition of the African 'extended family' system. Although Tanzania's socialism obviously owes a great deal to the Chinese model, it has never been a slavish copy; it has involved adapta-tion, rather than adoption, of Chinese methods – perhaps the greatest lesson Nyerere learned from China was the concept of self-reliance. He has described his attitude to other models in an essay on socialism:

Why should Tanzania not learn from the agricultural communes of China? Their experience could promote thought and ideas about our own rural organization, provided that we go to learn, and proceed to think-not to copy. Why can we not learn from the Korean success in rural transformation in comparison with continuing difficulties in other communist countries? Do the Cuban experiments in adult education have nothing to teach us? Agricultural organiza-tion, rural transformation, adult education, are all problems we have to deal with in Tanzania; why should we not study the techniques used by other men to see if they could usefully be adapted to meet our needs, or if they provide a clue to the solution of a difficulty we are experiencing?

Nor do we have to confine our attention to development in communist countries. The cooperative settlements of Israel, the cooperative organization of Denmark and Sweden, have all accumu-lated great experience which we could learn from. Even the most avowedly capitalist countries have something to teach us – for example, the techniques by which they encourage workers to increase their output . . .[8]

On his return from China Nyerere immediately impressed on his people, and more particularly on his officials, the need to emulate the Chinese examples of frugality and discipline, which he had so admired. There had, in any case, been criticism in the National Assembly and elsewhere of ministerial extravagance, and officials who rode around in expensive Mercedes Benz cars had been jokingly described as a new tribe – the 'Wabenzi' (Wa being the Swahili prefix for people, or tribe). A Member of Parliament recalled that during his visit to China, Nyerere had been astonished to learn that China's Foreign Ministry possessed only ten cars, and he urged the Wabenzi to cut down their purchases. Nyerere had also been impressed by the fact that in Peking he had toasted Sino-Tanzanian friendship in orange juice, and thenceforth no hard drinks were served at Tanzanian official functions. Later, Nyerere and his ministers reduced their own salaries.

Whereas frugality, at any rate official frugality, could be imposed from the top, discipline and hard work could only come from below. A sense of discipline and a love of hard work, it is true to say, have been engagingly absent from the Tanzanian character, and Nyerere has never lost an opportunity to stress that without them the task of nation-building is near-impossible. If you cannot force people to work hard, you can at least show them what can be achieved by hard work – Nyerere has himself set an example, and used others as examples. He praised, for instance, the speed with which the Italians constructed the Tanzania-Zambia oil pipeline, and told Tanzanian workers to follow their example. But it is the Chinese who have provided most 'hard work models', and at the ground-breaking or completion (usually ahead of schedule) of Chinese-aided projects, Nyerere and his ministers have drawn the Tanzanians' attention to the hard work and dedication of the Chinese experts. At the opening of the Friendship Textile Mill, Nyerere told the Tanzanian workers: 'Disciplined work is essential, and here once again our Chinese technicians have set us a great example.' He once said in conversation that the

Chinese example of hard work was probably their most valuable contribution to Tanzania's development.

The formalization of Nyerere's socialist thinking came in the Arusha Declaration of 1967, which nationalized foreign banks and certain other foreign-owned enterprises, but stopped short of total nationalization. At a meeting of the TANU party to discuss the Declaration, Nyerere, admitting that many people had said 'there's a lot of Mao Tse-tung in it', emphasized that Arusha was 'based on the Tanzanian people's needs, not on Chinese philosophies'. He later told a press conference that 'only a bunch of fools' would think it took Mao Tse-tung to tell him of his own country's social injustices – 'but if it is Mao Tse-tung, brothers, learn from it.'[9]

It was to be expected that in Tanzania's 'leftward march' some would march faster than others, and, in Nyerere's words, 'go all the way to Peking'. He therefore increasingly found himself in a middle position, criticized by the West and his own conservative wing for going too far, and by extremists in Tanzania for not going far enough. He was quite capable of defending his policies against both criticisms, which he did in his farewell speech at the end of his second visit to China in 1968, at the height of the cultural revolution:

The friendship between Tanzania and the People's Republic of China is a friendship between most unequal equals. Perhaps for that reason some other nations of the world find it hard to understand: they are always trying to suggest that Tanzania is a satellite of China, or – alternatively – that our friendship is about to break up. This is probably an expression of wishful thinking, or else it is a misunderstanding of the nature of friendship and an assumption that friendship is exclusive – that you cannot be friends with many nations if these are not themselves close friends.

I admit that in the modern world real friendship between very big nations and very small nations is a comparatively rare thing. For friendship in these circumstances means a recognition on both sides that the difference in size, wealth and power are irrelevant to the equality which exists between sovereign nations. It means that both sides recognize the differences, but treat them as facts which have relevance only when the friendship itself needs them, or can benefit from them.

Mr Premier, the friendship between China and Tanzania is based on these principles of respect and equality. It is not an exclusive thing, and we do not interfere in each other's affairs. When we feel able to cooperate we do so; if either of us feels reluctant, then we move on to some other matter. I can state quite categorically that Tanzania is enriched by this friendship, and we value it. No outside nation will be able to interfere with it; only we ourselves, by our own actions to one another, could destroy it. I have therefore no reason to believe that friendship between Tanzania and China will not continue indefinitely, and grow stronger as time passes.

Having said that I would like to say further, Mr Prime Minister, that my colleagues and I have not come to China to ask China to place a protective nuclear umbrella over Tanzania. Colonialism in Africa passed under many labels. Some of our countries were called colonies; others, protectorates; some provinces; and yet others, trust territories. In fact they were all colonies, and all of them rightly rejected their colonial status. If therefore I had come to ask China to declare Tanzania to be her nuclear protectorate, the people of Tanzania would have every right to denounce me as a lackey of nuclear neo-colonialism.[10]

Students

As in many other countries, the extreme left of Tanzanian opinion has been found amongst students. At Dar es Salaam University I was handed in 1970 a leaflet, reproduced below, from the Tanzanian Friends of China 'Revolutionary Committee'. The possibility that it was a fake, planted either by Nyerere's conservative opponents or even by friends of the Soviet Union, should not be discounted. Certainly I heard nothing more of the group.

FELLOW TANZANIANS

We, a group of young Tanzanians, armed with the ideas of Mao Tse-tung, have decided to found the organization 'TANZANIAN FRIENDS OF CHINA' (TFC).

We consider that the People's Republic of China is our only friend and comrade in the battle against modern revisionism and US imperialism.

We consider that many of our leaders merely talk of socialism while in reality they have come to terms with modern revisionism and US imperialism.

We do not want Nyerere's type of socialism!

Our main task is to fight the clique in power which has taken the capitalist path, overthrow it and create a real people's Tanzania, permanently friendly to China.

LONG LIVE THE ALL-ILLUMINATING
IDEAS OF MAO TSE-TUNG!
DOWN WITH THE REACTIONARY AND
REVISIONIST CLIQUE!
MAY THE RED SUN RISE OVER OUR COUNTRY!

TFC Revolutionary Committee

As far as I am aware, there was little direct contact between the Chinese embassy and students, although there were always considerable quantities of Chinese literature at the university, both bought locally from the Friendship Bookshop or mailed direct from Peking. (Chinese literature was also freely on sale in the town, and capitalistically minded children used to buy Mao's *Red Book* at the Chinese bookshop for resale, at a modest profit, to tourists.)

But however spontaneous the students' enthusiasm for China, Nyerere found it necessary to warn them in his inaugural speech as Chancellor of the University that

... we have always known that London University and Moscow University must each try to understand, and be understood by, their respective societies in order to serve their nation's people. Yet it is only recently that we have realized a similar necessity in Africa. Our universities have aimed at understanding Western society, and being understood by Western society, apparently assuming that by this means they are preparing their students to be – and themselves being – of service to African society.

This fault has been recognized, and the attitude it involved has been in the course of correction in East Africa – and particularly in Dar es Salaam – for some time. But there is now the danger of an understandable – but nevertheless a foolish – reaction to it. The universities of Africa which aim at being 'progressive' will react by trying to understand, and be understood by, Russian, East European, or Chinese society. Once again they will be fooling themselves into believing that they are thus preparing themselves to serve African society. Yet surely it is clear that to do this is simply to replay the old farce with different characters. . . . The University of Dar es Salaam has not been founded to turn out intellectual apes whether of the right or of the left. We are training for a socialist, self-respecting and self-reliant Tanzania.[11]

China has also won some uncritical admirers amongst Tanzania's journalists, initially those working for the TANU party newspaper the *Nationalist*, and, after its nationalization and re-christening as the *Daily News* – the *Standard*. Journalists have visited China as guests of the Afro-Asian Journalists' Association and of other friendship organizations, and the NCNA office in Dar es Salaam has maintained close links with both newspapers.

Apart from using Chinese jargon, the newspapers have taken an uncompromisingly pro-Chinese line on almost every major world issue. The *News* managed to defend China's actions over Bangladesh which even her most uncritical friends could interpret only in terms of blatant state opportunism and self-interest. In an article entitled 'The Capitalist Jihar' the *News* wrote that 'According to bourgeois political "analysts" the Bengali question has now been answered. They take the Indian view that Sheikh Mujib is the representative of the Bengali hopes and aspirations!'

For most people this indeed would have been the correct view, but, according to the *News*, Mujib was not only an out and out capitalist, but an exploiter of the masses; it went on to ask why India should be blamed for the situation more than Pakistan. Apparently because '... the Indian ruling class is richer and more powerful and therefore the greater of the two devils'. China's 'seemingly contradictory policy' is tortuously explained: 'Pakistani leaders are not socialists. But in the long run it might be better to have taken sides with less clever capitalists, rather than with Bangladesh under an outright and sophisticated capitalist.' Not even NCNA went to these lengths to explain China's actions, and the article betrays the sort of sychophancy which Nyerere is doing his best to discourage.

The *Nationalist* has expressed its admiration mainly through the use of Chinese jargon, although it, too, has not been averse to a gentle twisting of meaning. After the opening of a French-built textile mill in northern Tanzania in 1970, Nyerere gave a somewhat surprising interview to the *Agence France Presse*, the import of which was that if China thought she was going to interfere in Tanzania's internal affairs she had better 'watch out'. (There appeared to be no particular reason at that time for him to issue such a warning.) The *Standard* headline read, 'Nyerere warns Chinese'. The *Nationalist* said, 'Mwalimu [Nyerere's Swahili sobriquet, meaning Teacher] praises Chinese.'

The *Nationalist*'s caption writer also appeared to have come under Chinese influence. For example, under a picture of schoolchildren watering their vegetable garden was written the stirring caption: 'Under the revolutionary banner of "Education for Self-Reliance" an unprecedented all-round spirit of love for manual labour has developed among the nation's pupils and students.' My own favourite was an account of a road accident. Under a picture of a battered motor-cycle was the simple description: 'An oppressed scooter.'

THE CHINESE IN TANZANIA

If, for friendship's sake, it was necessary for the Tanzanians to be circumspect in their criticism of China, the Chinese on their part behaved with meticulous correctness in their relations with Tanzania. We have already seen that in the early part of the relationship there were good state reasons why China wished to be on good terms with Tanzania: through Tanzania she transported arms and other supplies to Burundi, and so on to the Congolese rebels; Dar es Salaam was a centre of contact with the liberation movements, and the Chinese embassy the centre of all Chinese operations in East and Central Africa. Tanzania was in fact a firm foothold (or 'bridgehead' as the South Africans would have it) on the African continent, and China was determined that through her good behaviour there it would remain so.

In practical matters China's sense of timing was perfect. Her offer to build the railway came at a time when Nyerere felt disillusioned with the West and without a rich and powerful friend to turn to, just as an earlier offer to help train the army came after the 1964 mutiny of the British-trained army. China also stepped in after the withdrawal of British aid following UDI in 1965 and offered to finance some of the plan projects which the Tanzanians had thought they would have to abandon. The farm implements factory (Nyerere has said an agricultural revolution could be effected in Tanzania if farmers could be persuaded to turn from the hoe to the plough) and the Friendship Textile Mill were both tailored precisely to Tanzania's needs. Later, China's offer to take over training of the armed forces, following the termination of the Canadian military training agreement, was yet another example of China proving that she was a 'friend in need'.

The range of aid to Tanzania has also been outstanding, and few sectors of the population have not benefited in one way or another from Chinese largesse. Apart from the large-scale development projects, there have been Chinese donations for the Tanzanian Red Cross, aid for the preservation of antiquities, a cash grant for a university complex, including a bookshop; and for the Youth League a mixed bag of gifts included a set of musical instruments, thirty footballs and a desk and chair for the Secretary-General.

But Tanzania has been more than a model country in which to demonstrate the aptness and disinterestedness of Chinese aid; it has also been a showcase for the whole Chinese ethos and way of life. The hard work and sense of discipline of the Chinese technicians has already been mentioned, but also on show have been their spartan living standards (six Chinese, in bunks, to a room in their Dar es Salaam hostel), simple clothes, physical fitness (all the embassy staff swam across a Dar es Salaam bay to celebrate Mao's swim in the Yangtse) and a generally inconspicuous, unflamboyant presence – contrasted favourably by Tanzanian leaders to the conspicuous consumption of some Western diplomats and aid personnel. Not all these qualities have necessarily been admired by the Tanzanian man-in-the-street, or even considered qualities. But to Tanzanian officials, and possibly to Tanzania's neighbours, they have served as an antidote to the sinister, revolutionary image conjured up by China's enemies and to a lesser extent by China's own disruptive activites. As an English journalist visiting Tanzania laconically remarked: 'They seem a very mellow peril.'

Secretive attitude

However, amongst Tanzanian officials at almost all levels, a highly defensive attitude about what the Chinese were doing has always prevailed. They have cloaked Chinese activities with an unnecessary veil of secrecy which has naturally aroused suspicion. I am aware that I speak as an 'outsider', a white journalist (and *all* journalists tend to be regarded in Africa as spies) who, on a number of occasions, was either thwarted from getting a story about the Chinese or arrested while trying to get one. For example, my written permission to visit the Tanzam marshalling-yard site in company with some Tanzanian and Zambian journalists was revoked at the last moment, after a suggestion that I could be 'spying' for the West. And a camera, as not only I but a number of far more innocent tourists discovered, was a lethal weapon if used within hundreds of yards of any Chinese project. Armed with written permission from at least five different authorities I was still arrested and my cameras confiscated while covering a story about Zambian copper being shipped through Dar es Salaam harbour – because there happened to be a Chinese ship unloading in the background. For the same reason any number of tourists had their cameras confiscated for taking what they thought was an innocent snap of a pretty harbour scene.

Far worse, was the case of a Nigerian student, Cornelius Ogunsanwo, who had applied to the Tanzanian embassy in London to visit Tanzania to do some field research for his thesis on the Chinese in Africa (some of his work is quoted in this book). The request was referred to Dar es Salaam where he arrived in December 1969. He had spent less than a month in the country before his arrest and illegal detention – 'in inhumane and animalistic conditions', according to him – for thirty-nine days. He became a *cause célèbre* in Tanzania because after his release he revealed the previously unknown existence of a large number of political prisoners improperly detained, but his case also illustrated the paranoid attitude of the Tanzanians to *anyone* (Ogunsanwo, after all, was an African) showing any interest, even an academic one, in Chinese activities. Typical of this was the Swahili newspaper *Ngurumo*'s editorial about the affair (which was partly sour grapes at the fact that they had been scooped over a very good story by their rival, the *Standard*), which blandly accepted that any acts could be perpetrated in the name of 'security' and that Ogunsanwo's allegations about degrading prison conditions and inhumane treatment could have been justified if he had been studying

Tanzania's developmental progress, but not since he was investigating the activities of the Chinese.

Shortly after the Ogunsanwo incident, the *Standard* took the opportunity of the fifth anniversary of the treaty of friendship between Tanzania and China to try and clear up some of the 'misconceptions that the agreement has engendered not only overseas, but to some extent in Tanzania as well'. The *Standard* commented:

The Western powers tend to regard all relations between the developing countries of Africa and the socialist world as sinister in its implications. This arises understandably from the post-war conflicts and is a part of the history of the contradictions between capitalism and socialism.

Yet Tanzania has had no part in the earlier conflicts, and is a country dedicated to a socialist ideal. It is extraordinary therefore that some official circles have developed a thin skin of sensitivity to any mention of China's role here; that an air of secrecy has been created where none should exist; and that a smokescreen of suspicion is thrown up when anyone attempts to discuss or analyse and evaluate Chinese aid to Tanzania . . .

Except where the interests of national security demand, the development in Tanzania arising from Chinese aid should be proclaimed, a matter of pride, not shame. The current air of spurious discretion is both unnecessary and immature. (20 February 1970)

It is difficult to say how much of this secrecy has been encouraged by the Chinese themselves; what does seem likely is that they have taken their cue from Peking: during China's own isolation the Chinese technicians did seem isolated, in the cultural revolution they were militant and during the diplomatic offensive they were diplomatic. In recent years there does certainly seem to have been a relaxation, both on the Tanzanian and the Chinese sides, and in some cases Western journalists have been able, for example, to inspect work on the railway. Earlier, however, the Chinese were partly responsible for the secrecy which surrounded their activities, screening their projects with high fences or bush and assuming near-police powers to eject or arrest strangers in the area. Having stressed the 'racial' nature of their relations with Tanzania (the Chinese chargé at the opening of the Friendship Textile Mill said the project was proof that Asians and Africans could stand by themselves without any help from Europeans), the Chinese seemed anxious to exclude white people completely from their dealings with the Tanzanians. I know that a senior white expatriate officer at the Ministry of Development Planning, technically responsible for liaison between the ministry and the railway authority, was asked to leave several key meetings on the grounds that the railway was an exclusively Chinese-African matter. Another incident involved a Canadian instructor who was training some Tanzanian soldiers at Naching-wea, in southern Tanzania. Nearby, other soldiers were being trained by a Chinese instructor, who ordered a canvas screen to be erected around 'his' area so that the white man could not see what was going on. In another incident the government revoked their previously given authority to a European businessman to develop as a tourist resort a small island outside Dar es Salaam harbour. The Chinese had apparently claimed that as it was close to a naval harbour they were building it constituted a 'security risk'. Finally, the (Asian) auditors asked to prepare the balance sheet of the Friendship Textile Mill were given only sufficient figures (in 1971) for them to conclude rather tentatively that the mill made a small profit the previous year, but they added the rider that 'the terms for the payment for the value of the above assets are covered by an agreement . . . the details of which were not available'.

The special relationship between the two countries has also been recognized by the Tanzanians granting, or the Chinese taking, what could best be described as quasi-diplomatic privileges. These, naturally, have infuriated and puzzled Westerners in Tanzania, as well as occasionally upsetting the Tanzanians themselves. It is not clear whether these privileges have been formally granted, whether the Chinese simply take them, or whether minor Tanzanian officials are in awe of the Chinese and turn a blind eye. Certainly the language barrier means that the Chinese could in any case get away with quite a lot. For the most part these privileges are petty – Chinese official cars, jeeps and lorries, for example, appear to be able to park in Dar es Salaam where they like, and never attract a parking ticket. I have also watched Chinese lorries blatantly jump long queues, and their drivers tend to monopolize the middle of the road, expecting all other traffic to get out of their way. In 1973 Tanzanian authorities were concerned about the effect increased traffic was having on the recently American-completed Dar es Salaam to Morogoro stretch of the Tanzania-Zambia road and set up a weighbridge to ensure that vehicles were not overloaded. Chinese drivers taking supplies down to the Tanzam railhead quite simply refused to stop. At the airport the Chinese were not prevented from greeting new arrivals on the tarmac, although everyone else was required to show a security pass. During a meat shortage in Dar es Salaam in 1972, Chinese invariably went to the head of long queues and often cleared out the shop's entire stock in front of the amazed gaze of other shoppers. I 'suffered' from this form of treatment myself once: I turned up for a National Assembly debate without a tie and was refused admission. A few minutes later the NCNA correspondent appeared, without a tie – and was welcomed profusely.

Every now and then these fairly regular privileges would be extended. In January 1968, the Chinese accountant at the Friendship Textile Mill refused to give evidence at a magistrate's court in the case of a clerk at the mill stealing 7000 shillings. Normally, the court would have ordered the arrest of a reluctant witness; in this case the charge was dropped. Then there was the case of the screening of the film *Shoes of the Fisherman*, which portrays a starving China proposing to invade South-East Asia to feed her population, a situation saved by the intervention of a Russian Pope pledging the Roman Catholic church's wealth to feed the Chinese people. The film featured a fictitious Chinese leader, Chairman Peng. The Chinese embassy had unsuccessfully requested cuts to be made in the film, and the full version was shown at the charity *première*. The next day the film was taken off before the general public had a chance to see it. reportedly after the Chinese embassy had appealed directly to Nyerere. This was one of the very few occasions when the Chinese actually criticized Tanzania – an embassy spokesman told me: 'This film is anti-China. We feel sorry it was shown. It was an unfriendly action to China.' A similar incident occurred when the embassy successfully persuaded the *Standard* to drop a series entitled 'Barbarians from the West' which portrayed a weak China being ravished by Western imperialists. The Chinese assumption that they were in a privileged position led also to a celebrated incident near Mbeya in south-west Tanzania, in which the Chinese railway builders became involved in a brawl with Americans building the Tanzania-Zambia highway. The Chinese had apparently asked the Americans to stop work in the area while they made a survey. When the Americans refused the Chinese surrounded their vehicles and shouted slogans at them for five hours. Police were called from Mbeya and the Chinese scuffled with them too. The Chinese involved were subsequently sent home.

Tanzania through Chinese eyes

Through their many cooperative ventures with Tanzania and daily contacts with officials, the Chinese would have built up a very comprehensive picture of Tanzanian political life. They were, and are, fully involved in the country's commercial, military and developmental life. The Chinese diplomats astonished everyone by their hard work, frequently making presentations, visiting project sites, holding and attending receptions and constantly broadening their range of knowledge and contacts. Embassy staff, for example, were often seen at parties of friendly countries such as North Korea, North Vietnam and Cuba, with whom it was assumed they had information-pooling arrangements; they were also very close to the Guinean and Egyptian embassies, from whom they must have gained African viewpoints about Tanzanian politics and about their own position in Tanzania.

In one way, what they would have seen of the government machinery and learned about the general 'feel' of political life could not have pleased them. It might be instructive to look at the situation as it must have appeared to the Chinese. First was Tanzania's considerable reliance on foreigners, mainly British, to staff the senior and middle-grade civil service posts. In 1968, for example, there were 1619 non-Tanzanians in the Tanzanian government apparatus. In State House, Nyerere filled a number of key positions with long-serving British officials, such as Joan Wicken, his own personal assistant. Throughout the country there were British teachers, British farmers, missionaries, businessmen and minor officials. An

Englishman, Derek Bryceson, was even a member of the cabinet. The educational and judicial system were British. The vast bulk of trade was conducted with Britain. Finally, the language spoken was English. As the Chinese ambassador once, somewhat despairingly, told a senior British diplomat: 'You even have your own newspaper here (the *Standard*)!' No Chinese has ever held a government position in Tanzania, and it seems unlikely one ever will. A position of privilege, even of prestige, should not therefore be confused with one of influence. One recalls once again Nyerere's remark that 'the whole influence of this country is Western'. Chinese influence does not extend in Tanzania to substantive matters, and propaganda asserting that it does is quite false.

Tanzania's friendship with China has stimulated various responses from her neighbours and from African countries further afield, ranging from outright hostility to genuine interest. These reactions have in no way influenced Sino-Tanzanian bilateral relations – as Nyerere said in another context 'Tanzania would not allow her friends to choose her enemies for her.'

Apart from South Africa, Rhodesia and Portugal five independent African governments with varying degrees of inaccuracy have held the Chinese in Tanzania responsible for adverse developments in their own countries. As we saw earlier, President Banda of Malawi accused the Chinese embassy in Dar es Salaam of being behind a plot to oust him in 1964, but he produced no evidence to back up the charge.[12] In the whole of Black Africa Banda's anti-communism has been paralleled only by that of President Houphouet-Boigny, and his accusations against the Chinese should be judged in the light of an interview he gave in 1965, in which he stated that

We should be blind if we failed to realize that China, which is overpopulated and would soon have a thousand million mouths to feed, looks enviously at our huge continent populated by only 300 million. If we are not careful we shall be served up as Chinese soup.[13]

Nevertheless, it should be remembered that Banda's policy of cooperation with the apartheid regimes, extending even to the provision of military facilities which could be regarded as a direct threat to Tanzania, has made him a neighbour beyond the pale as far as Nyerere is concerned, and for years the two countries have been in a state of semi-hostility. They have a border dispute on Lake Malawi which flares up intermittently, and the granting of exile to Banda's dismissed ministers was an obvious provocation. Thus, the story told by a captured dissident at a press conference arranged by Banda in 1967, that he and sixty other supporters of the exiled ministers had been trained at a Chinese-run guerrilla camp near Dar es Salaam and that others had gone for training in Peking, Cuba and Algeria, should probably not be discounted. If true, Nyerere's actions could hardly be described as an enlightened example of brotherly African solidarity, but until a slight détente in 1973, the Tanzanian President regarded Banda as an intrinsic part of the white power bloc and his removal therefore of service to Black Africa. This then was essentially an internecine African dispute, and the alleged use of Chinese instructors to train Malawian dissidents was neither here nor there. Banda's emphasis on the supposed role of the Chinese was simply a device to try and minimize the real indigenous opposition to his rule and win sympathy from the anti-communist camp, a trick presumably learned from the South African advisers in his information ministry.

Two other cases of African governments blaming the Chinese in Tanzania for subversion in their own countries have already been discussed: the Congolese, with justification, held that the rebellion in eastern Congo could not be sustained without Chinese arms, shipped through Tanzania. Until Mobutu established relations with China in 1973, the Chinese in Tanzania were openly regarded as a 'threat' to the security of Zaire; the second case was Nigeria's belief, almost certainly mistaken, that China herself was supplying arms directly to Biafra – via Tanzania (see page 160).

Tanzania's relations with her two partners in the East African Community, Uganda and Kenya, have also been affected by her friendship with China. Until the coup which brought General Amin to power in 1970, President Milton

Obote, a close friend of Nyerere's, seemed in some ways to be taking his cue from Tanzania. A gradual swing to the left culminated in the Poor Man's Charter, Uganda's version of the Arusha Declaration, while in foreign policy an initial lukewarmness towards China was replaced by increasingly friendlier relations, marked by substantial aid and trade agreements. But Nyerere's refusal to recognize the Amin régime put the whole future of the Community in jeopardy and led to rapidly worsening bilateral relations between Tanzania and Uganda.[14] During one of the skirmishes between Amin's troops and supporters of Obote – who was living in Dar es Salaam – the Ugandan army claimed to have killed a 'Chinese colonel', whose body, in a Tanzanian army uniform, was subsequently put on display outside the Kampala international conference centre. The dead man turned out to be a Tanzanian policeman of mixed Tanzanian/German parentage. Amin may have been genuinely misled by the man's physiognomy but, whether he was or not, he, like Banda, recognized the propaganda potential of raising a Chinese spectre. He had earlier, without any apparent evidence, told a press conference in London when on a visit to seek military equipment and military training that 'three Chinese' had been amongst guerrilla groups infiltrating from Tanzania. South Africa joyfully seized on the incident, and Radio Johannesburg predictably commented that it could not

... be viewed as an isolated incident without military or political significance. Against the background of the intense Communist Chinese penetration of Tanzania it is a significant pointer to the role China can be expected to play in the future in subversion in east and southern Africa through the auspices of the Tanzanian government.

Because of her own unhappy experiences with China, Kenya's attitude towards a large Chinese presence in Tanzania has been understandably cautious, although relations between the neighbours have never been directly exacerbated as a result of Tanzania's friendship with China. However, because of Kenya's own attitude towards China and, to a lesser extent, her lukewarm relations with which she regards as her 'radical' neighbour, Nairobi has often been used as a launching pad for anti-

Chinese propaganda, aimed at Tanzania. One obvious forgery, a picture purporting to show a recruitment drive in China for workers on the Tanzam railway and with a caption suggesting that after completion of the project they would be 'settled' in Tanzania, was fully publicized in the Kenyan press – 'never loth to portray events in Tanzania in an unfavourable manner', as the *Standard* commented. Another anti-Chinese propaganda pamphlet, entitled 'Revolution in Africa' and describing China's plans to subvert Africa, was also distributed in Nairobi, while 'Nairobi sources' were credited with starting a preposterous rumour – that Chinese toys on sale in Kenya were coated with poisonous lead, 'to kill capitalist children'. Tanzania also reacted angrily when the Kenyan-based *Reporter* magazine claimed the Chinese had duped the Tanzanians into naming the first ship of the Sino-Tanzanian line after Cheng Ho, by describing him simply as a great Chinese admiral and omitting to mention that he was a eunuch and an 'expansionist'. The line's general manager retorted that the ship was to be named *Ushirika* and that 'this vexing story about the admiral's physical condition and dreams of empire is a naked and contemptuous provocation'.

On a governmental level, it will be recalled that Kenya's invitation to Chou En-lai to visit Nairobi was cancelled in 1965 as a direct result of his speech in Dar es Salaam emphasizing that 'an exceedingly favourable situation for revolution' still prevailed in Africa.

But Chinese activities in Tanzania have not everywhere stimulated adverse reactions. Partly because of the correctness of China's behaviour in Tanzania, partly because of the great personal influence of Nyerere on Kaunda, Zambia's attitude towards China has altered radically. Immediately after Zambia's independence, Kaunda, with both a Christian and a Western-inspired distrust of communism, adopted a distant attitude towards China.[15] The delay in finally accepting China's offer to build the railway was generally attributed to Kaunda's unwillingness to deal with the Chinese and his hope that a counter offer would be forthcoming from the West, and the preliminary survey was reportedly only conducted on the Tanzanian side, due to the Zambians' fear of 'letting the Chinese in'. Nyerere's insistence that the Chinese offer was

10

genuine, and that Africa had nothing to fear from China's friendship, was instrumental in changing Kaunda's own attitude – and he is now amongst the most vocal admirers of the Chinese.

Other African countries must have observed, more indirectly, the benefits to be won from establishing relations with China, and noted Nyerere's success in hosting a large Chinese presence in his country. Although we do not know, it is quite possible that leaders of other African countries may have asked him at meetings of the OAU or in other forums for his opinion of the Chinese, and whether they should establish relations. He would certainly have encouraged them to do so. Some of these leaders paid state visits to Tanzania, and could see for themselves how beneficial and relevant Chinese aid was. Faced with the decision whether or not to recognize China, a leader like Haile Selassie, for example, who had visited Tanzania, might well have been swayed by what he had seen there and heard from Nyerere. Even visitors, from further afield, like Forbes Burnham of Guyana who was most impressed by Chinese projects, were able to see what the Chinese were doing in Tanzania and form their own opinions.

Another distant state whose relations with Tanzania were very much affected by Sino-Tanzanian friendship was, of course, the Soviet Union. Tanzania has posed something of a problem for the Soviets, a radical country, acknowledged by their own theoreticians to be 'on the road of non-capitalist development', yet beholden to China and severely critical of the Soviet Union's foreign policies. Their response has been to adopt a low profile in Tanzania, content to maintain a watching brief on the Chinese and as cordial as possible relations with the government. Just how low this profile has been can be measured by the Soviet Union's aid commitment to Tanzania, limited to a £7 million loan made in 1966 and even now scarcely drawn on. With the obvious Chinese determination to make a considerable impact with aid, and the Tanzam railway a clear rival to the Aswan Dam as a prestige project, the Soviet Union has probably calculated that it would be a waste of effort and money to try and compete, just as China would not attempt seriously to challenge the Soviet aid effort in Egypt.

Apart from the squabbling at the Moshi AAPSO conference and the propaganda use made by the Soviet Union of Chinese aid to Tanzania as an example of how aid should not be given (and by China of how it should) neither side has sought to impose the Sino-Soviet dispute on Tanzania.[16] The Chinese have refrained partly because they learned early on of Nyerere's resentment at attempts to do so, partly because their very presence and preponderance in Tanzania is in itself propaganda victory enough. They have also been well served by the Soviet Union's own actions, notably the invasion of Czechoslovakia, which produced such sharp reactions from the Tanzanian government; and by the lukewarm reception given to Nyerere when he visited Moscow in 1970, a visit described to me by one of his party as 'a complete waste of time – we just marched down long corridors at the Hermitage'. The only occasion, to my knowledge of the Chinese 'using' Nyerere was when he (very unusually) accepted a Chinese embassy invitation to attend a 'private' party, at which an anti-Soviet film about the Sino-Soviet border dispute was shown. Radio Peking broadcast news of this visit, implying Nyerere's approval for the Chinese position. He was apparently upset when told about this, and complained to the embassy.

On a more philosophical plane, I feel that the somewhat cold, 'economic' Soviet communism would be alien to Nyerere, for whom socialism must be 'people-centred'. And on a practical level China's policies of self-reliance and rural development have far more attraction for Tanzania than do the heavy industrialization policies of the Soviet Union.

On Zanzibar Karume appeared to be more tolerant towards anti-Sovietism; he was, for example, prepared to listen to Vice-Consul Liu Ching-yu describe the Czechoslovakian invasion and Biafran 'genocide' as examples of collaboration between Soviet revisionism and Western capitalism in a speech on the nineteenth anniversary of the founding of the PRC. Karume later echoed the insult by referring to 'socialist countries where socialism is not practised'.[17] But even in Zanzibar Chinese doctors have to practise in a hospital built by the Soviet Union, and still called the Lenin Hospital. Still, according to them, Lenin's mantle has fallen, not on Brezhnev, but on Mao.

'The Quid pro Quo.'

One can understand the curiosity of journalists in wanting to know 'what's in it for China', as well as the frustration felt by Nyerere and other Tanzanian leaders at the frequency of the question. Almost every interviewer or group of journalists from all parts of the world have tried to discover, from what they take to be Tanzanians hiding a guilty secret, what is the 'quid pro quo' for China's friendship. On their part they cannot conceive of an altruistic, disinterested relationship between two sovereign states of such unequal size. Nyerere cannot see why they do not believe him when he says that China has never pressurized him to do anything he did not want to, or even demanded a substantial 'return' for her 'investment' in Tanzania – that nothing, in short, but good has come from the relationship. In fact, of course, as we have seen throughout this book, the friendship of African nations has of itself been of considerable benefit and encouragement to China. The misunderstanding about the friendship between Tanzania and China arises, I think, because the benefits to China are intangible, whereas those to Tanzania are tangible, and Westerners find it very difficult to equate the two. On the one hand, they see a great railway project with thousands of technicians from a powerful state 'swarming' – as they would put it – over the countryside, they see the huge involvement of China in the Tanzanian economy and in the armed forces; on the other hand, they see a poor and weak African state, desperate for help. When they ask her leader what China expects in return for all this help he ingenuously replies: 'Friendship'. They shake their heads in disbelief – it cannot be so. Either he has been misled or he is misleading.

He is not misleading, and he is in fact answering their question, because the 'friendship' of Tanzania is precisely 'what's in it for China'. This friendship enables China to attain other goals, not always directly connected with Tanzania. Firstly, as we have seen, it can be held up by China to other states as a model of China's friendship; it can be used internally to demonstrate that China is carrying out her internationalist duty and it can even be used to train Chinese in selflessness, much as the Americans use the Peace Corps in a similar way. Finally, in a more practical way, Tanzania's friendship, and more particularly the building of the Tanzam railway has ensured a Chinese presence in a part of the world which for Sino-Soviet, strategic, trade and revolutionary reasons China must regard as important. For the Chinese must have calculated that once a project as important as the railway was started not even a reactionary leader thrown up by a possible coup against Nyerere would request its abandonment; it therefore virtually guaranteed their presence until the mid-1970s, and probably beyond.

Tanzania's tangible gains from China's friendship are more obvious, but not necessarily greater. Apart from the material benefits of Chinese-aided projects, Tanzania has been able to draw on Chinese developmental experience and use her friendship to demonstrate the validity of her claim that she was pursuing a truly non-aligned foreign policy. But that Nyerere realized the dangers of over-reliance on one source of aid, was demonstrated in 1972 when he said that Tanzania would not seek further aid from China until after completion of the railway.[18] To a cynical world, the relationship has truly been remarkable, but until there is evidence to prove the contrary this friendship between most unequal equals will simply have to be taken at its face value.

Notes

1. *People's Daily*, 18 June 1968, in article entitled 'Welcome to President Nyerere'.
2. Ogunsanwo, op. cit., p. 183. He was told this by a Tanzanian minister.
3. Nyerere's speech in Peking, 17 February 1965.
4. Nyerere's press conference. Dar es Salaam, 24 February 1965.
5. Nyerere's speech in Peking, 17 February 1965.
6. Press conference, 24 February 1965.
7. *Peking Review*, No. 9, 26 February 1965.
8. *Freedom and Socialism*, an essay by J. K. Nyerere, pp. 21–2.
9. Reuters dispatch from Dar es Salaam, 4 March 1968.
10. Tanzania Information Services, 21 June 1968.
11. Tanzania Information Services, 29 August 1970.
12. An authoritative source, however, has told me that the Chinese did definitely channel funds to Malawian dissidents through the Dar es Salaam embassy.
13. *Le Progrès*, Leopoldville, 20 September 1965.

14. In February 1971, shortly after Amin took power, Somalia and Tanzania were preparing to back an invasion of Uganda to reinstate Obote. But according to a well-informed British journalist resident in Dar es Salaam Chou En-lai sent a message to Nyerere through the Chinese ambassador in Tanzania firstly drawing his attention to the principle of non-interference in the internal affairs of other countries. 'Secondly he warned that if African countries intervened to unseat Amin, whom the British initially preferred to Obote, they were creating the risk that British troops stationed in Kenya and elsewhere might be put in to support the Ugandan soldier against them.' (David Martin, *General Amin*, Faber and Faber, London, 1974, p. 55.) Nyerere evidently heeded the advice for the invasion was called off.

15. For example, he appealed to *China* to act in the spirit of Bandung over the Sino-Indian border dispute, betraying his belief in China's guilt.

16. But Russians and Chinese never mixed in Tanzania. The Tass news agency correspondent in Zanzibar told me that in three years on the island the NCNA man had only ever once approached him to make conversation – about the 'errors of revisionism'. And once at a press conference at TANU headquarters the NCNA 'team' unleashed a verbal attack on their unfortunate Soviet colleagues, to the surprise of assembled journalists.

17. Reuters, Zanzibar, 2 October 1968.

18. But see p. 224. Nyerere has not explained why he accepted the new loan, in apparent contradiction to this resolve. However, it is in fact unlikely that the £31 million will be *drawn* in before completion of the railway.

16
CONCLUSIONS

'We should take long range views. . . .'
SECRET CHINESE ARMY DOCUMENT

THE concept and conduct of an outward-looking foreign policy, based notionally on the equality of sovereign states, is alien, and possibly repugnant, to the Chinese mentality. Until the end of the last century there was no bureaucratic machinery in Peking for dealing with foreign governments on an equal basis. People who lived beyond the boundaries of the Empire – the world, in Chinese eyes – could come, as was fitting, to pay tribute to the Emperor and to acknowledge his authority. China sent no ambassadors abroad and had virtually no dealings with foreign governments.

The European and Asian invasions, the imposition of humiliating 'unequal treaties', the plundering and sequestration of Chinese territory, the ineffectual attempts to adapt Western forms of government and Western technology to counter these threats to the existence of the Empire, the horrors of a prolonged civil war, in which one side was backed by a foreign power, and finally, real or imagined betrayal by the one foreign ally she thought she could trust, rudely introduced China to modern 'diplomacy'. It is against this background that the foreign policy of the People's Republic must be judged. The most urgent concern has been the security of the state; internally the most important consideration has been consolidation of the authority of a strong, central government. Thirdly has been the psychological need to re-establish China's self-respect, allied to a commendable determination not to treat weaker states in the way she herself was treated. Then, partly as a by-product of her dispute with the Soviet Union, has been a desire to have her revolutionary and developmental models copied by countries of the Third World. Whether the ancient conviction of the innate superiority of the Chinese race and the belief that China and the world are synonymous have survived the traumatic events of the last eighty years is not revealed by the official pronouncements of the communist mandarinate. But it is unlikely that the thought patterns of thousands of years could be rubbed out in so short a time.

Diplomacy in Africa has played an important part in the educative process of Communist China's foreign policy makers and of her emissaries. When contact was established between the two regions nearly twenty years ago China's ignorance of African personalities and political conditions was almost total.[1] Since then she has built up an experienced African corps,[2] has established cordial relations with the majority of countries on the continent and would seem to have achieved many of the goals which we presume she must have set herself. There have been failures and disappointments, but on these and on the successes of their African diplomacy the Chinese bureaucrats have kept their traditional silence. Except in the case of the captured PLA Bulletin of Activities, we have no sure indication of China's expectations of Africa or of her strategy for the continent; and if we judge her failures and successes by Western standards we cannot be sure that the criteria we use, especially the time factor, would be the same as those employed in Peking.

Nevertheless, it is clear by *any* standards that Africa has played a major supporting role in China's post-revolution foreign policy. That distant continent, 'shrouded in a mist of blue vapours', as it was described by the fifteenth-century navigator Cheng Ho, could obviously never be as important to China as her Asian neighbours. But until the recent détente with the West, Africa was the area of greatest secondary importance: China has diplomatic relations with more countries in Africa than in any other continent; the bulk of her economic aid, including the communist world's greatest-ever project, has gone to African countries and the greatest numerical support for her entry to the UN came from Africa.

Western commentators have tended to assume that rigid principles have guided China's African policies. Since many of these have also until recently subscribed to the conspiratorial theory of China's role in the world, some fanciful and Machiavellian theories of China's aims in Africa have been evolved, ranging from continent-wide subversion to a desire to settle and populate the region with Chinese. More sober judgements now prevail and there is general agreement that Chinese foreign policy in Africa has been very flexible and by no means as sinister as its erstwhile critics maintained.[3]

In her worldwide diplomacy, China has used three methods to extend her influence: official diplomacy, including the establishment of diplomatic relations, provision of aid and trade relations; 'popular' diplomacy, an appeal over the heads of governments to individuals and groups friendly to China, and including support for dissident groups; and thirdly, relations with communist parties. The few un-proscribed communist parties in Africa are without exception pro-Soviet, so in her African diplomacy China has only employed the first two methods.

Why did China interest herself in dealing with African countries on the basis of equality when the ethnic, cultural, intellectual and historic backgrounds of the two continents were so vastly different? Although the first contact in the modern era between the two was virtually an accident, the result of a meeting between Chou En-lai and Nasser, Mao had declared as early as 1936 that when the Chinese revolution was victorious the masses of many colonial countries would 'follow the example of China and win a similar victory of their own'. And in 1940 he wrote that revolutions in colonial and semi-colonial countries would have a 'new democratic' character like that of China. Later, as the rift with the Soviet Union grew wider, China advanced the claim that her revolution was *the* model for dependent countries and that Marxism as interpreted by Mao was the only true communist doctrine. Africa, with its plethora of colonies, was bound to become an important battleground for these ideological differences. The advocacy of armed struggle as the instrument for gaining independence can also be seen as a personal attempt by Mao to consolidate his own 'line': he himself had once been under attack by the

CCP as a 'military adventurist' and even Chou had denounced his old-fashioned 'guerrilla-ism' in the early 1930s. Eventually Mao's methods proved right for China; their successful application to other revolutionary situations would strengthen his internal standing and enhance his international reputation.

In the event, with one main exception, African independence gave the lie to both Chinese and Soviet prescriptions, and the quiet withdrawal of the European powers left China and the Soviet Union first to rationalize events, then to compete with each other in the more prosaic fields of economic assistance.

Both communist powers perceived that the ending of empire, and the apparent indifference of the US towards Africa, had created a political vacuum. Both moved to fill this vacuum, first in a spirit of grudging cooperation, later in a spirit of bitter rivalry. Both miscalculated the hostility this rivalry would arouse in what they seemed to regard as a passive factor – the Africans themselves – who resented the 'second scramble for Africa' just as much as the earlier European scramble of the nineteenth century.

It was possible the communists underestimated the strength of nationalism among the newly independent countries; certainly the Soviets seemed to ignore it when putting forward Pan-Africanism as the panacea for post-independence ills. For African independence had been won, sometimes spuriously, under the banner of nationalism. No policy, or ideology, which ignored this fervent nationalism that guided, and still guides, Africa's rulers, could possibly be acceptable. As President Senghor of Senegal, a leading left-wing African thinker, once said:

The nation is the primary reality of the twentieth century. Europe can afford to abandon the idea of sovereign nationhood today because it has outgrown the national stage of its history. We have not done that yet. That is the tragedy of our situation.[4]

Religious feeling, as well as nationalism, was an opposing factor which both communist powers had to take into account. The atheism of China and the Soviet Union perturbed many Africans, as did the alleged mistreatment in the two countries of religious minorities.[5] President Sekou Touré himself, who spent several years studying in Czechoslovakia and is on the extreme left of the African political spectrum, has said:

In my view Marxism offers us important ideas concerning the history of mankind. Dialectical and philosophical materialism offers us a possibility of interpreting social and economic reality, but it involves the denial of the existence of God. Now nowhere in any African country, and particularly not in Guinea, will you find a single man or woman who does not believe in the existence of God. Even if you find someone who tells you that he is a fetishist, or that he hasn't any religion, nevertheless he is a believer.[6]

Similar views were expressed by the Ghanaian politician, Kofi Baako:

I should like to draw your attention to the religious feelings of our people. No native of Ghana, or of any other African country, is an atheist. Deep down within him are hidden spiritual forces which move him to honour the god of his ancestors ... It would therefore be well to bear in mind that no political ideology that fails to take these basic facts into account can be regarded as acceptable, and that if it is nevertheless imposed on the people it will lead to nothing but trouble and social revolt.[7]

During his visit to China in 1974 Nyerere reminded his hosts that, being a Christian, he could interpret their view of social progress as a kind of 'divine discontent.'

The 'second vacuum'

There was not only a second scramble for Africa; there was also, I contend, a 'second vacuum' which occurred after the Soviet invasion of Czechoslovakia. The invasion confirmed many African leaders in their fears that the Soviet Union was just another imperialist power, no better than the former colonialists and possibly even a little worse because of the poorer quality and harsher terms of her economic aid. The West (excluding the less powerful nations such as Canada and the Scandinavian countries, whose 'neutral' aid was increasingly welcomed) was also not trusted. Britain appeared impotent to deal with the Rhodesian crisis and her close economic ties with South Africa made her suspect in the eyes of a Black Africa committed to liberating the southern part of the continent. Many African countries at this stage might have been prepared to move closer to the US – despite her Vietnam policies which were strongly criticized. The glow of the Kennedy era, when many Africans believed the US might even mount some sort of Marshall Plan for independent Africa, had not quite died down; there was talk of the need for closer ties between Africans and American negroes; the US suffered in Africa no colonialist taint. But despite oratorical declarations about keen US interest in Africa and her ardent desire to improve relations, the Vietnam engagement became America's overwhelming foreign preoccupation. The chance, if chance it was, was lost. And, like Britain, the US came under a cloud because of her continued trade with, and investment in, South Africa and the Portuguese territories. Later, the Byrd Amendment, which enabled the US to ignore UN sanctions and import Rhodesian chrome, thus giving considerable comfort to the Smith regime, and the manufacture under licence in the US of the joint French-South African Cactus missile – a *de facto* breach of the declared US arms embargo to South Africa – confirmed suspicions about the cynical nature of the US's African policies.

It was at this stage that the 'new China' emerged from the turmoils of the cultural revolution. Untarnished – unless her most hostile critics were to be believed – by contact with Africa's white south (in fact, actually aiding the forces opposed to the racialist regimes), she professed to disclaim big power status, which she characterized as bullying of smaller and medium-sized nations by superpowers, and offered instead a friendship based on the equality of sovereign nations. It was to be a relationship based on the fellowship of poverty, but China was not so poor that she could not give substantial economic assistance to the poorer members of the 'club'. Her considerable aid commitments made during the diplomatic offensive in the early 1970s convinced many previously dubious countries that, while Chinese aid would never be a complete substitute for Western and Soviet aid, it was still very substantial and could effectively be used as a lever. Some countries, notably Tanzania and Congo-Brazzaville, found that Chinese aid allowed them to all but dispense with other donors. The quality of Chinese aid, its aptness for African conditions, and China's impeccable record of not interfering in the internal affairs of recipient countries, made her aid doubly welcome.

China gradually emerged as a true friend and a credible alternative as an ally, particularly in the UN, to Africa's traditional European allies, from whom the majority of countries – mainly because of the wealth gap – increasingly felt alienated.

The Sino-Soviet dispute

The Czechoslovakian invasion had been a traumatic event for China's as well as for Africa's leaders. It, and the subsequent 'Brezhnev doctrine' which sought to justify Soviet intervention in any socialist country judged to have 'bad tendencies', convinced the Chinese of the imperialist intentions of the Soviet Union. The border incidents in 1969 confirmed these convictions.

Chinese officials impressed 'Post Nixon' visitors that China genuinely did fear a Soviet invasion, a version of the Sino-Soviet dispute that was lent credence in 1970, and to a lesser extent in mid-1973, when China virtually went on a war alert. An American journalist reported[8] after talks with Chinese leaders that their 'primary preoccupation continues to be their unshakeable belief in a Soviet threat to their country's independence'.

But that what China says and what China does are two different things has been a theme of this book. China's leaders *may* believe in a direct Soviet military threat (or more likely Soviet pressure at a critical time in the future), and they behave as if they do. But just as the emphasis on People's Wars in the 1960s was a holding operation, a tactic designed hopefully to divert the attention of the then main enemy, the US, away from China while the Communist party was consolidating its hold on the country, so the constant emphasis on the threat from the 'new Tsars' is also an attempt to buy time – time during which by 'occupying minds with foreign quarrels', Chou and the moderates can work to ensure continuity of policy after the old guard has departed, and during which China can continue to develop her nuclear capabilities.

Nuclear strategy

It is China's nuclear programme which gives the lie to her

disclaimers about not seeking big power status; or to be more charitable she is using big power methods – nuclear parity – in an attempt to abolish the distinctions between the big powers and herself. Doubtless, when China's nuclear programme has reached a stage when she feels she can deal more or less equally with the Soviet Union, much of the tension will go out of the Sino-Soviet dispute, just as tension between the US and the Soviet Union slackened as they reached nuclear parity. At the moment the Soviet Union's nuclear lead over China is equivalent to the unequal treaties imposed on her in the last century; but communist China, unlike the Empire, refuses to be 'blackmailed'.

In 1974, according to US intelligence, China was deploying about fifty medium-range (1000 miles) ballistic missiles carrying a small 20-kiloton warhead, and was beginning to deploy intermediate (1500 miles) ballistic missiles, with a larger warhead. In that year, Chinese scientists under Dr Tsien Hsueh-shen, who did rocket research in the US during the Second World War, were developing an inter-continental ballistic missile (ICBM) with a range of 3000 miles. A constant, unconfirmed, rumour was that it would be tested from pads in Sinkiang with a splashdown in the Indian Ocean off Zanzibar.

The apparent détente with the US and the development of a nuclear programme does not invalidate Mao's theories on People's Wars and the primacy of rifles over bombs, as the Vietnam war amply proved. But it does obviously diminish the importance of foreign revolutions, particularly as a diversionary tactic. And if Mao really believes the spiritual atom bomb is greater than the nuclear variety, one would be justified in asking why China is devoting so much of her resources to a nuclear missile programme. The Sino-Soviet dispute and the consequent desire to enlist as many supporters, of whatever political inclination, in a broad united front against big-power hegemony (in other words the Soviet Union) has narrowed the scope for Chinese support of revolution. Correct relations with legitimate African governments, from empires to military dictatorships, has entailed abandonment of support for their oppositions, however ideologically worthy. Even 'just' wars of liberation, such as those being fought in southern Africa, which do not involve China in direct state considerations, are viewed with little enthusiasm in Peking. As early as November 1971 a Western military analyst predicted a shift in Chinese strategy:

Before guerrilla groups in the Middle East and elsewhere put all their hopes for the decade on backing from Peking, they should consider how contingent and equivocal this support might prove to be.

To cast this doubt is not to deny the continuing ability of the CPC to feel an affinity with the revolutionary left elsewhere. It is merely to make the point that it is now bound to decide its commitments primarily in relation to the geostrategic situation of its own nation-state. Thus, it cannot be an accident – to use a favourite Marxist phrase – that the apparent approach of what some are sure to see as a great missile breakthrough is coinciding with a diminution of overt hostility toward certain Western countries and also the UN.[9]

The Indian Ocean

Geostrategic considerations have played a part in China's attitude towards supposed Soviet naval expansion in the Indian Ocean, but it seems likely that China, like the West, has deliberately exaggerated the dangers for her own purposes. Although the re-opening of the Suez Canal activates the possibility of the Soviet Union servicing an Indian Ocean fleet from the Black Sea, the reality in 1974 was that in terms of ship days the West's presence was far greater in the Ocean than the Soviet Union's. And while the Soviet Union had limited facilities, amounting virtually to mooring rights, at a few ports, notably Berbera in Somalia, and Aden, the US and Britain were building a major base on the island of Diego Garcia. Nevertheless, the build-up of military activity has given China ammunition for propaganda – she even viewed the July 1973 coup in Afghanistan as part of a grand Soviet strategy to dismember Pakistan and establish her influence firmly on the shores of the Indian Ocean.[11]

China signalled her preoccupation by expressing approval of the line taken by many delegates at the Commonwealth Conference in Singapore in January 1971, against the expansion of superpower military strength in the Indian Ocean. NCNA's quoting of Ceylonese Prime Minister Mrs Bandaranaike's suggestion for a 'zone of peace' in the Ocean was the first official Chinese mention – however oblique – for many years of a limited measure of arms control. Later, the Soviets were attacked directly;

Donning the mantle of the old Tzars, the Soviet revisionist leading clique ambitiously set out its expansionist activities in the Indian Ocean long ago with the aim of establishing a sea-lane arch stretching from the Baltic Sea to the Japan Sea, through the Mediterranean, the Red Sea, the Indian Ocean and the West Pacific, linking Europe, Asia and Africa in order to attain sea hegemony. Since Brezhnev took office, Soviet revisionism has tried to get hold of the right to use naval bases and ports of certain countries on the shores of the Indian Ocean by providing 'economic aid' and 'military aid' and other bait. (*Peking Review*, 14 January 1972)

China was openly delighted when the OAU adopted a Declaration on the Issues of the Law of the Sea, recommending an exclusive maritime economic zone of 200 nautical miles for member states, and commented that

This is not only an important measure to safeguard the marine resources of the African countries but also a tremendous support for the common struggle of the small and medium-sized countries against the rivalry of the superpowers for maritime hegemony. (*Renmin Ribao*, 1 June 1973)

Typically, China's response to this new threat has not been only verbal. Western journalists[12] in China have reported that she is now building a new naval force, mainly consisting of anti-submarine vessels, to counteract the Soviet presence off her waters.

China's navy – perhaps because Mao was a soldier – has always been the weak link in her defensive system. Although it musters over 1200 surface vessels, forty conventional submarines and an estimated strength of nearly 200000 men, the navy is capable of undertaking only short-range, coastal operations. Half of the ships are under 100 tons, and China has only four destroyers. It seems likely that for many years to come China's navy will continue to be used for defensive purposes only; but if she did decide to show the flag with a few ocean-going ships there is no reason to suppose they would not be welcomed by her riparian African allies – Tanzania, Zanzibar, Congo-Brazzaville, Cameroon etc – as well as by other Indian Ocean friends, such as Mauritius, Shri Lanka, Pakistan and Madagascar.

Leader of the Third World

By persuading the non-superpowers to accept her thesis that the world is divided between the superpowers and the 'small and medium-sized countries' China can also serve some of her own state interests. Her encouragement of an 'independent' Rumania, closer relations with Yugoslavia and her approval of the EEC all serve, she hopes, to undermine big power hegemony. In Africa, encouragement given to the North African countries to make the Mediterranean a 'sea of Mediterraneans' might one day conceivably deny the Mediterranean to both the US and to the Soviet Union. And in the continuing, but now more peaceful, battle with the capitalist West the replacement of Britain as chief exporter to Tanzania and a loan of £30 million to Cameroon, enabling her to gain greater independence of France, are but two examples of how China can 'shake up' traditional and established relationships to her own advantage. In many ways this is Mao's guerrilla tactic of constantly harrying the enemy on all fronts, applied on a global scale.

Although she would deny it, China does see herself, and is accepted by many, as champion of the Third World. This is particularly true in the economic sphere, where, in the UN and in other international forums, China has articulated the frustrations of the poorer countries against the inequalities of the present world economic system. She has put forward pleas for: trade on a basis of equality, an end to 100 per cent foreign exploitation of natural resources, the removal of developed countries' tariff barriers, the end of one-crop economies kept going for the benefit of industrial nations, an end to dumping, the breaking of the monopoly of a few countries in shipping, insurance and other services, but above all, for the application of the principles of self-reliance to the problems of development. A typical statement of China in this role would be the speech of Wang Jun-sheng to the 55th session of the UN Economic and Social Council:

In the course of developing our national economies, we developing countries are faced with practical difficulties such as inadequacy of funds and lack of technical know-how. However, so long as we proceed from the specific conditions of our own countries, rely mainly on our own efforts while seeking for aid as an auxiliary, properly handle the relationship between the development of agriculture and that of light and heavy industry and between the vigorous expansion of production and the improvement of the people's livelihood, we can accumulate funds for construction by increasing production and practising strict economy. (*Peking Review*, 29 July 1973)

THE CHINESE MODEL

There is very little in that with which leaders of developing countries could take issue. But it is an obvious invitation to copy China's own model, and insofar as African and other Third World countries perceive China's development to have been successful and balanced, they will borrow from the Chinese model. Thoughtful leaders will not slavishly follow China's example, and indeed, the Chinese emphasis on self-reliance specifically allows for local solutions to local problems. Just as Mao had to adapt Marxism to Chinese conditions, so African leaders will have to adapt useful Chinese (and other) examples to African conditions: the evolving concept of African socialism, based on the traditional extended family system and incorporating some aspects of foreign models, is one example of how this is happening already.

President Nyerere, whose country has enjoyed such a fruitful relationship with China, has shown the value of a selective approach to China's political and economic model. Since independence Tanzania, like China, has worked to reduce the differences in the standard of living in the urban and rural areas; she has organized isolated peasant communities into more viable 'Ujamaa' villages, based partly on Chinese communes, partly on kibbutz; she has injected a practical element into schooling; government officials have been encouraged to go into the countryside to see what the country's real problems are; a people's militia has been formed. But Tanzania, unlike China, has tried to de-politicize her army, which is based therefore on the English model. Nor has the Tanzanian state taken over all the means of production – private enterprise still has a role, albeit a minor one, to play in the economy.

Despite China's public pronouncements of the great similarities between China and developing Africa, many would argue that the differences are even greater. China's 'political consciousness', as she has stressed, was moulded and strengthened by foreign invasion and years of revolutionary struggle, factors which were absent in the majority of African independence movements. China's successes are, to a large extent, based on an efficient, incorrupt bureaucracy and a disciplined, hard-working people – again, factors which are lacking in most African countries. China, although undoubtedly not united at all levels, is at least not split along tribal or religious lines, nor has she had to experiment with different forms of government. The apparent strength and cohesion of China contrasts strangely with the fragmented, élite-conscious, coup-prone appearance of many African nations.

Nevertheless, China must feel that the attempt, however nugatory, of African states to copy the Chinese model reflects well on her system: and states which admire China enough to try and copy her example are less likely to be hostile. She does not, at this stage anyway, seek direct influence, and one is reminded of the ancient Chinese emperors who did not ask the tributary states to copy the Chinese system, but only to acknowledge their authority.

The moral force

This authority of the Ming Emperors rested, not on force, but on virtue. Cheng Ho was dispatched, not to conquer or settle the lands of Azania, but to impress on the barbarian peoples living there the 'transforming power of the imperial virtue'. Arthur Huck has described this connection between China's foreign relations and her own system of government:

In the eyes of the mandarins the superiority of China has always rested on a superiority of doctrine. Their ancient system of government was not superior simply because the empire was vast, populous and unified; its material strength on the contrary flowed from its virtue and the basis of its virtue was immutable [Confucian] doctrine. Because the Emperor embodied certain immutable moral truths his country was powerful and prosperous. Indeed, if the condition of the country worsened and the populace suffered, this was a sign that the Emperor had abandoned the path of virtue and forfeited the heavenly mandate. *The basis of all superiority was moral superiority founded on true doctrine.* Representatives of foreign potentates who arrived bearing tribute were supposed to be showing their recognition of this fact and therefore of the Emperor's superior place in the scheme of things.[13]

Historical analogies can be taken too far. Conditions change – even most Chinese would acknowledge now that China is not synonymous with the world – but the belief that authority (leadership of the Third World, acceptance by other nations of China's world view) rests on moral superiority, which in turn rests on true doctrine (Maoism), seems to have survived. Like religious sects who know they have found the true way, the Chinese see situations in simplistic terms. Their propaganda writing is full of such phrases as '. . . (whoever is being criticized) has done a bad thing', or 'This is a good which we must fight for.' There is a very strong moral, almost puritanical, streak in Chinese society – the cult of unselfishness, sexual strictness, sobriety – which the Chinese undoubtedly believe lends weight to their authority in the outside world. Again, like religious conviction, this can lead to obstinacy: to paraphrase Chesterton, orthodoxy is Mao-doxy. Externally this sense of moral sureness can give offence – foreigners can hardly be expected to agree that the Chinese are right all the time. Internally it is a source of great strength. A British politician commented on his visit to China that the humiliations of the last century, the civil war and twenty years of vigorous development have

bred leaders of exceptional toughness and resilience and integrated them deeply and personally with their people in a way that is hard for outsiders to understand. The result is what one can only call moral force based on a cultural and psychological revival of a kind that simply cannot be ignored as a source of China's internal cohesion and energy.[14]

Translated into political action this moral force produces an ingredient in foreign policy which is virtually unknown to Western diplomacy: altruism. Perhaps it would be fairer to say that the political return for a foreign initiative can be less for Chinese leaders – admittedly untroubled by a questioning electorate[15] – than for Western ones. The more cynical might argue that China expects her dividends to be paid later than Western political investors; but to present appearances a project like the Tanzam railway has a higher 'moral' content than, for example, the parallel American road. China's system, like those of the Scandinavian countries, allows for a fairly high moral ingredient in foreign policy, with the obvious proviso that it does not interfere with state considerations.

A PRAGMATIC PROGRAMME

China's stated aims are revolutionary, but her foreign policy towards Africa, except for the aberrant period of the cultural revolution, appears to have been evolutionary and pragmatic. Specifically, it appears to have evolved towards an accommodation with regimes which can hardly be ideologically satisfactory to Peking – whose overthrow ten years ago she might well have advocated – and towards a relationship with African countries based on such non-revolutionary links as mutual economic advantage. If the establishment of relations with Zaire, Ethiopia, Nigeria and Cameroon, the abandonment of support for such opposition groups as the ELF, the UPC and extremist elements in Kenya and the lukewarm enthusiasm for the liberation movements of southern Africa is simply an appearance, then even discerning critics could be forgiven for thinking that China must be very good at appearances. This, Chinese policy-makers might conceivably argue, is to ignore the connection between the short-term and the long-term, or, to use Maoist terminology, to overlook the 'tactical flexibility, which allows the guerrilla fighter to take one step backward before moving two forward. It could be argued, for example, that establishment of relations with a right-wing government gives China greater opportunities to contact and cultivate opposition elements within that country dedicated to the regime's overthrow; economic aid, likewise, could build up a constituency within an African country favourable to the Chinese economic model and therefore more likely to adopt her political one; less convincingly, it could be argued that the sparse allocation of resources to revolutionary movements encourages the Chinese ideal of self-reliance, which constitutes an – admittedly oblique – tribute to Chinese theory.

Although any nation could use long-term, vaguely defined ideological goals to justify apparently contradictory short-term policies, China's present leaders have more justification than most for asserting that this is true. Their own struggle for power, conducted in adverse conditions over a period of nearly thirty years, convinced them of the virtues of patience and of the need to wait for the right circumstances. With their penchant for historical analogies (and a corresponding weakness for assuming that Chinese history will repeat itself in other parts of the world), Chinese planners have equated the post-independence phase of Africa's development with pre-revolution events in China:

At present some parts of Africa are going through experiences similar to what we experienced in China sixty years ago in the Boxer uprising. Some of the events were like those which occurred during the Hsin-hai Revolution, while others resembled what happened around the May 4th Movement (1919). We had not yet begun the period of the Northern Expedition and that of the War of Resistance against Japan, and we were still far from the events of 1949 in China. Africa is at present mostly occupied with fighting imperialism and colonialism. Its fight against feudalism is not so important, and moreover, its role in the Socialist revolution is in a dormant phase . . .

We must tell [the Africans], in order to help them, about the experience of the Chinese revolution, pointing out the significance of the Taiping uprising, the Boxer uprising, Dr Sun Yat Sen, and the revolutionary experience of the Communists in this generation. They must depend mainly upon their own personal experience, for foreign assistance can only come second; their victory will come eventually but no immediate results should be expected . . . We should take long range views of this problem.[16]

Africa, in this theory, has still, therefore, to experience the equivalent of the Chinese revolution, which was primarily a military revolution. This is where theory and reality become divorced: China's revolution was stimulated by foreign invasion and foreign occupation; no African country is threatened by either. Yet because China's independence was won by struggle, she is reluctant to acknowledge the legitimacy of an independence won by non-violent means. In this sense, Africa still is, in Chinese eyes, 'ripe for revolution'. Evidence that this is a correct interpretation of Chinese thinking would seem to be given by the fact that China, unlike the Soviet Union, has yet to write prescriptions for Africa's *social* revolution, which in the Chinese case succeeded the nationalist revolution. This social revolution – which Africa's present leaders believe they themselves are now leading – is for China in the distant future:

. . . the embryo of national people's revolution in these countries will become a genuine people's revolution, give rise to Marxists, form political parties of the proletariat, and go towards social revolution.[17]

A 'genuine people's revolution' has yet to be acknowledged by China in any African country: no true Marxists, in Chinese eyes, have yet arisen and no Communist party has received Chinese endorsement. Social revolution is a distant goal, not to be achieved in this generation.

The visionary future, which presumably at its optimum would envisage a Maoist Africa, a client area like the Empire's tributary states, is not allowed to obscure present realities – China must make the best of what is, not dream of what might be. A convincing case can be made that China has in fact already had the best of Africa. African support, however meagre it might have appeared to the outsider, boosted internal morale at a time when the new government felt itself isolated and contained by the outside world, and as it struggled to assert its authority within China. African support helped secure a seat at the UN and eventual recognition by that same hostile world. And the acceptance of and praise for Chinese assistance by African countries earned China further recognition and respect, and raised her standing in the eyes of other countries of the Third World. There seems little else that Africa can 'give' China. Support for China in the Sino-Soviet dispute is unlikely to be forthcoming from any truly independent African country, there is no 'African Albania'. Africa cannot help physically with the problem of Chinese security, its countries being neither rich, technologically capable nor militarily powerful; apart from its natural resources and somewhat vague 'moral support' Africa has little to give for China's friendship. This is not to suggest that China will therefore pack up and leave; in fact, in the immediate future, China is as likely to over-compensate – not least in terms of aid commitments – as to scale down her activities, for what she herself regards as a diminishing interest in the continent. Just as the US found it difficult to abandon Chiang Kai-shek, so would Mao be reluctant to take no further interest in China's African allies.

Policies might be altered with Mao's death, as they undoubtedly will with Chiang's. Second generation ministers might advise a new chairman, as a fifteenth-century minister advised the Emperor, not to

. . . glorify the sending of expeditions to distant countries. Abandon the barren lands abroad and give the people of China a respite so that they [could] devote themselves to husbandry and to the schools.[18]

Leaving behind no institutions and no language the Communist Chinese could withdraw from Africa virtually without trace, just as their forebears did over five hundred years ago. Future archaeologists might idly pick over pieces of crockery made in the People's Republic and speculate what prompted China's renewed interest in that distant continent.

Notes

1. China's early predictable mistake was to paint Africa in her own image. In 1964, for example, a Chinese playwright had been told to write a play about West African peasants and had been instructed that their problems were the same as pre-revolutionary Chinese peasants – i.e. they were exploited by a feudal class and were landless. There being no Chinese books on Africa, he approached a Western friend, who gave him Gunther's *Inside Africa* to read; the playwright was astonished to learn that there were no landless poor in Africa, and that Africa's problems were entirely different to China's. His play was eventually based on an American journalist's impressions of Africa. Many visitors to China (see e.g., Huck, op. cit., p. 15) were impressed by the ignorance and lack of interest of Chinese in the outside world, many of them knowing only whether a certain country had a pro-Peking Communist party or not.

2. But China, unlike the Soviet Union, has not contributed to African scholarship, and seems not to want to do so, declaring that African studies should be undertaken primarily by Africans. For a more detailed discussion of this topic see Larkin, op. cit., p. 240.

3. The exception, for obvious reasons, has been South Africa; a recent 'theory' was advanced by a Johannesburg physician, Dr Jack Penn, described as an expert on the African guerrilla movement, who wrote in the *New York Times* of April 1972 that 'At the completion of the Tanzam railway the Chinese hope to swamp southern Africa from the north. The coastlines are already patrolled by the Russians. It is obvious that the policy of the Chinese Communists is to eliminate the Europeans (whites) by using the black tribes for this purpose. If this were to succeed, they would encourage inter-tribal warfare and probably total subjugation of the blacks.' But the old prejudices, and the old language still linger in the West too – a semi-secret British Foreign Office report on Chinese foreign policy, dated November 1971, considered the Chinese would be 'awkward customers' in the UN on colonial questions, peace-keeping and disarmament.

4. Lecture to the Royal Institute for International Affairs, London, November 1959.

5. China was worried enough about African criticism of her treatment of Moslems to invite a Mauritanian delegation to investigate the allegations in 1967. The Mauritanians said they were satisfied freedom of worship was allowed in China. The China-Islamic Association, formed in 1953, organizes pilgrimages to Mecca and sends delegations to Islamic countries.

6. Fernand Gigon, *Guinée Etat-pilote*, quoted in Franz Ansprenger, *Politik in schwarzen Afrika*, Cologne, 1961, p. 292.

7. Kofi Baako, *Ghana's Conception of Socialism*, lecture to Christian students in Accra, 19 August 1961, quoted in Schatten, op. cit., p. 329.

8. Charles Yost, *Christian Science Monitor*, 26 July 1973.

9. Neville Brown, *Military Review*, November 1971.

10. On this issue, as on many others, South African propaganda appears to be unable to distinguish between the policies of China and the Soviet Union. Commenting on a visit to China of Mauritian Prime Minister, Seewoosagur Ramgoolam, Radio Johannesburg (16 April 1972) said China, whose ultimate aim was world domination, had considerable influence in East Africa through her foothold in Zanzibar – 'but add Mauritius, (and) the picture changes considerably. It is a stepping-stone to Madagascar, and the two islands could provide perfect bases for the control of the entire southern Indian Ocean and potentially southern Africa.'

11. See e.g., *The Times*, 2 August 1973.

12. See e.g., the *Daily Telegraph*, 28 July 1973.

13. Huck, op. cit., p. 18 (italics mine).

14. Anthony Wedgwood Benn in the *Sunday Times*, 26 September 1971.

15. However, during Nyerere's March 1974 visit to China a film showing construction of the Tanzam railway was accompanied by a similar film on a railway built four years previously in south-west China. *The Times* correspondent commented that '. . . it could be seen as an answer to people in China who have asked why so many resources should be devoted to building a railway in Africa.' (*The Times*, 31 March 1974)

16. J. Chester Cheng, op. cit., pp. 484–5.

17. Ibid., p. 484.

18. Jung-pang Lo, *The Decline*, p. 153.

Postscript: The Portuguese Coup

The Portuguese army coup in April 1974 had its roots in the frustration felt by young officers at the hopelessness of the African campaign, as well as their doubt in its moral justification. The coup's consequences were immediately felt in Africa: Guinea-Bissau was given full independence in September, with the PAIGC forming the independent government. Mozambique will be given full independence in June 1975; in the meantime the government is comprised of nine FRELIMO appointees and three named by Portugal, with a prime minister appointed by FRELIMO. Angola's future at present remains uncertain, because it is the wealthiest of the colonies, because it has a relatively high proportion of white citizens and because it has no one united nationalist group representing the entire population. Portugal's offer of a two-year transitional period prior to a referendum was rejected by both FNLA and MPLA, which despite internal differences were trying to form a common front. UNITA was portrayed by these two as collaborating with white interests. China's immediate reaction to the coup was to castigate the Soviet Union for recognizing the new regime before it had acknowledged the principle of independence for the three territories. Later FRELIMO was warned (*People's Daily*, 14 September 1974) against 'the busy activity of the Soviet revisionist social-imperialists in their efforts to divide and weaken the African national liberation movements'. In Angola China made clear her support for the FNLA, and before the ceasefire in October over 100 Chinese guerrilla instructors were training FNLA groups at camps in Zaire.

The Tanzam Railway

The new 'respectability' of Angola and Mozambique somewhat dented the economic viability of Tanzam, for without political embarrassment Zambia was able to utilize the cheaper options of the Benguela line through Angola, or send copper by road to the Malawian railhead of Salima for railing to either Nacala or Beira in Mozambique. Port delays at Dar es Salaam throughout 1974 forced Zambia increasingly to use the Benguela option – in June she exported nearly the entire month's copper production through Angola, and the viability of Tanzam remains very much tied to the ability of Tanzania to decongest Dar es Salaam port.

Bibliography

Note: African newspapers and specialized magazines (listed over-leaf) give limited coverage of Sino-African relations. The best single source for factual information, but limited to arrivals, departures, official notes, banquet speeches and editorials is the Survey of the Chinese Mainland Press (SCMP), published by the US Consulate, Hong Kong, and available in most major libraries. The following list is limited to publications strictly relevant to the subject dealt with in this book, and does not attempt to include the vast literature on China's wider foreign relations.

Attwood, William, *The Reds and the Blacks*. London: Hutchinson, 1967.

Brzezinski, Zbigniew, Ed., *Africa and The Communist World*. Stanford: Stanford University Press, 1959.

Cheng, J. Chester, Ed., *The Politics of the Chinese Red Army*. Stanford: Hoover Institution on War, Revolution and Peace, 1966.

Filesi, Teobaldo, *China and Africa in the Middle Ages*, Trans. David Morison. London: Frank Cass, 1972.

Halpern, A. M., Ed., *Policies Towards China: Views From Six Continents*. New York: McGraw-Hill for the Council on Foreign Relations, 1965.

Hamrell, Sven, and Widstrand, Carl, Eds., *The Soviet Bloc, China and Africa*. Uppsala: The Scandinavian Institute of African Studies, 1964.

Hevi, Emmanuel, *An African Student in China*. New York: Praeger, 1963.

Hevi, Emmanuel, *The Dragon's Embrace*. London: Pall Mall Press, 1967.

Larkin, Bruce, *China and Africa, 1949–1970*. Berkeley: University of California Press, 1971.

Lessing, Pieter, *Africa's Red Harvest*. New York: John Day, 1962.

Okello, John, *Revolution in Zanzibar*. Nairobi: East African Publishing House, 1967.

Ogunsanwo, Cornelius, *China's Policy in Africa, 1958–1971*. Cambridge: Cambridge University Press, 1974. (This is the thesis quoted in this book – see p. 71 – and now published in book form.)

Schatten, Fritz, *Communism in Africa*. New York: Praeger, 1966.

Thompson, W. Scott, *Ghana's Foreign Policy 1957–1966*. Princeton: Princeton University Press, 1969.

Tung Chi-ping, and Evans, Humphrey, *The Thought Revolution*. New York: Coward-McCann, 1966.

Yu, George, *China and Tanzania: A Study in Cooperative Interaction*. Berkeley: University of California Centre for Chinese Studies, 1970.

The following journals also occasionally have articles on Sino-African relations.

Africa. London.
Africa Confidential. London.
African Development. London.
Africa Report. New York.
Afrique Asie. Paris.
China Quarterly. London.
Current Scene. Hong Kong.
Far Eastern Economic Review.
Foreign Affairs.
International Affairs. Moscow.
Jeune Afrique. Tunis.
Mizan Newsletter. London.
Peking Review. Peking.
Race. London.
Red Flag. Peking.
West Africa. London.

INDEX

Compiled by Gordon Robinson